Python® FOR DUMMIES®

by Stef Maruch and Aahz Maruch

WILEY

Wiley Publishing, Inc.

Python® For Dummies®

Published by
Wiley Publishing, Inc.
111 River Street
Hoboken, NJ 07030-5774
www.wiley.com

WILEY

About the Authors

Stef Maruch got her hands on an original 128K Mac in 1984 and has been writing about computers ever since. She has over fifteen years' experience in instructional design, writing, and editing end-user computer manuals, including tutorials and user's guides for Apple Newton, HyperCard and HyperTalk, and DVD Studio Pro.

Aahz Maruch is a writer, trainer, and consultant who has been using Python for more than seven years. He has been using computers professionally for 20 years, and his background includes stints of high-end tech support, systems administration, and programming. Aahz is currently working as a programmer for a company with a Web-based application.

The authors can be reached at authors@pythonfood.com.

Dedication

Stef: I dedicate this book to my parents, Don and Betty Jones. You have always believed in me, even at times when I was quite improbable.

Aahz: I dedicate this book to the Python community. I hated programming until I learned Python (yes, for more than 20 years). I hope this book brings the joy of Python to many people.

This book is also dedicated to the Flying Spaghetti Monster.

Authors' Acknowledgments

Many people have helped us and supported us in writing this book. There are too many to mention all of them by name, so we want to start by thanking all the people we don't name here — all the family and friends and community who have sustained us.

Paula Anderson, Naomi Tilsen, Joyce Wermont, and Maggie Young provided much appreciated emotional support.

Thanks to our editors at Wiley:

- ✔ Acquisition editors Terri Varveris, Tiffany Franklin, and Kyle Looper, who shepherded these first-time *For Dummies* authors with just the right balance of patience and whip-cracking.
- ✔ Project editor Pat O'Brien, who provided invaluable assistance in e-mails that were often time-stamped with hours well past the time any less-dedicated person would have been in bed.
- ✔ Copy editor Andy Hollandbeck, who improved the book with his keen grasp of the beginner's mind, light-hearted prose, and Monty Python quotations.

High praise also to the production staff at Wiley, who are doing such great work with an extraordinarily complex and flexible book design.

Our technical editor, David Goodger, vastly improved our book with his edits and suggestions.

We feel fortunate to have our agents, David Fugate, who supported us expertly and patiently through the lengthy acquisition process, and Carole McClendon, who provided support at a critical juncture. Thanks also to the efficient staff at Waterside Productions.

Many people gave us advice and help while we were writing:

- Don and Betty Jones provided invaluable advice from the point of view of programming beginners
- Aahz's coworkers at Printra (`http://printra.net/`), especially Tony Lownds

The community of Python programmers on `comp.lang.python` and `tutor@python.org` not only helped Stef learn Python but also tirelessly work every day to promote Python and help make it accessible. This book wouldn't be possible without them.

The folks who maintain `www.python.org` and run the Python Software Foundation provide a critical service without which Python would be poorer.

Millions of people volunteer their time and efforts to make the Open Source movement a powerful force for good in the computer industry.

We also want to thank each other. Living together and writing a book is stressful, but we're glad we did this.

And, of course, none of it would be possible without Guido.

Publisher's Acknowledgments

We're proud of this book; please send us your comments through our online registration form located at www.dummies.com/register/.

Some of the people who helped bring this book to market include the following:

Acquisitions, Editorial, and Media Development

Project Editor: Pat O'Brien

Acquisitions Editor: Kyle Looper

Copy Editor: Andy Hollandbeck

Technical Editor: David Goodger

Editorial Manager: Kevin Kirschner

Media Development Specialists: Angela Denny, Kate Jenkins, Steven Kudirka, Kit Malone

Media Development Coordinator: Laura Atkinson

Media Project Supervisor: Laura Moss

Media Development Manager: Laura VanWinkle

Editorial Assistant: Amanda Foxworth

Sr. Editorial Assistant: Cherie Case

Cartoons: Rich Tennant (www.the5thwave.com)

Composition Services

Project Coordinator: Tera Knapp

Layout and Graphics: Claudia Bell, Denny Hager, Jake Mansfield, Barbara Moore, Barry Offringa, Heather Ryan

Proofreaders: Laura Albert, Susan Moritz, Techbooks

Indexer: Techbooks

Publishing and Editorial for Technology Dummies

    Richard Swadley, Vice President and Executive Group Publisher

    Andy Cummings, Vice President and Publisher

    Mary Bednarek, Executive Acquisitions Director

    Mary C. Corder, Editorial Director

Publishing for Consumer Dummies

    Diane Graves Steele, Vice President and Publisher

    Joyce Pepple, Acquisitions Director

Composition Services

    Gerry Fahey, Vice President of Production Services

    Debbie Stailey, Director of Composition Services

Contents at a Glance

Table of Contents

Introduction

· ·

Congratulations! You're ready to discover the easiest-to-read powerful programming language — or maybe the most powerful, easy-to-read programming language. That's Python, of course.

With *Python For Dummies*, you can ferret out just a little or a lot. And with Python, you can write a little program that picks a random quote from a file, or you can write a set of programs that runs a complex business.

This book is for you whether you're a student, you're a hobbyist, you need to understand more about what your programmer co-workers are talking about, or you're taking the first steps on a new career path.

Python For Dummies gives you everything you need to get to an advanced-beginner level of Python programming. And it points you to other resources so you can take your Python programming skills even further.

About This Book

Python For Dummies is a reference book, which means you can read it in any order, and you don't have to read every chapter or section. However, to some extent, later chapters about more complex Python features rely on information introduced in earlier chapters. So if you don't understand something you see in a later chapter, go to Chapter 3, or go to the chapter on that feature to find out more. You can also look in the index to find a term or feature you want to know more about.

Conventions Used in This Book

This book contains Python code examples. All code examples are in `monospaced font` so they are easy to recognize. Anything that you need to type is also indicated in `monospaced font` so you know exactly which commas should be typed and which commas are part of the surrounding sentence.

Python interactive mode examples include this prompt: >>>. If you don't see the prompt, you can assume the code was written in a text editor.

Foolish Assumptions

We make the following assumptions about readers of this book:

- ✔ **You know how to use your computer and its operating system.**

  It's helpful but not necessary to know how to set environment variables on your computer. It's also helpful to have a Web browser with access to the Internet.

- ✔ **You have and know how to use a text editor that can produce plain ASCII text or files that end with the .txt extension.**

  If you don't have a text editor that can do this, we include instructions for setting up Python's IDLE programming environment to work with the examples in this book.

- ✔ **You have had a minimal amount of exposure to programming.**

  We really do mean *minimal*. If you had a programming class in high school, or wrote a few BASIC programs at one time, or even if you have used HTML tags, that counts.

  If you have absolutely no experience with programming, you can still find out plenty from this book, but we recommend that you also look at a book or Web tutorial designed to introduce programming to beginners. You'll benefit from the extended explanations of some concepts that we don't have the space to discuss in detail here.

- ✔ **You might have done some programming in another language.**

  Programming knowledge is not required for this book, but people who have programmed in other languages have their own sets of issues when transitioning to Python, and we provide some material for such people.

- ✔ **You know little to nothing about Python.**

  If you know Python, this book will still be helpful as a reference or a source of tips and tricks you may not be aware of.

How This Book Is Organized

This book gives you an overview of Python; the lowdown about all of its major parts, structures, and libraries; and a glimpse into some more advanced features. You also find out where to go to discover more.

Part I: Getting Started

In this part, we introduce Python and situate it among the myriad other programming languages available. Python is good for some things and not for others; you find out which is which. We provide a hands-on introduction to some of Python's abilities, using its helpful interactive mode and its IDLE programming environment. We briefly describe each of Python's basic building blocks and show how all these blocks come together by dissecting a working program. We sketch an overview of how professional programmers design programs and debug code and show you how to put these practices to work to make your own programming life easier.

Part II: Building Blocks

Python has six basic data types and many ways to work with each of them. In this part, we describe how to work with strings (chunks of text), numbers, lists and tuples (both of which store multiple data elements), dictionaries (which associate one element with another), and sets (which always contain unique elements, never duplicates).

Part III: Structures

Python code usually comes in chunks, both small and big, and each chunk does a particular thing. This part also includes a brief introduction to some advanced features and the new features of Python 2.5.

Part IV: Libraries

Python comes with everything you need to write a very powerful program, and other people have already solved lots of programming conundrums for you. Its libraries include primary services such as communication with the operating system, text processing tools, various ways of reading and writing information to disk, and Internet access methods.

Part V: The Part of Tens

All *For Dummies* books include The Part of Tens. In this part, we give you ten useful but not-so-obvious programming idioms and ten resources where you can find out more about Python.

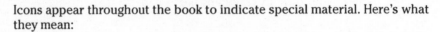

Part VI: Appendixes

Here you find instructions on how to install Python and its documentation, as well as a list of new features introduced with each new version of Python since 2.0.

Icons Used in This Book

Icons appear throughout the book to indicate special material. Here's what they mean:

A Tip explains how to do something a little bit more easily and efficiently.

A Warning gives you a heads-up about tricky stuff or common mistakes that might cause data loss or some other sort of headache. It's best to read Warnings to make sure a tricky feature doesn't "getcha."

A Technical Stuff icon flags text that's of interest to readers who like to know about the inner workings or history of a subject. You don't need to read Technical Stuff material. After you've internalized a little about a subject, reading this text might help you understand it from a different angle.

Remember icons highlight important concepts or pieces of information to keep in mind.

Where to Go from Here

If you want an overview of Python's history and what it can do, go to Chapter 1. If you're new to Python and want to start working with it right away, go to Chapter 2. If you want a brief overview of all of Python's building blocks, go to Chapter 3. If you know some Python and you want a refresher or additional info on some of its tools, go to the specific chapters you're interested in.

Part I
Getting Started

The 5th Wave   By Rich Tennant

"The engineers lived on Jolt and cheese sticks putting this product together, but if you wanted to just use 'cola and cheese sticks' in the Users Documentation, that's okay too. We're pretty loose around here."

In this part . . .

You get an overview of the Python programming language, an introduction to its interactive and developer
environment, and a walkthrough of the building blocks
that make up Python programs.

Chapter 1 describes the history of Python and all the
exciting things it's being used for today. You find out why
computers are both the fastest and dumbest things around.
Best of all, you discover why it's called *Python* anyway.

Chapter 2 lets you talk to Python via its interactive mode
and IDLE environment. You write a few basic programs
and find out how to get Python to carry out commands
for you, how to get Python to tell you things, and how to
import tools that let you do even more.

Chapter 3 introduces you to Python's data types and code
blocks, the chunks you use to build programs.

Chapter 4 shows you a working program. You see how all
the chunks of a Python program talk to each other, and
you find out something about the design philosophies
behind Python programs.

Chapter 5 lets you try on a programmer's hat to understand
how programmers work and why they make the design
decisions they do. (Unfortunately, it doesn't explain the
relevance of caffeinated sodas to this process — you'll
have to figure that out for yourself.) There's also a very
useful section on strategies for debugging programs, which
is a huge part of every programmer's job.

Chapter 1

Introducing Python

*W*elcome to Python! If you're the type of person who wants to know what you're getting into, this chapter is for you. We give you a quick history of Python and its community of developers. You find out what Python is and isn't good for (the "is" section is much longer than the "isn't" section) and the most important principles of good Python programming. If you're new to programming, you'll see how it's very similar to a task you're probably familiar with.

The Right Tool for the Job

Python is a general-purpose, high-level language that can be extended and embedded (included in applications as a tool for writing macros). That makes Python a smart choice for many programming problems, both small and large, and not so good for a couple of computing tasks.

Good uses of Python

Python is ideal for projects that require quick development. It supports multiple programming philosophies, so it's good for programs that require flexibility. The many packages and modules already written for Python provide versatility and save you time.

The story of Python

Guido van Rossum created Python and is affectionately bestowed with the title "Benevolent Dictator For Life" by the Python community. In the late 1980s, Guido liked features of several programming languages, but none of them had all the features he wanted. Specifically, he wanted a language that had the following features:

- **Scripting language:** A *script* is a program that controls other programs. Scripting languages are good for quick development and prototyping because they're good at passing messages from one component to another and at handling fiddly stuff like memory management so that the programmer doesn't have to. Python has grown beyond scripting languages, which are used mostly for small applications. The Python community prefers to call Python a *dynamic programming language.*

- **Indentation for statement grouping:** Python specifies that several statements are part of a single group by indenting them. The indented group is called a *code block.* Other languages use different syntax or punctuation for statement grouping. For example, the C programming language uses { to begin an instruction and } to end it. Indentation is considered good practice in other languages also, but Python was one of the first to *enforce* indentation. Indentation makes code easier to read, and code blocks set off with indentation have fewer begin/end words and punctuation to accidentally leave out (which means fewer bugs).

- **High-level data types:** Computers store everything in 1s and 0s, but humans need to work with data in more complex forms, such as text. A language that supports such complex data is said to have *high-level data types.* A high-level data type is easy to manipulate. For example, Python strings can be searched, sliced, joined, split, set to upper- or lowercase, or have white space removed. High-level data types in Python, such as lists and dicts (which can store other data types), encompass much more functionality than in other languages.

- **Extensibility:** An extensible programming language can be added to. These languages are very powerful because additions make them suitable for multiple applications and operating systems. Extensions can add data types or concepts, modules, and plug-ins. Python is extensible in several ways. A core group of programmers works on modifying and improving the language, while hundreds of other programmers write modules for specific purposes.

- **Interpreted:** Interpreted languages run directly from source code that humans generate (whereas programs written in *compiled languages,* like C++, must be translated to machine code before they can run). Interpreted languages run more slowly because the translation takes place on the fly, but development and debugging is faster because you don't have to wait for the compiler. Interpreted languages are easier to run on multiple operating systems. In the case of Python, it's easy to write code that works on multiple operating systems — with no need to make modifications.

People argue over whether Python is an interpreted or compiled language. Although Python works like an interpreted language in many ways, its code is compiled before execution (like Java), and many of its capabilities run at full machine speed because they're written in C — leaving you free to focus on making your application work.

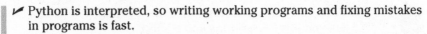

> Guido began writing Python during his Christmas vacation in 1989, and over the next year, he added to the program based on feedback from colleagues. He released it to the public in February 1991 by posting to the Usenet system of newsgroups. In Guido's words: "The rest is in the Misc/HISTORY file."

Fast development

High-level features make Python a wise alternative for prototyping and fast development of complex applications:

- ✔ Python is interpreted, so writing working programs and fixing mistakes in programs is fast.

   Programs written in interpreted languages can be tested as soon as they're written, without waiting for the code to compile.

- ✔ Python takes care of such fiddly details as memory management behind the scenes.

- ✔ Python has debugging features built in.

All these features make Python a good language for

- ✔ Off-the-cuff, quick programming

- ✔ Prototyping (sketching the design basics of complex programs, or testing particular solutions)

- ✔ Applications that change, build on themselves, and add new features frequently

Programming styles

Python is a *multi-paradigm* language (meaning it supports more than one style or philosophy of programming). This makes it good for applications that benefit from a flexible approach to programming. Python includes tools for the following paradigms:

- ✔ Object-oriented programming (OOP for short) is one of the popular programming styles that Python supports. OOP breaks up code into individual units that pass messages back and forth.

   Object-oriented programming is good for applications that have multiple parts that need to communicate with each other.

- ✔ Python has features in common with the following languages. If you know these languages, you'll find features in Python that you are familiar with, making Python easier to learn:

- **Java:** An object-oriented language especially for applications used over networks

- **Perl:** A procedural language used for text manipulation, system administration, Web development, and network programming

- **Tcl:** Used for rapid prototyping, scripting, GUIs, and testing

- **Scheme:** A functional programming language (a language that focuses on performing actions and calculations by using functions.

    For more about functions, see Chapter 11, and for an intro to functional programming, see Chapter 16.)

Python For Dummies includes a brief introduction to object-oriented programming (Chapter 13), an overview of using Python for Web development (Chapter 20), and tips for scripting and testing.

Versatility

Python *modules* (collections of features for performing tasks) let Python work with

✔ **Multiple operating systems and user interfaces**

     With *Python For Dummies*, you can write and run programs on Windows, Mac, and Unix (including Linux). Python programmers have also written code for other operating systems, from cell phones to supercomputers.

✔ **Special kinds of data (such as images and sound)**

Python comes with dozens of built-in modules. New modules can be written in either Python or C/C++.

Companies that use Python

The main portal to Python and the Python community is www.python.org. This portal contains a page that lists some companies that use Python, including

✔ Yahoo! (for Yahoo! Maps)

✔ Google (for its spider and search engine)

✔ *Linux Weekly News* (published by using a Web application written in Python)

✔ Industrial Light & Magic (used in the production of special effects for such movies as *The Phantom Menace* and *The Mummy Returns*).

Other commercial uses include financial applications, educational software, games, and business software.

Convenience

Most programming languages offer convenience features, but none boast the combination of convenience and power that Python offers:

- **Python can be embedded in other applications and used for creating macros.** For example, Python is embedded in Paint Shop Pro 8 and later versions as a scripting language.

- **Python is free for anyone to use and distribute (commercially or non-commercially),** so any individual or company can use it without paying license fees.

- **Python has powerful text manipulation and search features for applications that process a lot of text information.**

- **You can build large applications with Python, even though it doesn't check programs before they run.** In technical terms, Python doesn't have *compile-time checking*. Python supports large programs by connecting multiple modules together and bundling them into packages. Each module can be built and tested separately.

- **Python includes support for testing and error-checking both of individual modules and of whole programs.**

Sometimes, Python isn't so hot

Python by itself isn't best for applications that need to interface closely with the computer's hardware because

- **Python is an *interpreted language.***

  Interpreted languages are slower than compiled languages.

- **Python is a *high-level language*** that uses many layers to communicate with the computer's hardware and operating system.

Python might not be the best choice for building the following types of applications and systems:

- **Graphics-intensive applications, such as action games**

  But some games use Python because specialized modules can be written to interface with hardware. The pygame module is one such package. (Modern computers are extremely fast, which means it's more important to be able to write clean code quickly than to get maximum speed out of the software, except for the most graphics-intensive games.)

- **The foundations of an operating system**

The Python developer community

Python has attracted many users who collectively make up a community that

✔ Promotes Python

✔ Discusses and implements improvements to the language

✔ Supports newcomers

✔ Encourages standards and conventions that improve Python's usability and readability

✔ Values *simplicity* and *fun* (after all, Python was named after Monty Python, the British comedy troupe)

The Python community has created words to describe its philosophy:

Pythonic identifies code that meets the following criteria:

It includes interfaces or features that work well with Python.

It makes good use of Python *idioms* (standard ways of performing tasks) and shows understanding of the language.

Unpythonic code is roughly translated from other languages instead of following Python's philosophy.

Pythonistas are knowledgeable users of Python (especially users who promote the language).

Cooking Up Programs

Writing programs is a little bit like working with recipes. For example, you can

✔ **Write a recipe to make bread from scratch.**

In Python, you can build a program from scratch, writing all your own code and using only Python's basic built-in functions.

✔ **Use the product of one recipe in another recipe (for example, a recipe for turkey stuffing uses bread as an ingredient).**

After you write program that performs a basic task, you can insert it into other programs the same way you add any ingredient to a recipe.

✔ **Buy premade bread.**

Python comes with many *modules,* which are sets of programs other people have written that you can plug into your program, just like you can buy bread at the store without baking it yourself.

Python's even better than bread because most Python modules are *free!*

When you write a program, you are telling the computer to do something. *Python For Dummies* gives you step-by-step instructions that help you understand how to write the way a computer "thinks."

Unlike you, computers are pretty stupid. They can do only a few things. All the actions that humans make them do are the result of the computer's doing those few things over and over, in different combinations, very quickly.

Training your assistant

Imagine that you're a baker, and you have taken on an apprentice baker who is as stupid as a computer. If you want to show your baker how to make bread from scratch, you need to start with very basic steps. You've already started by putting warm water and sugar in a small bowl. Then you and the apprentice have this conversation:

> **You:** "Add a package of yeast."
>
> **Apprentice:** "I can't find a package of yeast."
>
> **You:** "The refrigerator is over there. Inside the refrigerator is a little package labeled *Yeast.* Go get it."
>
> The apprentice gets the package and says, "Now what?"
>
> **You:** "Put the package in the bowl."
>
> The apprentice puts the package in the bowl.
>
> **You:** "Hey! Open the package first!"

By now you might doubt the wisdom of hiring an apprentice baker who needs to be told things that seem completely obvious to you. But if you persevere, you'll come out ahead. If this apprentice is like a computer, then after finally figuring out how to bake bread in your kitchen, your new baker will be able to prepare 100 loaves a minute!

Combining ingredients

When your apprentice baker knows all the procedures involved in baking bread, such as finding the ingredients on the shelves, finding the pots and pans, mixing ingredients, and operating the oven, you can assign other tasks that use those same procedures. Baking bread involves combining ingredients in a bowl, so if you need to combine ingredients for another recipe, the apprentice already knows how to do that. So when you want to explain how to make cookies, you can now say "combine sugar, flour, and butter in a bowl" without explaining where to find the bowls or the sugar.

In Python, after you've written a program to do something, you can import it into another program. So the more you work with Python, the faster you'll be able to write programs.

Chapter 2

Getting Your Hands on the Keyboard: Using Help, Interactive Mode, and IDLE

....

In This Chapter

▶ Seeing two ways to work with Python

▶ Checking out the help system

▶ Getting interactive

▶ Writing your own scripts and modules

▶ Going native with Python's own programming environment

....

*E*ven if you haven't used Python or another programming language before, it's easy to get up and running with Python. You don't even have to know how to write a complete program because you can run Python in *interactive mode.* In interactive mode, you can tell Python what to do one instruction at a time, or you can write small portions of code to see how Python handles them. In this way you can learn by doing, trying things out at your own pace.

If you've worked with other programming languages, you're probably eager to get into the workings of Python and see how it compares. This chapter introduces you to some of the tools you'll use as you develop Python programs, as well as some of Python's basic syntax.

Ready for a full-on development experience? Or just curious what a *debugger* is? Then go on to the "IDLE Musings" section about Python's very own development environment, IDLE (Integrated DeveLopment Environment). This comprehensive set of tools supports you when you are writing, testing, and finding or fixing mistakes in programs.

In most of this book, you read and experiment on your own; it's structured so that you can pick up information without reading sequentially. However, if you're new to programming, you might find it useful to read all of this chapter and try some examples before going on to the rest of the book. In the following sections, you get a good "hands-on" foundation with Python's interpreter, which will make you more comfortable when you move on to writing your own programs.

If you want to get an overview of Python's features, jump ahead to Chapter 3. We'll be waiting for you here when you want to find out more about interactive mode or the IDLE editor/debugger.

If you need to install Python, Appendix A has the instructions.

Two Ways to Interact with Python

One of the reasons Python is easy to use is that it comes with tools that help you design, write, and debug your programs.

This chapter describes two of these tools:

- **Interactive mode:** In interactive mode, you type instructions to Python one line at a time — much the same way that an operating system (shell) accepts instructions from a command line. You can also write short multiline programs or import code from text files or from Python's built-in modules. Interactive mode includes extensive help, too. With interactive mode, you can explore Python's abilities.

- **IDLE:** The IDLE development environment includes Python's interactive mode and more — tools for writing and running programs and for keeping track of names.

  IDLE is written in Python and shows off Python's considerable abilities.

Going One-on-One in Interactive Mode

You can do most anything in interactive mode that you can do in a Python program — even write multiline programs. Think of interactive mode as

- A sandbox for experimenting safely with Python
- A tutor
- A tool to find and fix problems (bugs) in your programs

You can't save what you type in interactive mode. If you want to keep a copy of what you wrote, save your code and results in a file on your computer.

You can use interactive mode as a calculator. You can manipulate text and make assignments in interactive mode. Finally, you can import modules, functions, or parts of a longer program and test them. These features can help you

✔ Experiment with Python objects without writing long programs.

✔ Debug programs by importing parts of your program one at a time.

Starting interactive mode

To start Python's interactive mode, follow these steps:

1. **Open a command window.**

    • If you're using Mac OS X, *open the Terminal application* and *select File⇨New Shell.*

    • If you're using Windows, *open the Command Prompt window.*

    • If you're using UNIX, either *open a new shell window* or *just type in your existing shell window.*

2. **Type python.**

    When Python opens, you see the text shown in Figure 2-1.

Figure 2-1:
Python's
interactive
mode in a
Terminal
window.

```
Last login: Sun Jun 25 14:20:24 on ttyp2
Welcome to Darwin!
$python
Python 2.5b1 (r25b1:47038M, Jun 20 2006, 16:17:55)
[GCC 4.0.1 (Apple Computer, Inc. build 5341)] on darwin
Type "help", "copyright", "credits" or "license" for more information.
>>> []
```

When Python's interactive mode starts up, it tells you what version is running, the date the version was released, and a few hints about what to do next. Then it displays the Python prompt: >>>

Why computers are always saying "Hello, World!"

"Hello, World" programs are a computer programming tradition. According to the free Internet encyclopedia Wikipedia (`http://wikipedia.org`), the first instance of a computer program that printed "Hello, World" occurred in 1973, in a book called *A Tutorial Introduction to the Language B,* by Brian Kernighan. Since then, a "Hello, World!" program has been written for almost every computer language. Wikipedia lists more than 170 "Hello, World!" programs written in languages from 4GL and ActionScript to UNIX shell and XUL.

One reason that "Hello, World" programs are popular is that a program that prints a single statement is usually the shortest working program in a language.

✔ In Python, the shortest working program is one line long.

✔ In Java, the program is five lines long.

Aren't you glad you're using Python?

Following the rules of engagement

The basic method for working with interactive mode is simply this:

1. **Type a statement or expression.**

2. **Press the Return or Enter key.**

When you press Return, Python interprets your input and responds if what you typed calls for a response or if the interpreter doesn't understand what you typed.

In the following example, the statement tells Python to print a string. Because the statement doesn't specify where to print the string, Python prints it to the screen (the default behavior in interactive mode).

```
>>> print "Hello, World!"
Hello, World!
```

This statement is a whole Python program! Pretty simple, eh? When you use interactive mode, Python processes each line of code you type as soon as you press Return (unless it sees that you are writing a multiline chunk of code), and the results appear underneath.

Seeing information about a Python object

In interactive mode, there are two ways to see information about an object:

✔ Type the object (or its name) and press Return.

✔ Type the `print` command and the object (or its name) and press Return.

What you see depends on what the object is.

✔ With some data types (integers and lists, for example), the two methods of seeing the value give the same result — as in this example, in which the name stores a list:

```
>>> x = [3,2]
>>> x
[3, 2]
>>> print x
[3, 2]
```

✔ With strings, the result of typing `print` *name* and pressing Return is slightly different from the result you get by typing *name* and pressing Return. When you just type *name* and press Return, the value is surrounded by quotation marks, but when you type `print` *name* and press Return, there are no quotation marks. (To find out why, see the sidebar, "Representing data".)

This example shows the difference between using just the name and using the `print` statement with the name:

```
>>> x = "mystring"
>>> x
'mystring'
>>> print x
mystring
```

✔ When the name refers to a code block (for example, a function, module, or class instance), looking at the name shows you information such as the kind of data, the name, and the storage location.

This example creates a class called `Message` and displays information about the class:

```
>>> class Message:
...     pass
...
>>> Message
<class __main__.Message at 0x58db0>
>>> print Message
__main__.Message
```

Representing data

Why do you sometimes see different results when you type *name* and when you type print *name*? Just typing *name* and pressing Return is a shortcut for using the function repr() to display the result, whereas the print command uses the function str() to display the result.

In technical terms, when you type an object name, literal, expression, or statement and press Return, Python *evaluates* the object. That is, Python runs the code and returns/displays the result.

According to Python's built-in documentation, the function str() returns a "nice" string representation of an object. The function repr() returns the "canonical" string representation of the object. Here's the difference between a "nice" and a "canonical" representation of a floating point number:

```
>>> 3.2              # canonical
3.2000000000000002
>>> str(3.2)         # nice
'3.2'
>>> repr(3.2)        # canonical
'3.2000000000000002'
>>> print 3.2        # nice
3.2
```

The canonical representation usually tries to be a chunk of text that, when pasted into the interpreter, re-creates the object. This example shows how:

```
>>> mytuple = (3, 4)
>>> mylist = [1, "2", mytuple]
>>> print repr(mylist)
[1, '2', (3, 4)]
>>> mylist == [1, '2', (3, 4)]
True
```

(Note that some objects, such as files, can't be re-created by repr(). You can still use the output of repr() as debugging info when working with such objects.)

Here's an example of what str() and repr() return when you give them a class as an argument:

```
>>> class Message:
...     pass
...
>>> str(Message)
'__main__.Message'
>>> repr(Message)
'<class __main__.Message at 0x58e40>'
```

Seeing the result of the last expression

When you type an expression by itself in interactive mode, or when Python returns an expression as a result of something you typed, Python also stores the value of the expression in a special name: _ (an underscore character). This name is available only in interactive mode. To see the value stored, type _.

```
>>> "Hello, World!"
'Hello, World!'
>>> _
'Hello, World!'
```

Note that _ doesn't store the results of any *statements* (assignments such as x=25 or commands such as print). In the following example, _ continues to hold the value of the expression even after a statement was typed:

```
>>> "Hello, Nurse!"
'Hello, Nurse!'
>>> x = 35
>>> _
'Hello, Nurse!'
```

Don't rely on _ in long segments of code. The value stored in _ may change unexpectedly if you aren't paying close attention to the difference between statements and expressions.

Manipulating strings and lists

You can use Python's interactive mode to see a few of the interesting tricks Python can do with string and list data. (We cover strings and lists in Chapters 6 and 8.)

Of printing, commas, and space

When you want to print several strings, or a string and the value of a name, you can use a comma to stand for a single space in the printed output. The following example shows the comma in action:

```
>>> y = "The meaning of Life, the Universe, and Everything is"
>>> x = 42
>>> print y, x
The meaning of Life, the Universe, and Everything is 42
```

Measuring and splitting strings

The function len() returns the length of a string, as illustrated here:

```
>>> x = "supercalifragilisticexpialidocious"
>>> len(x)
34
```

len() works with other sequence data types, too — for example, if you give it a list as an argument, it returns the number of items in the list.

The method split() breaks a string into separate words and returns a list of the words, like this:

```
>>> x = "This is an ex-parrot!"
>>> x.split()
['This', 'is', 'an', 'ex-parrot!']
```

The split() method actually breaks a string wherever it finds white space, so sometimes it doesn't break the string where you expect — for example:

```
>>> 'one and/or two'.split()
['one', 'and/or', 'two']
```

Using interactive mode as a calculator

The Python interpreter can be used like a calculator. If you just want to do simple calculations, you can type numbers and operators and press Return to see the result, as in the following example:

```
>>> (1 + 3) * (2 + 2)
16
>>> 1 + 3 * 2 + 2
9
```

Don't use an equals sign (=) when doing calculations like these. In Python, an equals sign gives a name to a value. If you use = to try to get the result of a calculation, Python gives you an error message:

```
>>> 1 + 3 * 2 + 2 =
  File "<stdin>", line 1
    1 + 3 * 2 + 2 =
                  ^
SyntaxError: invalid syntax
```

You can also use names to do math in the Python interpreter. This is easier when doing calculations with several steps, like the following:

```
>>> x = 1 + 3
>>> y = 2 + 2
>>> x * y
16
```

If you type all whole numbers (integers) when you're doing arithmetic, Python returns the result in integers. If you want precise results in calculations involving division, be sure that at least one of the numbers in a calculation is a decimal number, or type the statement from __future__ import division before doing your calculations. Doing the latter imports the true division feature from a special module called __future__, which contains improvements that will be automatically activated in later versions of Python. To find out more about using Python to do division, see Chapter 7.

These examples show how to get correct division results:

```
>>> 13/3      # That can't be right.
4
>>> 13.0/3    # That's more like it.
4.333333333333333
>>> from __future__ import division
>>> 13/3
4.333333333333333
```

Working with built-in functions

In addition to the standard arithmetic operators such as + and *, you have access to a number of math functions and other functions built into the Python interpreter, and more such functions are available in the math module.

Functions are pieces of code that

✔ Carry out specific operations.

✔ Return the results of those operations.

To work with a function, you need to *call* it, and you usually need to pass it one or more *arguments* — data you want it to act on. You call a function by adding parentheses at the end of the function name. Any arguments you pass to the function go inside the parentheses.

Getting help on a function

To get help on built-in functions, type `help` with the name of the function in parentheses.

The help usually tells you how many arguments the function takes. If an argument is in square brackets (`[]`), it's an optional argument. If you leave out an optional argument, a default value is used.

The help for `round()`, displayed here, shows that `round()` takes one required argument and one optional argument (the number of digits to the right of the decimal point, which defaults to 0):

```
>>> help(round)
Help on built-in function round:

round(...)
    round(number[, ndigits]) -> floating point number


    Round a number to a given precision in decimal digits (default 0 digits).
    This always returns a floating point number.  Precision may be negative.
```

The following examples call a built-in function named round(), which takes a decimal (or floating point) number as an argument. It rounds off the number to the nearest whole number and returns the result.

```
>>> round(9.9)
10.0
>>> round(9.3)
9.0
```

Examining names

When working in interactive mode, you sometimes need to be reminded what names you've given to objects. The dir() function, which is built into interactive mode, lists the names (such as names of data objects, module names, and function names) that are stored in the interactive mode's *namespace* at any particular point in your coding session. (*Namespace* is a Python term for a list of names that a particular part of a program knows about.)

You can also use the dir() function to examine the contents of modules.

Examining the namespace

The following example shows what happens when you start Python's interactive mode (so you have not defined anything yet), use dir() to see what is defined, and then give a value to a name and use dir() again:

```
% python
Python 2.5b1 (r25b1:47038M, Jun 20 2006, 16:17:55)

>>> dir()
['__builtins__', '__doc__', '__name__']
>>> too_many_cats = "Impossible!"
>>> dir()
['__builtins__', '__doc__', '__name__', 'too_many_cats']
```

After you give a value the name too_many_cats, the namespace remembers that name and gives you the value if you ask for it, like this:

```
>>> too_many_cats
'Impossible!'
```

Examining a module

The __builtins__ module defines some exceptions (error-handling code), functions, and constants. To see what's in the __builtins__ module, simply type dir(__builtins__).

There are a lot of things in that __builtins__ module! The following example shows the contents of the credits *constant* for Python 2.5. (A constant, like a name, stores data, but the data inside a constant shouldn't be changed.)

```
>>> credits
    Thanks to CWI, CNRI, BeOpen.com, Zope Corporation and a cast of thousands
    for supporting Python development.  See www.python.org for more information.
```

The capitalized names in the __builtins__ module are *exceptions*, messages that Python sends when it encounters errors and other unusual conditions. These are all part of a module called exceptions, which you can see if you type one of the names into interactive mode:

```
>>> ArithmeticError
<type 'exceptions.ArithmeticError'>
```

Writing multiline programs in interactive mode

You can write multiline programs or parts of programs in interactive mode. However, note that interactive mode doesn't let you save your work, so you might also want to save the code in a text file.

The following example program prints some kilometer/mile conversions. Here's how it looks when typed into a text editor. (If you don't understand everything the code does, don't worry. String formatting is explained in Chapter 6.)

```
for miles in range(10, 70, 10):
    km = miles * 1.609
    print "%d miles --> %3.2f kilometers" % (miles, km)
```

Note that some lines are indented. Indentation is very important in Python because it's how Python tells when you are using a code block (several lines of code that are grouped together). Four spaces is standard for one level of indentation (the lines starting with km and print), eight spaces for two levels, and so on.

Here's how the same program looks when you start to type it in interactive mode. When you press Return after the first line, the interpreter recognizes that you're writing a code block and displays a continuation prompt: . . . (three dots). Even though you see a continuation prompt, you still need to indent the lines that are part of the code block, so don't forget to add four spaces before starting the km assignment and the print statement.

```
>>> for miles in range(10, 70, 10):
...     km = miles * 1.609
...     print "%d miles --> %3.2f  kilometers" % (miles, km)
...
```

Okay, we admit it: We sometimes make our thumbs happier by adding only two spaces when we're working in interactive mode. For actual programs that others might see, though, it's a Good Idea to use four spaces.

When you are finished with the code block, you press Return at the continuation prompt without typing anything. The interpreter runs the code, which gives this result:

```
10 miles --> 16.09  kilometers
20 miles --> 32.18  kilometers
30 miles --> 48.27  kilometers
40 miles --> 64.36  kilometers
50 miles --> 80.45  kilometers
60 miles --> 96.54  kilometers
```

When you run a code block in interactive mode, the names you've defined in the namespace retain the values they were given last.

```
>>> print km
96.54
>>> print miles
60
```

Quitting interactive mode

To exit Python's interactive mode, press Control-D (on Mac or UNIX) or Ctrl-Z (on Windows).

If you type quit, Python reminds you what to do, like this:

```
>>> quit
'Use Ctrl-D (i.e. EOF) to exit.'
```

If you have Python 2.5, you can still use Control-D or Control-Z (depending on your operating system) to quit, or you can type quit() or exit() (both work on all operating systems). The reminder if you type quit without the parentheses is a little different (this is the reminder on UNIX):

```
>>> quit
Use quit() or Ctrl-D (i.e. EOF) to exit
```

When you exit interactive mode, you return to the command prompt of your Terminal window or Command Prompt window.

When you quit the Python interpreter, all the values you've given names disappear. If you want to keep your work, copy any code you want to save into a text file.

Getting Help

Beyond *Python For Dummies,* many other sources of Python help are available to you. One of the most complete sources is Python's built-in help system.

The help built into Python assumes that you have some knowledge of programming and about Python. If you're new to programming, some of the help topics might look pretty daunting. But after you get a handle on some of the terminology, it gets easier!

Help in interactive mode

You can access Python's help system from interactive mode. There are two ways to use help.

Entering the help program

You can run the help system as a separate program inside the Python interactive mode environment. The help system has its own prompt. To go into help mode, follow these steps:

1. **Type** `help()` **at the Python prompt.**

   The help program opens, and you see a welcome message and some suggested topics. Then it displays the help prompt:

   ```
   help>
   ```

2. **Type the name of an item you want to know about.**

   For example, you can get help about the list data type and its methods:

   ```
   help> list
   ```

3. **To quit help mode, type** `quit` **at the help mode prompt.**

   When you quit help, you go back to Python's interactive mode, and you see the Python prompt again:

   ```
   >>>
   ```

Using help without leaving interactive mode

You can also use help to get a tip about a particular item without leaving interactive mode. To get help about a particular item, follow these steps:

1. **At the Python prompt, type** `help` **followed by the name of the item you want to find out about in parentheses.**

   For example, to get help about the `list` data type, type

   ```
   >>> help(list)
   ```

   If the information is less than one screenful, you go back to the interactive mode prompt automatically.

   If there's more information, follow Step 2.

2. **If the information is longer than one screen, press the spacebar to see more.**

   When you finishe, type `q` to go back to the interactive mode prompt.

Some installations of Python — for example, the installation on Mac OS X 10.3 (Panther) or 10.4 (Tiger) — don't come with all the Python help installed. If you see a message in the help program that documentation cannot be found, you can install the documentation (follow steps 1–3 in the next section, "Getting help in a Web browser") and tell Python where to look for it. One way to do this, if you're using Mac OS X or UNIX, is to set the PYTHONDOCS *environment variable* to the folder path containing the documentation. The way you do this depends on which UNIX shell (operating system) you are using. Here's how you do it in Mac OS X's Terminal window, using the default bash shell (replace the path with the correct path for your docs):

```
export PYTHONDOCS=/Library/PythonDocs
```

Getting help in a Web browser

If you want to keep Python documentation open in a separate window while you work, you're in luck. The Python documentation is in HTML format, so you can keep it open in a Web browser window.

Follow these steps to keep the Python documentation readily available for your use:

1. **Open your Web browser.**

2. **Type** `www.python.org/doc/` **in your browser's address box and press Return.**

This Web site archives documentation for every version of Python that has been released. The documentation for the most recent version is available at www.python.org/doc/current/.

3. **Follow the online instructions to download the correct version of the help files.**

4. **Make a bookmark in your Web browser to the location of the downloaded help files.**

   Doing this sets up the Python documentation so you can access it quickly.

5. **To open the help files in your Web browser while you're working with Python, just select the help file bookmark from your Web browser's bookmark list.**

Using Scripts and Modules

Because Python's interactive mode doesn't save any of your work when you quit, you'll want to store your important work in text files. Text files that contain Python code are called *scripts* (if they are whole programs) or *modules* (if they contain chunks of code meant to be imported into other programs).

Both scripts and modules end with the suffix .py.

Actually, the distinction between scripts and modules is fuzzier than that because some modules include code that lets them stand on their own or that gives information about their status . . . and some programs can be imported as modules.

Running a script from the command line

When you run a Python script from the command line of your shell or Terminal program, it behaves like other programs you run from the command line — when it's finished running, you get another command prompt. To run a script from the command line (indicated by the command prompt %), type python and the name of the script, like this:

```
% python script.py
```

If you run a script from the command line, you use the -i modifier to tell Python to go into interactive mode after you run it. To create a script and run it interactively on a command line, follow these steps:

1. **Use a text editor to write your script.**

   For example, you might type the following in a text editor:

   ```
   print "testing how scripts and interactive mode communicate"
   x = 500
   print "The value of x is ", x
   ```

2. **Save your script and give it a name.**

   Use the .py suffix for the name.

   Our script is called tinyscript.py.

3. **To run the script from the command line, type** python -i **followed by the name of the script (including the** .py **suffix).**

   When you run the script, Python executes its code and then enters interactive mode (you can tell because you see the >>> prompt).

   ```
   % python -i tinyscript.py
   testing how scripts and interactive mode communicate
   The value of x is  500
   >>>
   ```

   The names that are part of tinyscript.py are now available in interactive mode. To test this, type dir() and print the value of any of your script's names.

   ```
   >>> dir()
   ['__builtins__', '__doc__', '__file__', '__name__', 'x']
   >>> print x
   500
   ```

Importing a module in interactive mode

Modules are text files containing Python code that's designed to be used inside another program. To work with a module, you need to *import* it. When you import the module, Python runs the module's code and stores the module's name in the namespace.

There are two ways to import modules: You can *import the module name* or you can *import one or more of the names defined inside the module.*

The following examples import the module tinymodule.py, which includes the following function:

```
def tinyfunction(x):
    print "testing how modules and interactive mode communicate"
    print "You passed me the parameter", x
```

```
z = x**2
print x, "squared is", z
return z
```

Importing by name

Importing a module by name stores the module name in the namespace. But it does not directly import any names that are defined in the module.

To import a module by name, type `import` followed by the name of the module *without* the `.py` suffix, like this:

```
>>> import tinymodule
```

To make sure that the module's name has been imported, type `dir()`.

```
>>> dir()
['__builtins__', '__doc__', '__name__', 'tinymodule']
```

To use an item inside a module you've imported by name, you need to tell Python both the module name and the name of the item. (The items inside modules are collectively called *attributes* of the module.) This is similar to handing someone a book and telling them to find a chapter inside it.

To access an attribute of a module, type the module name, a dot, and the attribute name.

In this example, we call the `tinyfunction()` attribute in the `tinymodule` module, and we give a name to its result. This causes Python to run the code in the function. Here's the result:

```
>>> x = tinymodule.tinyfunction(2)
testing how modules and interactive mode communicate
you passed me the parameter 2
2 squared is 4
```

The `tinyfunction()` function also returns a value. To see it, we print the name we gave to the function:

```
>>> print x
4
```

Importing items from inside a module

Importing items from inside a module stores their names in the namespace, which gives you direct access to the items — you don't have to type the module name to use them. But this method doesn't store the name of the *module* in the namespace.

To import the function that's inside `tinymodule`, type this:

```
>>> from tinymodule import tinyfunction
```

To check what's stored in the namespace, type `dir()`. *Note:* If you didn't quit Python after doing the example in the previous section, "Importing by name," you might see other names as well when you type `dir()`.

```
>>> dir()
['__builtins__', '__doc__', '__name__', 'tinyfunction']
```

 Importing a module by name is the recommended way of getting access to a module and its functions. Although importing items from inside a module is useful in some situations, this can cause problems if the items have the same names as other items you're working with.

Using Python's standard modules in interactive mode

Python comes with dozens of modules that add functionality when you want it but stay out of your way when you don't.

Listing Python's modules

To see the list of built-in modules, follow these steps:

1. **In Python interactive mode, type** `help()` **and press Return to start the help utility.**

2. **At the** `help>` **prompt, type** `modules`, **like this:**

```
help> modules
Please wait a moment while I gather a list of all available modules...
```

Why modularizing is a good idea

Why doesn't Python automatically import all of its built-in modules? First of all, importing all of its modules would take a LOOOONG time. Second, if it did, there would be thousands of names stored in the namespace, and you wouldn't be able to give those names to your own data — or if you did use them, you might get unexpected results. Because you need to import modules, stuff you don't use stays out of your way, like storing your winter clothes in the attic until October.

Whoa! That's a lot of modules. But don't worry. You can drive a car without knowing exactly how everything under the hood works, and the same goes for working with Python. *Python For Dummies* explains the workings of many of Python's modules and shows you where to go to discover more about the rest.

The list of modules differs depending on your version of Python, your operating system, and the third-party modules that may have been installed for Python.

Listing the contents of an imported module

The names inside a module might include value assignments, other modules that the module imports, functions, classes, and so on.

To see the names that belong to a module you've imported — either a .py file you wrote yourself or one of Python's modules — type dir() with the name of the module inside the parentheses. For example, to import the math module that comes with Python and list its functions, follow these steps:

1. **At the Python prompt, type** import math.

2. **To list the names (functions and constants) that the** math **module defines, type** dir(math).

   Python displays the contents of the math module.

Getting interactive help for a module's functions

The help information for a large module can be many pages long. If you know the function you want, here's how to get help for that function specifically:

1. **Make sure the module has been imported.**

2. **Type** help(*module_name.function_name*).

   Be sure to include the parentheses and the dot between the module name and the function name.

This example shows the help for one of the functions in the math module:

```
>>> help(math.pow)
Help on built-in function pow in module math:

pow(...)
    pow(x,y)

    Return x**y (x to the power of y).
```

IDLE Musings

IDLE stands for *Interactive DeveLopment Environment.* (Other computer languages have such environments too, but they're usually called IDEs. Python's is called IDLE after Eric Idle of Monty Python fame.) IDLE is an editing program written entirely in Python by Guido van Rossum.

IDLE is installed when you install any recent version of Python, but it doesn't always come with versions of Python that are preinstalled on your computer, such as with the Mac OS X. You can find instructions for installing Python in Appendix A.

Opening IDLE

When you open IDLE, you see a window called Python Shell, as shown in Figure 2-2. Depending on your version of IDLE, you might also see other windows; you can safely ignore them for now.

Figure 2-2:
IDLE's
Python Shell
window on
Mac OS.

```
○ ○ ○                        Python Shell
Python 2.5b1 (r25b1:47038M, Jun 20 2006, 16:17:55)
[GCC 4.0.1 (Apple Computer, Inc. build 5341)] on darwin
Type "copyright", "credits" or "license()" for more information.

        *******************************************************************
        Personal firewall software may warn about the connection IDLE
        makes to its subprocess using this computer's internal loopback
        interface.  This connection is not visible on any external
        interface and no data is sent to or received from the Internet.
        *******************************************************************

IDLE 1.2b1
>>>
```

The Python Shell window runs in interactive mode; it displays the Python prompt, >>>.

Typing statements and programs in the Python Shell

Interactive mode in IDLE works much the same as interactive mode in a shell window running Python. Here are some differences:

✔ **The code you type is colorized to make it easier to distinguish one part of a statement from another.**

✔ When you write multiline statements, IDLE does not display the . . . continuation prompt.

✔ IDLE automatically indents lines for you.

Figure 2-3 shows IDLE's Python Shell window with the miles/kilometers conversion program we introduce in the section, "Writing multiline programs in interactive mode," earlier in this chapter (colorizing is not shown — it's a black-and-white book!).

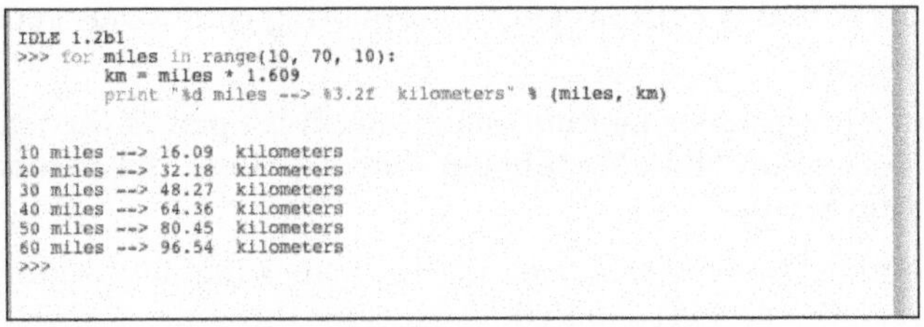

Figure 2-3:
A program
and its
result in
IDLE's
Python Shell
window on
Mac OS.

```
IDLE 1.2b1
>>> for miles in range(10, 70, 10):
        km = miles * 1.609
        print "%d miles --> %3.2f kilometers" % (miles, km)

10 miles --> 16.09  kilometers
20 miles --> 32.18  kilometers
30 miles --> 48.27  kilometers
40 miles --> 64.36  kilometers
50 miles --> 80.45  kilometers
60 miles --> 96.54  kilometers
>>>
```

Getting more help for IDLE

IDLE also has built-in help — look in the Help menu.

A good "getting started" Web page for a recent version of IDLE is here:

```
http://hkn.eecs.berkeley.edu/~dyoo/python/idle_intro
```

The following pages have additional documentation that you'll find useful, but they are based on earlier versions:

✔ www.ai.uga.edu/mc/idle/index.html (based on IDLE 1.0.2)

✔ www.python.org/idle/doc (based on IDLE 0.5)

Clever Python Shell features

Here are a couple of time-saving features of IDLE's Python Shell:

✔ Putting your insertion point or cursor in a line of code and pressing Enter inserts a copy of the code on a new line for editing.

✔ Typing the opening parenthesis for a function call or method call pops up a small box with a helpful tip or a list of expected arguments.

Writing and editing code with IDLE's text editor

IDLE includes a text editor for opening, editing, and creating modules and scripts. Here are some of its key features:

- ✔ **To open a new text editing window, choose File⇨New Window.**
- ✔ **To open an existing module or script for editing, choose File⇨Open.**
- ✔ **The Format menu available when you're working in the text editing window contains Python-specific formatting commands such as Indent Region.**
- ✔ **To run a program or module, make sure it is open in the text editor and choose Run⇨Run Module (on some versions, the command is File⇨Run Script).**

  The Python Shell restarts (clearing any names that it was storing from the previous session) and Python executes the code.

Briefly meet a few other IDLE commands

IDLE has Find commands (in the Find menu or Edit menu) to search for text in the frontmost IDLE window. It also has a Find in Files command that searches all files in the Python search path or a subset of those files.

With the Path Browser (available from the File menu), you can examine and open any Python code that is in the Python path. (The Path Browser is shown in Figure 2-4.) To navigate the path, click the + buttons to expand a folder. To open a .py file in the text editor, double-click it. To highlight a class or method in the .py file, double-click it in the Path Browser.

Figure 2-4:
The IDLE
Path
Browser.

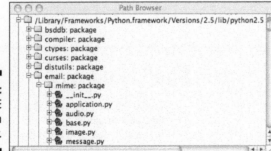

Debugging in IDLE

When you run code in IDLE's interactive mode, it informs you of errors the same way you've seen when using interactive mode in a Terminal or shell window.

When you run code from the text editor, IDLE also informs you of errors. Depending on the kind of error and on your version of IDLE, the error message appears in a dialog box or in the Python Shell window.

You can use the IDLE debugger to step through your program in various ways and display the values of names. The IDLE debugger is shown in Figure 2-5.

On the Mac OS, the IDLE debugger that comes with Python 2.4 and earlier has a bug(!). When you open the debugger window, you must immediately resize it; otherwise, IDLE will hang.

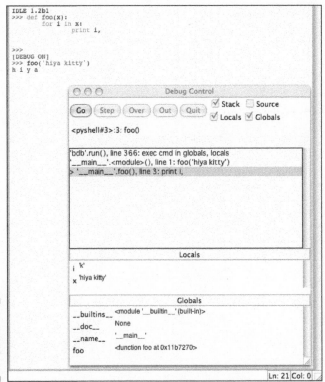

Figure 2-5:
The IDLE debugger at work.

Chapter 3

Basic Elements and Syntax

- -

In This Chapter

▶ Wading through some Python terminology

▶ Finding out about Python building blocks

▶ Getting used to Python syntax

- -

*T*his chapter briefly introduces some of the bits and pieces that make up the Python programming language. You find out about names and the differences between statements and expressions. We introduce several types of data and operators that work on these data types. We also explain how to include documentation in your program as well as how to understand error messages Python might give you. Finally, you get a taste of various kinds of control structures, loops, and other code blocks available in Python.

Making Names and Storing Values

In most programming languages, there are ways to associate a name or variable with a value. Here's an example of such a statement in Python:

```
num = 45
```

Many programming languages call a statement such as num = 45 "assigning a value to a variable." But Python doesn't really have variables (you don't need to know why), so this book uses the term *name* instead of *variable*.

In Python, a name *refers* to an object. A name is actually a label for a memory location in the computer that stores something — a value, a chunk of code, or any sort of thing Python understands. All these "things" — anything that's stored in a memory location — are called *objects* in Python. Therefore, Python programmers often say that when you enter a statement such as $x = 5$ in Python, you are *binding a name* (x) *to an object* (5). You can have multiple names for the same object.

The = symbol (a single equals sign) tells Python to associate a name with a value. When making an assignment, the name is always on the left, and the value is on the right, as in this example:

```
myname = "myvalue"
```

When you've given a name to a value, the name stands in for the value when you are writing code. For example, if you've already created the assignment myname = "myvalue", the following two statements do the same thing — they assign the name mynewname to the value "myvalue":

```
mynewname = "myvalue"
mynewname = myname
```

There are other ways to give a name to a value. For example, you can give a name to the result of a calculation or the information that a function returns. The def statement (which defines a function) and the class statement (which defines a class) also create names.

Naming rules

You can use any names you want, as long as they follow these rules:

✔ **Names must start with either a letter or an underscore character (_).**

✔ **You can't use any of Python's *reserved words* or *keywords*.**

These are words that have specific meanings to Python, such as if (which begins an if statement).

✔ **Names are case-sensitive.** num is different from NUM and nUm.

✔ **By convention, most Python programmers use lowercase for names that stand for values.** They use other rules for names that stand for functions and classes — you can find out more about these conventions in later chapters.

✔ **It's a Good Idea to use meaningful names.** If you name everything with a single letter, for example, you may have trouble remembering what the name stands for later.

Statements and expressions: Seeing the difference

Python code consists of *statements* and *expressions.* Knowing these terms isn't essential to writing basic code, but sometimes they help you to understand an error in your code (for example, you can't use a statement where an expression is required).

A *literal* is a chunk of text in a Python program that specifies the value for one of the basic Python data types (such as a string or number). When you run your program, Python creates an object with the literal's value.

A *statement* is like a command — it tells Python to do something. For example, the statement x = 25 tells Python to give the name x to the value 25, and print x tells Python to display the value of x.

An *expression* is one or more operations that produce a result. The operations can involve names, operators, literals, and function or method calls.

It's easiest to show the difference between expressions and statements by example. Note in these examples that when you enter an *expression* in the interpreter, the interpreter prints it, but when you enter a *statement* (which doesn't create any output — except for print statements), nothing visible happens:

```
>>> "monty python"   # This is an expression and a literal.
'monty python'
>>> x = 25            # This is a statement. 25 is a literal.
>>> x                 # This is an expression.
25
>>> 2 in [1, 2, 3]   # This is also an expression.
True
>>> def foo():        # This is a statement.
...     return 1     # return is a statement; 1 is an expression.
...
>>> foo()             # foo is a name; foo() is an expression.
1
```

Note that Python allows you to put multiple statements on a line by separating each statement with a semicolon, but you should avoid this because it makes programs less readable:

```
>>> x = 1; y = 2
>>> x, y
(1, 2)
```

Data Type Does Matter

When you write computer programs, you usually want to give the computer information (data) and have it do things with the data and give you results. Programming languages like Python have several *data types* that you do different things with.

You decide which data type to use depending on what you want to do. For example, if you want to do mathematical calculations, you might choose a number data type.

The following list briefly introduces some of Python's data types:

- ✔ **Numbers** are for data that you want to do math with.
- ✔ **Strings** are for text characters and for binary data.
- ✔ **Sequences** are for lists of related data that you might want to sort, merge, and so on.
- ✔ **Dictionaries** are collections of data that associate a unique key with each value.
- ✔ **Sets** are for doing set operations (finding the intersection, difference, and so on) with multiple values.
- ✔ **Files** are for data that is or will be stored as a document on a computer.

Numeric data

Python has four built-in numeric data types, as shown in Table 3-1.

Table 3-1	Python's Built-In Numeric Data Types	
Type (keyword)	*Example*	*Used for . . .*
Plain integers (`int`) and long integers (`long`)	7 6666666666L	Whole numbers (long integers are very large whole numbers.)
Floating point numbers (`float`)	1.1714285714285713	Real numbers
Complex numbers (`complex`)	(3+4j)	Imaginary numbers
Decimal numbers (`decimal.Decimal`)	decimal.Decimal("181.2")	Calculations requiring decimal arithmetic

Except when you're doing division with integers or using the `decimal` module (see Chapter 7), you don't have to worry about what kind of number data type you're using. Python converts numbers into compatible types automatically. For example, if you multiply an integer and a floating point number, Python automatically gives the answer as a floating point number:

```
>>> x = 5
>>> y = 1.5
>>> x * y
7.5
```

For more information about numbers and number data types, see Chapter 7.

Sequential data

Sequential data types contain multiple pieces of data, each of which is numbered, or *indexed*. Each piece of data inside a sequence is called an *element*.

The cool thing about sequential data types is that you can manipulate the whole sequence, chunks of the sequence, or individual elements inside the sequence.

Three sequential data types are built into Python:

✔ **Lists** can store multiple kinds of data (both text and numbers, for example). You can change elements inside a list, and you can organize the data in various ways (for example, by sorting).

✔ **Tuples,** like lists, can include different kinds of data, but they can't be changed. In Python terminology, they are *immutable*.

✔ **Strings** store text or binary data. Strings are immutable (like tuples).

Table 3-2 introduces Python's built-in sequential data types.

Table 3-2		Python's Built-in Sequence Data Types	
Type (Name)	*Kind*	*Example*	*Used for . . .*
`str` (String)	Immutable	`x = "monty python"`	Storing text
`tuple` (Tuple)	Immutable	`x = ("a", 2, "33")`	Storing a set of items you want fast access to
`list` (List)	Mutable	`x = ['here', 'is', 'my', 'list', 47]`	Storing a set of items you want to be able to change readily

To see the data type of a Python object, use the `type()` function, like this:

```
>>> type('foo')
<type 'str'>
```

Dictionaries

Python's dictionary (its keyword is `dict`) is a data type that stores multiple data items (*elements*) of different types. In a dictionary, each element is associated with a unique *key,* which is a value of any immutable type. When you use a dict, you use the key to return the element associated with the key.

You use a dictionary when you want to store and retrieve items by using a key that doesn't change and when you don't care in what order Python stores the items. (In dictionaries, elements aren't numbered.)

Here's what a Python dictionary is not: A Python dictionary bears only a small resemblance to the kind of dictionary that contains words and their definitions. In Python, a dictionary is more like a list of employees and their employee numbers. Because each employee number is unique, you can look up that employee by typing his or her number.

Dictionaries are mutable, like lists, but their keys are immutable.

Here is an example of a dictionary with two key:value pairs:

```
swallow_velocity = {"european" : "47", "african" : "69"}
```

You can find out much more about using dictionaries in Chapter 9.

Sets

A set stores multiple items, which can be of different types, but each item in a set must be unique. You can use Python sets to find unions, intersections, differences, and so on — just like the sets that probably annoyed you in school.

One use for sets is when you have repetitious data and you want to ignore the repetition. For example, imagine that you have an address database and you want to find out which cities are represented, but you don't need to know how many times each city appears in the database. A set will list each city in the database only once.

The syntax for a set is a little different from the syntax of the other data types described in this section. You use the word `set` followed by a name (or a group of elements) in parentheses. Here is a set that finds each unique element in a list. You'll notice that the elements are out of order in the set. That's because Python doesn't store set elements in alphanumeric order (the same is true for dicts):

```
>>> mylist = ['spam', 'lovely', 'spam', 'glorious', 'spam']
>>> set(mylist)
set(['lovely', 'glorious', 'spam'])
```

Files

Python uses the `file` data type to work with files on your computer or on the Internet. Note that the `file` type is not the same as the actual file. The `file` type is Python's *internal representation* of a computer or Internet file.

Before Python can work with an existing file or a new file, you need to open the file inside Python.

This example opens a file called `myfile`:

```
open("myfile")
```

You can do a lot with files in Python. Check out Part IV to find out more.

Data types have methods

In Python, each data type has built-in actions associated with it, which let you do various things with the data. These actions are called *methods*. Methods are tailored to work efficiently with their particular data types.

Calling a method — An example

Here's an example of how you use, or *call,* a method on a piece of data. Strings (text characters inside quotation marks) come with a method called `upper()`, which makes all the characters uppercase. To use the `upper()` method on a string, follow these steps:

1. **Give a name to the string, like this:**

```
>>> zed = "lowercase string"
```

2. **Type the name, a dot, the method name, and a set of parentheses.**

   This example changes the `zed` string's characters to uppercase:

   ```
   >>> zed.upper()
   'LOWERCASE STRING'
   ```

Incidentally, you can also use methods with values that haven't been given names. For example, the code `"hi".upper()` gives the result `'HI'`. One method that's commonly used this way is the string method `join()`, which combines strings. Most of the time, however, it's good practice to give names to values before using methods on them.

Passing information to a method

The parentheses at the end of a method — for example, `upper()` — tell Python to perform the action associated with the method (that is, to *call* the method).

If you forget the parentheses, Python gives you some information about the method object instead, as in this example:

```
>>> 'mystring'.upper
<built-in method upper of str object at 0x82071a0>
```

The parentheses have another use, too. When calling some methods, you sometimes need to include additional information about how the method should act. You put this information (also called the *argument*) inside the parentheses. This is called *passing data* (or *passing an argument*) to the method.

For example, here's how you would use a list method called `append()` to get Python to add an item to a list:

1. **Give a name to a list with several text strings like this:**

   ```
   >>> shopping_list = ['eggs', 'bacon', 'spam']
   ```

2. **To add an item to the `shopping_list` list, type the list name, a dot, the method name, and a new item inside parentheses, like this:**

   ```
   >>> shopping_list.append('butter')
   ```

   You can type the list name again to see the new contents of the list:

   ```
   >>> shopping_list
   ['eggs', 'bacon', 'spam', 'butter']
   ```

Operators Are Standing By

Operators are another tool for working with data. You'll recognize arithmetic symbols such as + and / for addition and division, but Python also comes with operators that cut up text, check whether two objects have the same value, and so on. This section introduces several kinds of Python operators:

✔ **Arithmetic:** The math symbols we're all familiar with as well as some less-well-known ones.

✔ **Comparison:** These operators tell you which of several things is bigger.

✔ **Logical or Boolean:** These operators test whether things are true or false.

✔ **Conditional:** This operator allows you to choose one of two values based on a logical test.

Arithmetic operators

Python understands a variety of math symbols. Here are a few of them:

✔ **Plus** (+): Addition

✔ **Parentheses** (()): Grouping

✔ **Asterisk** (*): Multiplication

✔ **Double asterisk** (**): Exponentiation (x to the power of y)

Some of these operators also work on data types other than numbers, but they may work differently. For example, + adds two numbers (2 + 2 gives the result 4), but it concatenates strings ('2' + '2' gives the result '22'). You can't use an operator with two incompatible data types. For example, if you try to use + with an integer and a string, Python returns an error.

We discuss arithmetic operators in greater detail in Chapter 7.

Comparison operators

Comparison operators test the relative sizes of two pieces of data and give either `True` or `False` as the result. The symbols for these operators are as follows:

- less than (<)
- greater than (>)
- equal to (==)
- not equal to (!= or <>)

You can use comparison operators by themselves or in combination. For example, you can test whether something is less than or equal to something else by using the operator <=.

You use == (two = symbols) to test whether something is "equal to" something else. A single = symbol gives a name to a value.

You know about comparing the sizes of numbers — for example, 3 > 2. But Python can compare values of most other data types, too. (There are a few types you can't compare, such as complex numbers.) When you compare items by using these operators, the result is either True or False (except or some special data types in third-party modules). Here are a couple of examples:

- Strings are compared using alphabetical order, but all capital letters come before (are smaller than) all lowercase letters.

```
>>> 'a' < 'b'
True
>>> 'Z' < 'a'
True
```

- Each item in a list or tuple is compared against the item with the same index number in the other list or tuple.

```
>>> [1] < [2]
True
```

Also, lists and tuples are compared by length.

```
>>> [1, 2, 3] > [1, 2]
True
```

Boolean operators

Python has three operators that test whether expressions are true or false. These are called *Boolean operators* (you might also see them referred to as *logical operators*).

The Boolean operators work as follows:

✔ and stops testing when it encounters a false condition.

✔ or stops testing when it encounters a true condition.

Python tests an expression with and and or operators from left to right and returns the last value tested. (These operators don't return True and False unless the expressions themselves use comparison operators.)

```
>>> '1' and 1 and 'one'
'one'
>>> '1' or 1 or 'one'
'1'
>>> (2 < 3) or (5 > 6)
True
```

✔ not returns True if the expression is false and False if the expression is true.

```
>>> not 'one'
False
```

(Stuff like this is why your grammar teacher told you to avoid double negatives.)

In Python, *false* has a special meaning. It refers to anything that is zero or "empty." For example, the number 0 is false, and so is a string with no characters (' ') and a list with no elements ([]). You usually use Boolean operators to test for "emptiness."

For more information about Boolean operators, see Chapter 10.

Conditional operations

Conditional expressions are new in Python 2.5. They use this form:

```
X if C else Y
```

They work like this: First, C is evaluated. If C is true, then X is evaluated to give the result. Otherwise, Y is evaluated to give the result.

This example prints 'bar' because False evaluates as false:

```
>>> print 'foo' if False else 'bar'
'bar'
```

For more information on conditional expressions, see Chapter 16.

Order, please!

You probably remember from math class that when you do arithmetic, multiplication takes place before addition (for example, $3 + 2 \times 5 = 13$ because 2×5 is evaluated first). Likewise, operations in Python happen in a specific order, which is called *operator precedence*. As in arithmetic, operations in parentheses come first.

Table 3-3 describes operator precedence in Python. Operators in higher rows are evaluated before operators in lower rows. If multiple operators appear in a single cell in the table, that means they are equal in precedence and are evaluated from left to right when they appear in an expression.

Table 3-3	Operator Precedence
Symbol	*Type of operator*
`(a,b), [a,b], {a:b}`	Creation of tuples (via the comma operator), lists, and dictionaries
`s[i], s[i:j], s[i:j:k]`	Index and slice operations (on sequence data types); brackets are also used to select mapping elements
`f(...)`	Function calls
`x**y`	Exponentiation (evaluated right to left)
`x*y, x/y, x//y, x%y`	Multiplication, division, integer division, modulo (remainder)
`x+y, x-y`	Addition, subtraction
`x<y, x<=y, x>y, x>=y, x==y, x!=y`	Comparison and equality
`x is y, x is not y`	Identity
`x in y, x not in y`	Membership
`not x`	Logical negation
`x and y`	Logical and
`x or y`	Logical or
`if/else`	Conditional expression

Special powers of the = symbol

The = symbol might look like an operator, but in Python, it isn't. The = sign is used for *assignment* — associating a value with a name.

In Python, don't use = to get the result of arithmetic operations in the way you do when you use a calculator. Python stores the results of such calculations automatically. Also, don't use = to test whether one thing is the same as another (for that, you use == or is).

If We May Comment . . .

Python, like almost all programming languages, lets you add *comments* to your program. Comments are text in your program that the Python interpreter ignores. Why would you want to add stuff that the computer ignores? Comments help other people understand how the program works. They also let you decipher your own code six months later!

To add a comment to your program, type # (a pound sign) and then type your comment.

You can type # either at the beginning of a line of code or after the code. If you write a comment that spans more than one line, use # at the beginning of each line.

The example below shows comments in action:

```
# These are lines from Monty Python's "Parrot Sketch".
live_parrot = "'E's pinin' for the fjords!"      # Michael Palin
dead_parrot = "Bereft of life, 'e rests in peace!" # John Cleese
```

It pays to be conventional

Python programmers have conventions for how they add comments to their programs. The conventions make the comments and code easier to read by other programmers.

Here are some of the guidelines for comments:

- Keep lines to fewer than 80 characters.

   (This convention applies to the whole program, not just the comments.)

✔ Indent comments the same amount the code is indented.

For more information on indenting, see "Deciphering Code Blocks," later in this chapter.

✔ Use inline comments (comments that come after a line of code) sparingly, and only to explain things that aren't clear from reading the code.

The most important convention for comments is this one from the Style Guide for Python Code (`www.python.org/dev/peps/pep-0008`):

Comments that contradict the code are worse than no comments. Always make a priority of keeping the comments up-to-date when the code changes!

Documenting your program

Python supports a special kind of comment called a *docstring*.

As with other comments, you use docstrings to help others understand your code. What's different about docstrings is that they work with Python's help utility so that someone can figure out what your code does without having to look at the actual file.

A docstring is always the first line in a function. It can be more than one line if you begin and end it with three quotation marks. Here's an example docstring for a function we made up called `printme()`:

```
def printme(me):
    """
    Prints its argument.
    """
```

Here's what you see if you ask for help on the `printme()` function:

```
>>> help(printme)
Help on function printme in module __main__:

printme(me)
    Prints its argument
```

For detailed instructions on writing docstrings, see Chapter 11.

Oopsies! Understanding Error Messages

When Python finds syntax mistakes or other errors in your code, it gives you error messages to help you figure out what the problem is. For example, you get this error message when you try to use an equals sign (=) to do an arithmetic calculation:

```
>>> 5 - 6 =
  File "<stdin>", line 1
    5 - 6 =
          ^
SyntaxError: invalid syntax
```

The messages differ depending on the type of error but usually include these types of information:

- ✔ **The filename**

  When you work in interactive mode, the file is always `"<stdin>"`.
- ✔ **The line of code where Python first figured out there was an error**
- ✔ **The kind of error**

For a syntax error, a caret (^) points to the problem character (or to the place where the interpreter first figured out there was a problem).

Some error messages include information about the conditions in which the error occurred (this is called *traceback* information). The message you get when you try to divide by zero is an example:

```
>>> x = 0
>>> 9 / x
Traceback (most recent call last):
  File "<stdin>", line 1, in <module>
ZeroDivisionError: integer division or modulo by zero
```

Deciphering Code Blocks

In Python, you can write chunks of code, or *code blocks,* that perform a single function or group together several related tasks. We discuss the several kinds of code blocks and how to write them in the following sections.

The big deal about indentation

In many programming languages, you're encouraged — but not required — to indent a chunk of code that works as a unit. Some programmers are notoriously lazy about making their code readable to humans, and that means programs in those languages may not include indentation.

In Python, however, indentation is built into the interpreter. Code that's part of a block must be indented, or else you get an error message. This is one of the features that makes Python especially readable.

Indentation is so important to Python that Pythonistas printed up a T-shirt:

```
Python:
        programming
        the way
        Guido
        indented it
```

Code block syntax

There are two simple syntax rules to remember about code blocks:

- ✔ The code on the first line of a code block always ends with a colon (:).
- ✔ The code underneath the first line of a code block is indented.

Python programmers almost always use four spaces for the first level of indentation, eight spaces for the next level (a code block nested inside another code block), and so on.

The indentation must be the same for every line of a block. You get an `IndentationError` message if you use, for example, four spaces on one line of a block and three spaces on another line in the same block.

Basic code blocks: Control structures and loops

Basic code blocks in Python begin by testing whether a condition or expression is true. Python carries out instructions depending on the result of the test.

In the following sections, we introduce several kinds of control structures and loops and provide an example of each. Don't worry if you don't understand every bit of the code in the examples right now; it's explained in more detail in Chapter 10.

If statements

An `if` statement carries out one or more tests in a specified order. The first line always begins with `if`; subsequent tests begin with `elif` (which stands for "else if"), and you can add an `else` clause that runs if all the tests fail.

Here's an example of an `if` statement that includes an `else` clause. The `else:` line is not indented under the `if:` line because it's part of the structure of the `if` statement, as opposed to being one of the blocks inside the statement:

```
if statement == "We're fresh out of red Leicester, sir":
    response = "Oh, never mind, how are you on Tilset?"
elif statement == "We have Camembert, yessir":
    response = "Fetch hither the fromage de la Belle France!"
else:
    response = "I'm going to have to shoot you."
```

For loops

A `for` loop repeats a block of instructions, usually a specific number of times.

This example takes each item in `little_list` one at a time and prints it.

```
>>> little_list = ['the', 'quick', 'brown', 'fox']
>>> for the_item in little_list:
...     print the_item, "*",
...
the * quick * brown * fox *
```

Check out Chapter 10 for the lowdown on `for` loops.

While loops

A `while` loop repeats an instruction as long as a particular condition is true.

The following example code prints a number as long as the countdown value is greater than zero. It also subtracts 1 from the countdown value each time around the loop.

```
countdown = 10
while countdown:
    print countdown,
    countdown -= 1
print "blastoff!"
```

Here's what it prints:

```
10 9 8 7 6 5 4 3 2 1 blastoff!
```

Try statements

A `try` clause attempts to run some code. It is accompanied by one of the following:

- ✔ One or more `except` clauses (which catch errors raised in the `try` block)

  A try/except statement can also have an optional `else` clause.
- ✔ A `finally` clause

  This clause runs automatically after the `try` clause and re-raises any errors.

Starting in Python 2.5, a `try` clause can have all the above elements at once: `try`, `except`, `else`, and `finally`.

Here's a `try` statement that receives some input, does one thing if the input is an integer, and does another thing if it isn't:

```
user_input = raw_input("Enter an integer: ")
try:
    number = int(user_input)
    print "You entered", number
except ValueError:
    print "Integers, please!"
```

With blocks

The `with` statement (new in Python 2.5) executes a block in a particular *context*. This is an advanced feature that we discuss in Chapter 16.

Code blocks that create a namespace

Some Python code blocks set up a special area to store the names they know about. (*Names* are labels for areas of computer storage that hold particular values or other objects.) These areas are called *namespaces*.

Each namespace is self-contained, so names from different parts of a program don't bump into each other. This feature lets Python programmers create modular code that can be extended in many different directions without having to worry about whether their new code uses the same names as code in other blocks, modules, or programs.

Several kinds of code blocks create namespaces. Here is a brief introduction to some of them.

Functions

A function is like a blender or a bread maker. You put data into it, it does things with the information, and it returns a result.

Here is a small function (you may note there are no spaces at the end of the text strings. The comma stands for a single space):

```
>>> def myfunction(x):
...     y = x**x
...     print x, "raised to the power of", x, "is", y
...     return y
...
```

And here's how you might call it.

```
>>> result = myfunction(5)
5 raised to the power of 5 is 3125
>>> result
3125
```

Modules

A *module* is a text file that can contain any kind of Python code, but a module usually organizes tools that work in a particular way. Sometimes it also includes names that store particular values. You can make a module available to another program by *importing* it.

Modules are the key to Python's portability and power. Python itself is made up of modules.

For example, Python has a `math` module that includes a number of specialized mathematical tools, and it also defines some names, including `pi`. Here's how you import it:

```
>>> import math
```

Here's how you access the name `pi` that it defines:

```
>>> math.pi
3.1415926535897931
```

This book covers many of the important modules that come with Python. For instructions on viewing the list of modules that Python comes with, see Chapter 2.

Classes

A class is similar to both a factory and a blueprint in that it makes copies of itself — but the copies are what do the actual work. Here is an example of a class:

```
class SayMyName:
    def __init__(self, myname):
        self.myname = myname
    def say(self):
        print "Hello, my name is", self.myname
```

You use a class to create objects called *instances* that can do specific things. This code creates an instance of the SayMyName class:

```
name1 = SayMyName("Aahz")
```

An instance has access to the class's *methods* (which are just functions attached to a class). This code applies the say() method to the name1 instance:

```
>>> name1.say()
Hello, my name is Aahz
```

Classes are useful because they can combine both data and methods that operate on that data. Python's data types — lists, strings, and so on — are based on classes.

Chapter 4

Grand Tour of the Python Language

In This Chapter

▶ Dissecting a spider

▶ Building a spider

▶ Improve on our work!

*I*n this chapter, we present and analyze a whole Python program so you can see how all the parts work together.

You may want to keep a bookmark on the program so you can flip back and forth between the whole program and the discussion.

The spider.py Program

Our sample program (Listing 4-1) finds all the pages within a Web site. When you run it from the command line, it prints the results to stdout (the operating system's standard output stream). You can also use it as a module to make it a building block in a larger program.

The program doesn't check links to Web pages external to the site.

This program has three parts:

- ✔ **The import statements**
- ✔ **The function and class definitions**
- ✔ **The body of the program,** which calls the functions and class

Listing 4-1:   spider.py

```
################################################
# program: spider.py
# author: aahz
# version: 1.1
# date: June 2006
# description: start on command line with URL argument.
# Finds pages within a web site.
################################################


# These modules do most of the work.
import sys
import urllib2
import urlparse
import htmllib, formatter
from cStringIO import StringIO


def log_stdout(msg):
    """Print msg to the screen."""
    print msg

def get_page(url, log):
    """Retrieve URL and return contents, log errors."""
    try:
        page = urllib2.urlopen(url)
    except urllib2.URLError:
        log("Error retrieving: " + url)
        return ''
    body = page.read()
    page.close()
    return body


def find_links(html):
    """Return a list of links in html."""
    # We're using the parser just to get the HREFs
    writer = formatter.DumbWriter(StringIO())
    f = formatter.AbstractFormatter(writer)
    parser = htmllib.HTMLParser(f)
    parser.feed(html)
    parser.close()
    return parser.anchorlist


class Spider:

    """
    The heart of this program, finds all links within a web site.

    run() contains the main loop.
    process_page() retrieves each page and finds the links.
```

```
    """

    def __init__(self, startURL, log=None):
        # This method sets initial values
        self.URLs = set()
        self.URLs.add(startURL)
        self.include = startURL
        self._links_to_process = [startURL]
        if log is None:
            # Use log_stdout function if no log provided
            self.log = log_stdout
        else:
            self.log = log

    def run(self):
        # Processes list of URLs one at a time
        while self._links_to_process:
            url = self._links_to_process.pop()
            self.log("Retrieving: " + url)
            self.process_page(url)

    def url_in_site(self, link):
        # Checks whether the link starts with the base URL
        return link.startswith(self.include)

    def process_page(self, url):
        # Retrieves page and finds links in it
        html = get_page(url, self.log)
        for link in find_links(html):
            # Handle relative links
            link = urlparse.urljoin(url, link)
            self.log("Checking: " + link)
            # Make sure this is a new URL within current site
            if link not in self.URLs and self.url_in_site(link):
                self.URLs.add(link)
                self._links_to_process.append(link)


if __name__ == '__main__':
    # This code runs when script is started from command line
    startURL = sys.argv[1]
    spider = Spider(startURL)
    spider.run()
    for URL in sorted(spider.URLs):
        print URL
```

Examining a Python Program

First, we discuss how the program is organized. Then we show you some of the Python features the spider uses.

Setting up the structure

The top of `spider.py` contains a bunch of `import` statements. Looking there gives you a quick idea of what the program does and how it works, because most Python programs rely heavily on imported modules.

If you know the modules that come with Python, you'll know from looking at the `import` statements that this program is designed to read and process information from URLs (Web site addresses). Here is what each module does in the program:

- ✔ The `sys` module retrieves a starting URL from the command line when `spider.py` is run as a script. (Chapter 17 covers the `sys` module.)
- ✔ `urllib2` retrieves data from URLs.(See Chapter 20.)
- ✔ The `urlparse` module slices and dices URLs and puts them back together. (See Chapter 20.)
- ✔ `htmllib` and `formatter` are imported on the same line because they're used together to parse information out of HTML files; in this program, we use them only to get the links (anchors or HREFs). (See Chapter 20.)
- ✔ `from cStringIO import StringIO` imports an object that pretends a string is a file. (See Chapter 18.)

Note the `from...import` syntax. We recommend avoiding `from...import *` because it can clutter up your program with conflicting names, but `from...import` syntax is appropriate when the module exports a single class, as here.

Initializing the spider

Down near the bottom of the program is this statement:

```
if __name__ == '__main__':
```

All the code after that statement runs only when you start the program from the command line.

In Python programs, this code often contains testing instructions. If ours did, typing `python spider.py` at the command prompt would cause `spider.py` to test itself. In our program, the code processes a command-line argument. You can start the program from the command prompt and give it a URL to examine:

```
% python spider.py http://pythonfood.com/spider-test/
```

Between the top (the `import` statements) and the bottom (the command-line code) lies the meat of the module. The `spider.py` script contains these blocks of code:

- ✔ Three functions: `log_stdout()`, `get_page()`, and `find_links()`
- ✔ One class: `Spider`

If you look back down at the bottom, you notice the following line:

```
spider = Spider(startURL)
```

This line creates an instance of the `Spider` class. This means the `Spider` class is the heart of this module.

When trying to understand what a Python script does, it's best to start at the bottom and work your way up because classes and functions have to be created and named before they are called (before the program asks them to run). So in a Python program, any `def` statements (which create functions) and `class` statements (which create classes) always come before statements that actually run the code inside the functions and classes they define.

Running the spider

Figure 4-1 shows which parts of the `spider.py` program talk to each other (pass information). You might find Figure 4-1 useful while reading this section or reading the program itself.

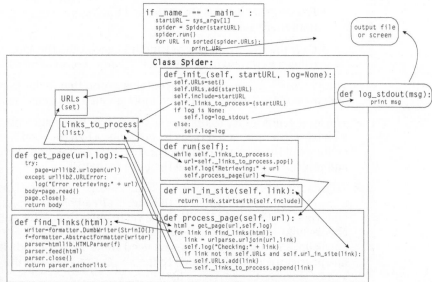

Figure 4-1:
Information
passing
in the
spider.py
program.

Reading the spider web

In the Spider class, the `process_page()` method is separate from `run()` because `run()` is easier to understand when you don't have to look at all the code in `process_page()` at the same time. This choice exemplifies two reasons behind Python's modular design philosophy.

It's a good idea to separate out chunks of code that do different things:

- ✔ Separating tasks into chunks makes it possible to use each chunk on its own.

- ✔ Reading a chunk of code that does only one thing is easier than reading a chunk of code that does multiple things.

The workings of the Spider class

To see how the heart of the `spider.py` program processes information, look at the Spider class. To use this class, you have to create an *instance* of it.

Instances are objects created from classes (see Chapter 13 for the details):

- ✔ A class is like a *template*.
- ✔ An instance is like a *document* created from that template.

The parts of the Spider class perform the following tasks:

- ✔ The `__init__()` method sets up the instance.

- ✔ The `run()` method does the real work. It's a simple loop that

  - *Processes* new pages (from the `self._links_to_process` list) until there are no more pages

  - *Calls* the `process_page()` method each time through the loop, using a new item from the `self.links_to_process` list.

- ✔ The `process_page()` method contains a loop that includes an `if` statement. (See Chapter 10 to find more about `if` statements and loops.)

- ✔ The loop sends a URL to the `get_page()` function, which opens the Web page, reads it, and returns its contents. Then the loop sends the contents of the Web page to the `find_links()` function, which logs and returns a list containing all the links in that URL.

- ✔ The statement `if link not in self.URLs and self.url_in_site(link):` checks whether this link is already in the `self.URLs` set and whether it's part of the Web site we're analyzing. (This spider only checks links internal to the Web site of the original URL. If you want to check links to other Web sites, you need some different code here.) If the link passes the tests, it's added to the `self.URLs` set and the `self._links_to_process` list.

Designing for expansion

To understand another design decision in the spider.py program, look at the url_in_site() method. It checks whether the link is part of the Web site.

Making url_in_site() a separate method doesn't make it easier to read the program, because the method has only one line of code. We decided to make a separate method for another reason: doing so makes it easier to *subclass* Spider. *Subclassing* is making a new class that shares most of the features of a class but either *overrides* or *extends* some of its functionality. (Chapter 13 has more about subclassing.) One way to subclass Spider is to extend the behavior of url_in_site() so that it works with both HTTP and HTTPS URLs at the same time. (The current program handles only one type at a time.) Having url_in_site() separate from process_page() means that such a subclass is easier to write. This illustrates another good programming practice.

When you're designing a program, think about the possibility that someone might want to customize or subclass your program in the future. (But don't overdesign or add features before they're needed. Python programs are easy to change, so you can quickly add features when necessary.)

The process_page() method combines the URLs returned from find_links() with the base URL specified by url. We could have put this functionality into the find_links() function. But leaving it out makes find_links() more generally useful — we (or others) can reuse it in programs that work with relative URLs in a different way from this one. This is an example of the design philosophy described in the preceding paragraph.

Using Building Blocks

This section describes how the spider.py program uses Python's most important building blocks and tools — functions and methods, loops, containers, names, strings, and error checking.

Function and method tidbits

The spider.py program illustrates key principles to keep in mind when writing functions and methods.

Understanding default parameters

The __init__() method has the parameter log=None. This is called a *default parameter*. (See Chapter 11.) It means that when you make an instance of the Spider class, you can specify a parameter for log, but you don't have to. If you don't, the instance automatically uses None as the value for log.

Default parameters give you choices and make your code more flexible. Because of the default log parameter, a number of different options for logging can be used with the Spider class.

The other side of the coin is that if you use a default parameter, you need to write code to test for the default value. In the Spider class, this code is part of the __init__() method. It assigns the log_stdout() function to self.log (if the user doesn't specify a value for log). In contrast, get_page() requires a log argument and therefore doesn't need to check for a default value.

Recognizing bare naked functions

Most function/method calls have self or a module name in front of them, followed by a dot. When you're reading a program, if you see a bare function or method (or class) — one without self or a module name — it usually means one of these:

- ✔ It was defined in the module (like get_page() and find_links() are in this program).
- ✔ It was imported by using the from ... import syntax (like StringIO).
- ✔ It is a built-in function (like sorted(), down at the bottom).

Functions and methods are essentially the same thing — a code block that performs an action and returns a result. Here's the difference:

- ✔ A function is by itself in a module.
- ✔ A method is part of a class.

Chapters 3, 11, and 13 describe how to use functions, methods, and classes.

Looping around

The spider.py script contains three loops:

- ✔ Two for loops

    Python programmers generally favor for loops, because for loops can both assign values and provide one element at a time.

✔ One `while` loop

A `while` loop is often better when you are both adding and deleting elements, so we used a `while` loop in the section where the `run()` method deletes elements from the `self._links_to_process` list (via the list method `pop()`) and also adds elements to the list (via `process_page()`).

Chapter 10 shows you more ways to use loops.

Collections of data

Sets, lists, and dicts are Python's data types for dealing with collections of data, especially if the data change while the program is running.

Lists

Lists (described more fully in Chapter 8) are most efficient, which is one reason we used a list (`self._links_to_process`) to keep track of all the links we're processing. Lists are also good when you need to

✔ Maintain elements in a particular order.

✔ Allow duplicate elements.

Sets

Sets are a good way of handling data when you want to ignore or avoid duplicates.

We used a set for the primary URL data in the `Spider` class (`self.URLs`) because we wanted only one copy of each URL. Chapter 9 shows more ways to use sets.

Dicts

Dicts are good for data that will be stored and accessed by keys rather than ordered alphabetically or numerically.

If we had wanted to associate some data with each URL in the Web page, we would have used a dict. Chapter 9 shows you how.

Naming names

If a good name is one that helps you understand what the named object is doing, then there are some good names and some not-so-good names in `spider.py`. An early draft of our program had functions named `get_links()` and `find_links()`. Those names don't really make clear the differences between the two functions, so we renamed `get_links()` to `get_page()`.

Programmers sometimes choose terse and not very explanatory names on purpose to indicate that you shouldn't pay much attention to the name because it's just a temporary name used to convey information (for example, it's used as an argument to a function or method). Sometimes a temporary name makes a few lines of code easier to read. Take, for example, the lines of code that use the name `f` in the `find_links()` function:

```
f = formatter.AbstractFormatter(writer)
parser = htmllib.HTMLParser(f)
```

We could have gotten rid of `f` by writing the code this way instead:

```
parser = htmllib.HTMLParser(formatter.AbstractFormatter(writer))
```

But that's kind of long and hard to read, so we decided it was better to split the lines and use a temporary name.

Give users of your modules information about which attributes, functions, classes, and methods they should avoid accessing directly, passing to other functions, subclassing, or rewriting. (Or, more colloquially, "Das ist nicht für gefingerpoken!") Sometimes this information is conveyed by using a single underscore character as the first character in a name, which means the object is *private*. (See Chapter 13 for more about private attributes.) For example, we chose to make `self._links_to_process` a private name because it's valid only inside the `Spider` class. We could have made `url_in_site()` a private name for the same reason, but we didn't in order to send the message that it's suitable for overriding in a subclass.

Managing strings

There are a lot of ways you can work with strings in Python:

- Python strings have many methods built in.

  For example, we use the `startswith()` string method in the `url_in_site()` function. (Unsurprisingly, `startswith()` checks whether a string starts with a particular substring.)

- Many Python modules include additional string-handling functions.

  We use one of these in the `process_page()` method: `urlparse.urljoin(url, link)`. The `urljoin()` function (as the name suggests — see the benefits of naming things well?) sticks together two parts of a URL, which we pass in as two strings, `url` and `link`.

Before you start writing some special functionality to process strings, check whether someone else has already done the work for you. The Cheat Sheet lists the most commonly used string methods.

Handling errors

One error-handling tool in the `spider.py` program is this block of code in the `get_page()` function:

```
try:
    page = urllib2.urlopen(url)
except urllib2.URLError:
    log("Error retrieving: " + url)
    return ''
```

This is called a `try/except` block (see Chapter 10). Its purpose is to catch errors from the `urllib2.urlopen()` function, which tries to open a remote URL.

What spider.py doesn't have

The `spider.py` program works as-is, but it's missing a few elements that are necessary to make it a fully functional Python program that follows the conventions of good programming:

✔ Docstrings for each function and class method.

✔ Error checking. For example, if you try to run the program from the command line without specifying a URL, the program fails messily. Here's what happens:

```
% python spider.py
Traceback (most recent call
   last):
  File "spider.py", line 91,
  in <module>
    startURL = sys.argv[1]
IndexError: list index out of
  range
```

Why are we showing a program without these features when we reiterate *ad nauseum* in this book that you should include these features in your program? Because lots of programmers talk about the benefits of comments, documentation, and error-checking, but lots of programs (some written by those same programmers) don't do as good of a job on those things as they should. This is a "Do as we say, not as we do" situation.

A complete version of the program with documentation and error checking is on our Web site:

http://pythonfood.com/

It's good practice to use `try` with I/O functions and user input or other external input. For example, we could improve our program by moving the `body = page.read()` line into the `try` block — because even if you can open a Web page, you might still have trouble reading it. Similarly, garbage in the HTML can cause the `htmllib` module's parser to choke, so the line `parser.feed(html)` should be in a `try` block as well, like this:

```
try:
    parser.feed(html)
except htmllib.HTMLParseError:
    log("Error finding links: " + url)
    return []
finally:
    parser.close()
return parser.anchorlist
```

The sidebar, "What spider.py doesn't have," describes another spot where error-checking would be useful.

Chapter 5

Working Like a Programmer

Professional programmers spend as little as 10 percent of their working time writing code. This chapter focuses on what they do the rest of the time. These practices generally consume about 60 percent of a programmer's time on a project:

- *Analyzing problems*

- *Designing solutions and documenting decisions*

- *Debugging*

- *Maintaining and improving code*

The final 30 percent of a programmer's time is taken by meetings and wasted time. (Sometimes, there's no difference between meetings and wasted time.)

The Three Ds

If you're writing a program that's more than a few lines long, don't just sit down and start coding. You need to take three steps to make your program the best it can be. These are *the three Ds*:

- **Document:** Making sure others can read your program

- **Design:** Making sure your program is solving the right problem and is organized so that it's efficient and potentially reusable

- **Debug:** Making sure your program doesn't have any mistakes in it and that it responds appropriately when given wrong input

Documenting

Documentation makes it possible to read, use, and maintain a program:

- ✔ In programming, documentation is all the writing associated with your program that isn't code.

- ✔ With a language like Python, readability is a prime virtue. That means your code is part of the documentation, too. For example, picking good names is part of documentation!

  Programming *starts* and *ends* with documentation:

- ✔ **Start by writing the problem that your program is intended to solve.**

  Before you even start writing your program, it's a good idea to write notes about the goal of the program. Pretend you need to explain it to someone else — and if you have someone to read the notes, so much the better.

- ✔ **End by making sure that the documentation still matches the program.**

If you don't write documentation, you will find it difficult to use or maintain your program after letting it sit for six months (even if you're the only person who uses the program).

Designing

Designing is actually shorthand for two intertwined parts of programming: *analysis* and *design*.

What do you really want?

Analysis is the process of determining what problem you're trying to solve. It's similar to the process an architect makes you go through to remodel your kitchen: "What do you *really* want?" For example, you might want to write a program to automate your data backups. That's a general description, but you need a more specific list of tasks you want the program to carry out, such as

- ✔ How often do you want to make backups?

- ✔ Do you want to back up all data or only data changed since the last backup?

- ✔ How long do you want to keep backups?

After you have some specific ideas of what you want, the design phase starts.

If you're remodeling your kitchen, then this is the point where the architect draws up a blueprint. The blueprint isn't the kitchen itself; it's the plan that needs to be followed to build the new kitchen. If you're writing a program, you start to build the outline of the program, which is similar to a blueprint. In fact, people who focus on the analysis and design of programs are often called *software architects*.

Pseudo-coding your thoughts

One way to design your program is to create an outline of sorts, using what is called *pseudo-code*. You write a sketch of what your program will do, using the structures you'll need to use when you write the program (such as class and function definitions and `if` statements), but you don't bother with the syntax details necessary to write working code.

Pseudo-code tends to resemble real Python programs, so it takes less effort to convert pseudo-code into working Python code. When the pseudo-coding process is finished, the details are easy to fill in.

Here's an example of pseudo-code that almost works as Python code:

```
if today == sunday:
    full_backup()
else:
    incremental_backup()
```

Debugging

A *bug* is a mistake in a piece of software that causes it to work improperly or to return incorrect results.

Teaching an old bug new tricks

This use of the word *bug* was already common before software was invented — for example, Thomas Edison used it in 1878 to describe problems with his inventions. Some people will tell you, though, that the term derives from an incident in which an actual insect was found to be causing glitches inside an early computer in 1947.

Although *bug* is older than writing programs, *debugging* has been an inherent part of writing software since people started writing software. One of the first computer scientists, Maurice Wilkes, is reputed to have said, "I can remember the exact instant when I realized that a large part of my life from then on was going to be spent in finding mistakes in my own programs."

The Zen of Python

Writing a complex program is something like designing a building. The architect's constraints include time, money, good taste, and the structural limits of the materials. Programming also requires balancing multiple needs — often including time, money, the feature requests of multiple groups of people, and the availability of sufficient quantities of caffeine.

Pythonista Tim Peters contributed 19 guidelines for good Python code. We consider them the best distillation of the Python philosophy of programming. They're on this Web page:

```
http://www.python.org/doc/humor/#zen
```

These are design principles, not rules to be followed blindly. They're meant to encourage you to think. In some cases the principles may appear contradictory. That's a reflection of the fact that programming sometimes requires balancing conflicting requirements. It's like the old saying: "Good, fast, cheap — pick any two." The principles can help you decide how to prioritize these requirements.

The principles were originally written to guide the development of Python itself, but they also apply to writing your own programs. That's how we discuss them here.

Some of the most important guidelines are these:

Explicit is better than implicit. Good code is as self-explanatory as possible:

- Use names that explain the purpose of the objects they represent.

- Include comments in your code when it isn't obvious what a particular line or block does.

- Avoid hidden effects. (For example, printing to the screen shouldn't erase your hard drive.)

Readability counts. A good program is easy for a human to read and understand. If two blocks of code produce the same result, consider using the one that's easier to read. (Sometimes cryptic code runs faster, but speed isn't the primary goal of most Python programming.)

Errors should never pass silently. If you write code that doesn't alert the user of errors, the errors might cause the program to give incorrect results:

- Build explicit error checking into your code.

- Write code to catch any errors that you haven't thought of.

- Report errors to the user of your program.

There should be one — and preferably only one — obvious way to do it. This guideline ("There's only one way," for short) is the most popular among people in the Python community. This is partly in response to the motto of Perl programmers, which is, "There's More Than One Way To Do It." The Python community creates and popularizes standard coding *idioms* (preferred ways of performing certain tasks). Using standard idioms saves time because the code is already mostly written; you just plug in your data and variables. *Python For Dummies* includes many standard idioms to get you started.

Typing `import this` at the Python prompt in Python 2.1.2 or higher will print the entire list:

```
>>> import this
The Zen of Python, by Tim Peters

Beautiful is better than ugly.
Explicit is better than implicit.
Simple is better than complex.
Complex is better than complicated.
Flat is better than nested.
Sparse is better than dense.
```

```
Readability counts.                          Now is better than never.
Special cases aren't special enough to       Although never is often better than
    break the rules.                             *right* now.
Although practicality beats purity.          If the implementation is hard to explain,
Errors should never pass silently.               it's a bad idea.
Unless explicitly silenced.                  If the implementation is easy to explain,
In the face of ambiguity, refuse the             it may be a good idea.
    temptation to guess.                     Namespaces are one honking great idea --
There should be one-- and preferably only        let's do more of those!
    one --obvious way to do it.
Although that way may not be obvious at
    first unless you're Dutch.
```

Most computer programs have bugs. When you discover problems with the way your program works or the results it gives, you *debug* to

✔ Find the source of the mistake.

✔ Fix the lines of code causing the problem.

As you get comfortable with programming and Python, you get a better sense for how the computer "thinks," which helps you figure out bugs more quickly. You'll become familiar with common causes for common problems like:

✔ **Syntax errors.** Missing punctuation is the most common syntax mistake. For example, if you try to create a string but forget a quotation mark, you'll get an error like this:

```
>>> mystring = "No! Not the Knights who say 'Ni'!
  File "<stdin>", line 1
    mystring = "No! Not the Knights who say 'Ni'!
                                                 ^
SyntaxError: EOL while scanning single-quoted string
```

You'll have fewer syntax errors in your programs if you use a Python-aware text editor that prints different syntax in different colors.

Tips for avoiding common syntax errors can be found throughout *Python for Dummies*.

✔ **Misspelled names.** If you name an object and then misspell the name when you refer to it later, you'll get an error. For example:

```
>>> lumberjack = "I'm OK"
>>> print lumbrejack
Traceback (most recent call last):
  File "<stdin>", line 1, in ?
NameError: name 'lumbrejack' is not defined
```

✔ **Using the wrong types of values.** For example, if you have a number in string format (perhaps from the `raw_input()` function, which converts the input into a string) and you try to do arithmetic with it, you'll get a result you didn't expect, like this:

```
>>> x = raw_input("Enter a number: ")
Enter a number: 45
>>> x * 2
'4545'
```

✔ **Creating infinite loops.** If you create a loop by using a condition that never terminates, your program will try to run forever, like the brooms that the Sorcerer's Apprentice creates:

```
sorcerer = "asleep"
def make_broom():
    print "another broom!"
while sorcerer == "asleep":
    make_broom()
```

Chapter 10 shows you how to create loops that you *can* control.

✔ **Trying to open files that don't exist or are empty, for example:**

```
>>> myfile = open('foo.doc')
Traceback (most recent call last):
  File "<stdin>", line 1, in <module>
IOError: [Errno 2] No such file or directory: 'foo.doc'
```

✔ **Incorrect logic for Boolean expressions**

To get the scoop on correct use of Boolean expressions in your programs, see Chapters 3 and 10.

The best way to find out about common bugs (other than writing your own programs) is to look at the bugs other people make. The `comp.lang.python` newsgroup or the Python tutor mailing list are good resources. (See Chapter 22 to find out how to access these resources.) The same errors come up over and over, and you'll soon be able to recognize them on sight.

For helpful debugging tips, see "Debugging Strategies," later in this chapter.

Maintaining Your Programs

Okay, you've written your program. Now what? Chances are you'll want to make some changes soon. In fact, most programmers spend far more time changing existing programs than writing new ones. When you want to update your code, you'll likely be tempted to change it in a way that doesn't take a lot of time. But that might not be the best way to go about it in the long run.

Suppose you've written a program to send yourself a daily e-mail with the top ten lines from your calendar file. It might look like Listing 5-1.

Listing 5-1: daily_calendar.py

```
import smtplib               # get the module for sending email
my_address = 'me@example.com'
headers = [ 'Subject: Daily calendar',
    'From: ' + my_address,
    'To: ' + my_address,
    ]                        # this list spans four lines for readability
entries = open('my_calendar').readlines()[:10]
msg = '\r\n'.join(headers) + '\r\n' + ''.join(entries)

smtp = smtplib.SMTP('mail') # replace 'mail' with the name of your mailhost
smtp.sendmail(my_address, [my_address], msg)
smtp.close()
```

Then you decide you want to send yourself a bigger chunk once a week. The simple, easy — and wrong — way to do it, illustrated in Listing 5-2, is called *cut-'n'-paste programming*. Note how most of the lines of the program are repeated in the `if` and `else` statements. (By the way, another change made in the program was the addition of `sys.argv` to get a command-line argument. That's not bad programming, we just wanted to point it out.)

Listing 5-2: calendar.py

```
import smtplib, sys
my_address = 'me@example.com'
if sys.argv[1] == 'weekly':
    headers = [ 'Subject: Weekly calendar',
        'From: ' + my_address,
        'To: ' + my_address,
        ]
    entries = open('my_calendar').readlines()[:50]
    msg = '\r\n'.join(headers) + '\r\n' + ''.join(entries)
    smtp = smtplib.SMTP('mail')
    smtp.sendmail(my_address, [my_address], msg)
    smtp.close()
else:
    headers = [ 'Subject: Daily calendar',
        'From: ' + my_address,
        'To: ' + my_address,
        ]
    entries = open('my_calendar').readlines()[:10]
    msg = '\r\n'.join(headers) + '\r\n' + ''.join(entries)
    smtp = smtplib.SMTP('mail')
    smtp.sendmail(my_address, [my_address], msg)
    smtp.close()
```

The right way to upgrade your code avoids this repetition by taking the repeated code and turning it into a chunk that gets called by another part of the program. This is called *refactoring* the code.

If you remember algebra, code refactoring is similar to algebraic factoring; for example, breaking the number 12 into its factors 3 × 4.

Refactoring a program works like this:

1. **Figure out the elements that are common to all the tasks the program performs.**

   In this example, the common element is that both tasks (*sending a daily calendar* and *sending a weekly calendar)* involve sending an e-mail.

2. **Put the common elements into one or more functions.**

   In this example, these tasks go into a function called send_calendar().

3. **Put the elements that are different for different tasks into an** if/else **block (or perhaps a loop).**

   In this example, the if/else block determines whether a daily or weekly calendar is being sent and how many lines of the calendar to include. It passes this information to the send_calendar() function as arguments.

Programming to the max

Smart programmers have come up with a variety of methods for writing better programs. Many of those methods are combined under the umbrella of *Extreme Programming* (XP). (Some programmers have always wanted to be as cool as skateboarders. Maybe using a term like this helps. Or maybe not.)

The idea behind XP is simple: If a programming method is a Good Idea, take it to the max! For example, one of the best ways of getting bugs out of a program is to have another programmer review the code. Well, why not have the second programmer review the code *while* you're writing it? That results in what "extreme programmers" call *pair programming*.

Similarly, if writing unit tests is good, maybe you should write the tests before you start writing code. That's called *test-driven development*. This Web page, "Test-Driven Development in Python" by Jason Diamond, has an example:

www.onlamp.com/pub/a/python/2004/12/02/tdd_pyunit.html

For more info about XP, see this Web site:

www.extremeprogramming.org

Not surprisingly, there is also a lot of hype about XP. Wikipedia to the rescue! Here is a balanced article about Extreme Programming:

http://en.wikipedia.org/wiki/Extreme_Programming

Why refactor?

Although refactoring will take you longer the first time you change your program, it will save you time in the long run, and it will also make your program more generally useful and easier to read. The refactored version of the `calendar.py` program in Listing 5-1 is easy to extend — all you have to do is write two-line `elif` blocks. Furthermore, if you want to change the `send_calendar()` functionality, you have to change only one chunk of code. But if you extended the program via the cut-'n'-paste method, your program would get longer very quickly, and if you made changes to the code that reads the calendar file and sends the e-mail, you'd have to make those changes multiple times.

A general rule to use: Refactor if at least three lines of code are duplicated in your program.

The refactored program looks like Listing 5-3.

Listing 5-3:   refactored_calendar.py

```
import smtplib, sys
my_address = 'me@example.com'

# set up and send the email
def send_calendar(address, num_entries, subject):
    headers = [ 'Subject: ' + subject,
        'From: ' + address,
        'To: ' + address,
        ]
    entries = open('my_calendar').readlines()[:num_entries]
    msg = '\r\n'.join(headers) + '\r\n' + ''.join(entries)
    smtp = smtplib.SMTP('mail')
    smtp.sendmail(my_address, [my_address], msg)
    smtp.close()

# parse the command-line argument
if sys.argv[1] == 'weekly':
    send_calendar(my_address, 50, 'Weekly calendar')
else:
    send_calendar(my_address, 10, 'Daily calendar')
```

Good Program Design Practices

There are a few good practices to keep in mind while you're designing and writing your program. They'll help with documenting, debugging, and maintaining the program later.

Naming names

The names of values and functions should be self-explanatory to make your code easier to read.

For example, if you want to write code that extracts a zip code from a customer entry in a database, you might write this:

```
customer_zip = get_zip(Pandora)
```

It is easier to figure out what the preceding line of code is doing than it is to figure out the following code:

```
z = getz(Pandora)
```

Following conventions

Python itself doesn't require you to write your code this way, but these conventions make programs easier for programmers (and you) to read.

The conventions are available on the `python.org` Web site under the name "PEP 8: Style Guide for Python Code." See them here:

```
www.python.org/dev/peps/pep-0008
```

The following conventions are the most critical guidelines.

Naming rules

Follow these guidelines when naming objects in your program:

- ✔ **Give modules and packages short, lowercase names without underscores:**

  ```
  likethis
  ```

  The name of a module or package is also the name of a file on the computer. Some computers don't handle long filenames or names with special characters. This practice makes it easier for users of other operating systems to use your program.

- ✔ **Start class names with a capital letter and use embedded caps:**

  ```
  LikeThis
  ```

  This format is sometimes called "StudlyCaps". Because, well, geeks have to feel studly about something.

- ✔ **End the names of error-type exceptions with** `Error`.

  This helps anyone reading or debugging your program to recognize exceptions right away.

✔ **Name functions and methods by using all lowercase characters.**

Underscores, `like_this`, are OK.

Using different styles for names of different types of object helps distinguish functions and methods from modules, packages, and classes at a glance. The underscore character helps people read the name of the function or method if the name includes more than one word (for example, `get_zip` is slightly easier to read than `getzip`).

✔ **Use all uppercase characters for constants,** `LIKETHIS`.

Formatting rules

To improve readability, follow these guidelines when formatting your code:

✔ **Indent each code block four spaces. Avoid tabs.**

✔ **Continue long lines by surrounding them with** `()`, `[]`, **or** `{}`.

✔ **Continue strings by ending the line with** `\`.

   • Use `\` to continue strings only when necessary.

   • Make sure to use an extra indent for continuation lines, like so:

```
parrot = "This parrot is no more! He has ceased to be! He's expired \
         and gone to meet his maker!"
```

✔ **Put spaces before and after** `=`.

But don't use spaces around `=` in default parameters of functions and methods.

Don't forget to comment!

Include comments as you write the program. Comments should describe why the code is written the way it is and not just what it does.

Chunks of code, such as functions, are usually preceded by comments that describe the whole chunk (not comments that go with each line).

If you've added comments to the program, collect them together when it's time to write

✔ **The main *comment block* at the beginning of the program.**

This block includes the type of file, the name of the programmer, the date of creation, the purpose of the file, and usage instructions.

✔ **The *docstrings* that are used to build the program's help file.**

Debugging Strategies

Some strategies that programmers use to debug their code are as follows:

- ✔ **Three built-in functions —** `repr()`, `type()`, **and** `dir()` **— aid debugging by helping you figure out what values and types your program uses.**

  See the following section, "Built-in functions," to find out about these three useful functions.

- ✔ **Traceback logs,** `print` **statements, and commenting out lines of code help you keep track of what's going on when your program runs.**

- ✔ **Debugger tools let you step through your program one line,** or one code block, at a time. See "Using a debugger" later in this chapter.

The following sections describe ways to use these strategies effectively.

Built-in functions

Your three best friends in debugging are the built-in functions `repr()`, `type()`, and `dir()`.

The `repr()` function gives you useful information about what Python really thinks is in a value; it is essential for debugging problems with strings because it shows the special escape characters in strings, like this (see Chapter 6 for a full explanation):

```
>>> mystring = "the knights who say 'Ni!'"
>>> repr(mystring)
'"the knights who say \'Ni!\'"'
```

The `type()` and `dir()` functions give you additional information about a value. Even when the bug in your program is a logic error, the symptom is often a wrong value getting passed around. Finding out what that value is and where it came from usually allows you to figure out the bug.

Here's a trivial case. Python's exception points you in the right direction for figuring out the error:

```
>>> price = raw_input('Enter price: ')
Enter price: 12.99
>>> qty = raw_input('Enter quantity: ')
Enter quantity: 3
>>> price * qty
Traceback (most recent call last):
  File "<stdin>", line 1, in <module>
TypeError: can't multiply sequence by non-int of type 'str'
```

The error message is clear enough, but it doesn't tell you what the "sequence" and the "non-int" are. What you might do next is check what `price` and `qty` are by using `repr()` and `type()`, as shown in the following example code. (So where's `repr()`? In interactive mode, if you just type the name, Python automatically uses `repr()`. You need to actually type `repr()` only when you're debugging in scripts.)

```
>>> price, type(price)
('12.99', <type 'str'>)
>>> qty, type(qty)
('3', <type 'str'>)
```

Ah-ha! Both `price` and `qty` are strings. (That's because the `raw_input()` function always returns a string.) In order to multiply them, you need to turn them into numbers. Here's how you do it:

```
>>> price = float(price)
>>> qty = int(qty)
>>> price * qty
38.969999999999999
```

Now suppose the user enters something that can't be turned into a number. This will create another problem in the program:

```
>>> price = float(raw_input('Enter price: '))
Enter price: Good dog!
Traceback (most recent call last):
  File "<stdin>", line 1, in <module>
ValueError: invalid literal for float(): Good dog!
```

The way to handle this problem is to write code that *catches the exception* and reminds the user to enter a number. We discuss how to do this in Chapter 15.

Print statements and traceback logs

When debugging, add `print` statements whenever you give a name to a value or manipulate something. You'll quickly discover at what point the name takes on the wrong value.

Don't suppress *tracebacks* (Python's information about errors or unusual conditions it encounters). If you want your program to continue after an error has occurred (instead of quitting), *log* or *print* the traceback and go back later.

Although `print` statements are useful in simple programs, wading through the output is difficult if you have a lot of them. It's also difficult to selectively turn `print` statements on and off. The `logging` module directs your debugging output to a file for later perusal. To control the amount of output, just change the logging level.

Chapter 17 shows how to use the `logging` module and also shows how to use the `>>` operator with `print` to redirect output to a file.

Comments

To use comments for debugging, add lines to the code that print the values of various names throughout the program. Then append a comment like `# for debugging` to these lines of code so you know to remove them later.

Using the comment character (#) at the beginning of a line of code disables that line. In some cases, disabling individual lines helps you track down which line of code is the source of a problem.

Using a debugger

A debugger lets you step through your code one line at a time or one code block at a time. It displays all the values Python keeps track of, showing exactly where values change.

pdb

The `pdb` module is a debugger that's built into Python.

The program we're debugging is called `x.py`, and it looks like this:

```
print "This function creates a list."
def makelist():
    a = []
    for i in range(1, 20):
        a.append(i)
        print "appending", i, ":", a
    return a
makelist()
```

To use `pdb` from the command line, follow these steps:

1. **At the command prompt, type** `python -m pdb x.py`**, where** `x.py` **is the name of your module.**

   You'll see something like this: The `(1)` on the first line indicates the first line of the program. The text following `->` is the actual code of this line. `(Pdb)` is the prompt.

   ```
   > /Users/stef/x.py(1)<module>()
   -> print "This function creates a list."
   (Pdb)
   ```

2. **To run the current line of the program and go to the next line, type** s.

    Each time you press s (which is short for "step"), you see the next line number and its code. In this example, you also see the result of the print statement on the first line.

    ```
    (Pdb) s
    This function creates a list.
    > /Users/stef/x.py(2)<module>()
    -> def makelist():
     (Pdb)
    ```

    If you type s again at this point, the program jumps to line 8:

    ```
    (Pdb) s
    > /Users/stef/x.py(8)<module>()
    -> makelist()
    (Pdb)
    ```

    That's because the first time Python sees a function definition, it reads (*defines*) the whole function. This process is considered a single step.

3. **When you want to check that the program is storing the correct values, type** p **and the name to see its value.**

    We got this result after we'd stepped through the program ten times:

    ```
    (Pdb) p a
    [1, 2]
    ```

To see available commands while you run pdb, type help. For help on a single command or topic, type help and the name of the command or topic, like this:

```
(Pdb) help a
a(rgs)
Print the arguments of the current function.
```

The most useful pdb commands are:

s (step) — Run the current line of the program and go to the next line.

If the line is a def statement for a function, define the function (if it hasn't already been defined), then go to the first line after the function. If the line is a *function call,* go to the first line inside the function.

n (next) — Run the current line of the program and go to the next line. But if the line is a function call, run the whole function and go to the next line after the function call.

c (cont) — Continue running the program until the next break point (see the following section, "Break points").

r (return) — Run the program until the current function returns.

l (list) — Display the source code around the current line.

a (`args`) — Display the current function's arguments.

p (`print`), pp (`pretty-print`) — Display the value of an expression.

q (`quit`) — Quit the debugger and the program.

Break points

If you know that most of your program is working but you suspect a problem in one part, you can set a *break point* where you think the problem is. In pdb, you do this by typing b and the line number you want to set a break point at:

```
(Pdb) b 3
Breakpoint 1 at Users/stef/x.py:3
```

In pdb, to run the program until it comes to the break point, type c (for "continue"). To see the values your program is storing at this point, type p and the name whose value you want to see.

The following example sets a break point at line 5 of our program, runs the program until it reaches the break point, and examines the values at that point. Note that the break occurs *before* Python runs line 5.

```
(Pdb) b 5
Breakpoint 2 at /Users/stef/x.py:5
(Pdb) c
appending 2 : [1, 2]
> /Users/stef/x.py(5)makelist()
-> a.append(i)
(Pdb) p a
[1, 2]
(Pdb) p i
3
```

Part II
Building Blocks

The 5th Wave   By Rich Tennant

"Ms. Gretsky, tell the employees they can have internet games on their computers again."

In this part . . .

Vou discover how to manipulate Python's many data types, from simple text strings, through all the different kinds of numbers you can work with (but don't worry, you won't have to remember high school algebra), to lists, tuples, dictionaries, and sets.

Chapter 6

So This String Walks into a Bar

*I*n most computer languages, including Python, a *string* consists of text characters — just one character, a few lines, or a whole text file. In this chapter, you find out how strings work in Python, including

✔ The various ways to use quotation marks to delimit strings

✔ How to use index numbers and slices to get at parts of strings

✔ Magic ways of formatting string output

We also introduce you to the mysteries of Unicode.

Stringing Them Along

Inside Python, a string *literal* is surrounded by quotation marks, which distinguish it from other kinds of data, such as integers or names. You see the quotation marks when you type the name of a string in the interpreter. But when you *print* a string, the quotation marks don't appear.

```
>>> y = '234'
>>> y
'234'
>>> print y
234
```

The Python interpreter calls repr() to display the result of an expression — this display itself is usually a valid expression. The print statement uses str(), which displays a "prettier" version. (Chapter 2 has more details.)

The following sections describe several ways to quote strings and how to use special characters inside strings (or how not to use them).

Just the quotes, ma'am

You can surround a string with single, double, or triple quotes. Which you use depends on the string contents and formatting you want.

One quote or two

When you create a string, Python lets you to use either a pair of single quotes or a pair of double quotes. Both mean "a string is inside." This example shows a double-quoted string and a single-quoted string:

```
>>> penguin = "on top of the television set"
>>> what_it_is_doing = 'standing'
```

If your text includes single quotation marks or apostrophes, it's easiest to make it into a string by surrounding it with double quotes, like this:

```
>>> knights = "We are the Knights Who Say 'Ni'!"
>>> print knights
We are the Knights Who Say 'Ni'!
```

Likewise, if your text includes double quotes, it's easiest to make a string by surrounding it with single ones.

Triple-scoop

To make a string that prints exactly as you type it, use triple quotes, either single (''') or double ("""). Python prints the string with line breaks and spaces exactly as you enter them, as shown:

```
>>> spam = """
...     spam spam spam spam spam
...     and spam
... """
>>> print spam

    spam spam spam spam spam
    and spam
```

Triple quotes are most commonly used to create *docstrings*. A docstring is a short description of a code block, such as a function. Python's help function automatically formats and returns the text of the docstring when you ask for help on the code block. For more about docstrings, see Chapter 11.

Triple quotes are also useful for surrounding text that has both single and double quotation marks.

Ways to escape

To tell Python to give special treatment to a character in a string literal, precede it with a backslash character (\), also called the *escape character.*

Table 6-1 lists some of the characters that do special things when preceded by a backslash. (These are commonly called *escape codes.*)

Table 6-1	Some Python Escape Codes
Character	*Meaning*
\ as last character on a line	Text on the next line goes with the text on this line.
\\	Backslash
\'	Single quote
\"	Double quote
\e	Escape key
\n	Linefeed
\t	Tab
\0nn	Octal character (*nn* is a two-digit number)
\xnn	Hexadecimal character (*nn* is a two-digit number)

One way to use the backslash is to tell Python to treat a quotation mark as a regular character rather than as a "string starter or ender," as in this example:

```
>>> whiteRabbit = 'Where\'s my pocket-watch?'
>>> print whiteRabbit
Where's my pocket-watch?
```

It's easier to read strings that don't have escape characters within the code, so avoid them if you can. If you have text with both single and double quotes, consider using triple quotes to designate it as a string.

To tell Python that a backslash is part of your string and not an escape character, precede it with a second backslash, as shown:

```
>>> path = "C:\\Applications"
>>> print path
C:\Applications
```

Raw strings

To tell Python not to look for any escape codes in a string, specify the string as a *raw string*. You might want to do this when handling Windows pathnames, which include the backslash character.

Raw strings also simplify *regular expression* searches, which also use backslashes as special characters. See Chapter 18.

To specify a raw string, type r before the first quotation mark, like this:

```
>>> path = r"C:\Applications"
>>> print path
C:\Applications
```

There's one case in which raw strings aren't completely raw. It's an error to end a raw string with a backslash because Python thinks you're using the backslash to escape the quote mark that ends the string. To type a string that ends with a backslash, you must use a regular string. You can add it to the raw string simply by typing it on the same line. If you type several strings on the same line, you don't need to use a concatenation operator:

```
>>> print r'C:\data\myprograms' '\\'
C:\data\myprograms\
```

Being wordy

There are several ways to create a string that will span more than one line.

- ✔ To write a string that will print exact as you entered it, surround the string with triple-quotes (''' or """).

- ✔ To write text that will print on several lines, add the linefeed escape code \n where you want a new line to start, like this:

```
>>> cheese = "cheeses available:\nsavoyard\nboursin"
>>> print cheese
cheeses available:
savoyard
boursin
```

✔ To turn two strings on two lines into a single string, surround them with parentheses. We recommend this method for entering long strings because it's easy to read. For example:

```
>>> x = ("hello"
... "world")
>>> print x
helloworld
```

✔ To create a long string, type a backslash character (\) at the end of a line. What you type after you press Return counts as part of the same line.

```
>>> longline = "this is a very long line a very long \
... line a very long line"
>>> print longline
this is a very long line a very long line a very long line
```

The end-of-line backslash doesn't work if you add spaces after the backslash.

How a string looks inside Python

To see how Python internally represents a string, type the name of the string and press Return. In this example, Python represents a newline character with the escape character \n:

```
>>> modernlife = "as i was surfing on the air\n\
... i saw a spam that wasn't there"
>>> modernlife
"as i was surfing on the air\ni saw a spam that wasn't there"
```

When you ask Python to *print* a string, it interprets the newline character. So the modernlife string is printed on two lines, like this:

```
>>> print modernlife
as i was surfing on the air
i saw a spam that wasn't there
```

"Please repeat": String operators

Several of Python's operators work with strings. This section covers the following operators:

✔ **Concatenation** (+): Sticks strings together.

✔ **Repeating** (*): Copies a string several times.

✔ **Size testing** (<, >): Determines which of two strings is bigger or smaller.

Combine and repeat

To concatenate strings, type the first string, the + symbol, and the second string, like so:

```
>>> hello = "hello"
>>> world = "world"
>>> hello + world
'helloworld'
```

If you're working with string literals rather than strings that have names, you don't have to use the + operator to stick them together. You can just put them next to each other on a line, like so:

```
>>> "It don' mean a thing " "if it ain't got that swing!"
"It don' mean a thing if it ain't got that swing!"
```

To repeat a string, type the string, the * symbol, and the number of times you want to repeat the string, as shown here:

```
>>> "It don' mean a thing " * 3
"It don' mean a thing It don' mean a thing It don' mean a thing "
```

To concatenate and repeat at the same time, combine the operations, like so:

```
>>> toaster1 = "would you like some toast? "
>>> toaster2 = "or how about muffins??? \n"
>>> annoying_toaster = (toaster1 + toaster2)* 3
>>> print annoying_toaster
would you like some toast? or how about muffins???
would you like some toast? or how about muffins???
would you like some toast? or how about muffins???
```

The augmented assignment operators += and +* also work with strings. These operators let you perform an operation and give the result to a name at the same time. They are very useful in loops because they make the assignment statement easy to read.

The + and * operators work differently on strings than they do on numbers. You can't add a string and a number together — you must first convert the string to a number (for example, by using the int() or float() functions). And if you try to use * on a string and an integer, you get a repeated string, not multiplication, like this:

```
>>> "5" * 6
'555555'
>>> int("5") + 6
11
```

Mine's bigger than yours! Comparing strings

When you're working with numbers, it's usually obvious what the smallest and largest numbers are. But it's less clear what *smallest* and *largest* mean when you're talking about characters.

A character's ASCII or Unicode value (a number) determines the character's order. So it would also be correct to talk about one character coming "before" (smaller) or "after" (larger) another character in a numbered list of characters. The following list describes how Python orders (assigns sizes to) characters:

✔ **Letters at the beginning of the alphabet are smaller than letters at the end.**

A is smaller than Z.

✔ **Capital letters come before (are smaller than) lowercase letters.**

Y and Z are both smaller than a.

✔ **Digits are smaller than letters.**

5 is smaller than A.

✔ **Most punctuation marks come before digits or letters.**

! is smaller than 5. The exceptions are curly braces ({ }), the pipe character (|), and the tilde (~), which are larger than letters.

To determine which of two strings is larger, use the < and > operators.

```
>>> 'A' < 'Z'
True
>>> 'b' > 'a'
True
>>> 'a' > 'Z'
True
```

Looping through strings — You can, but why would you want to?

Because a string is a sequence data type, you can use it in a loop; that is, you can *iterate* over it. But there are very few reasons to do this. In fact, code that does this probably has a bug. Python doesn't have a built-in error or warning message for iterating over a string, but external debugging tools such as PyChecker often flag it as a bug.

The PyChecker tool looks for common problems in Python code. It doesn't come with Python, but you can download it from http://pychecker.sourceforge.net/.

A few more methods for working with strings

You use a *string method* to perform actions on a string. To use a string method, type the name of your string, a dot, and the method. Then inside parentheses, pass any parameters that the method needs. In this example, the parameter is the string you want to count the occurrences of:

```
>>> mystring = "mississippi"
>>> mystring.count('s')
4
```

Testing the content of strings

Python lets you test whether strings have certain content. These tests return `True` or `False` (Boolean results).

To test whether text is anywhere in a string, type the text you're searching for in quotation marks, followed by `in` and the name of the string. This example gives a name to a string and tests for the string `'goose'` inside the string.

```
>>> mystring = 'the quick brown fox'
>>> 'goose' in mystring
False
```

To test whether text is *not* in the string, use `not in` rather than `in`.

Python 2.2 and earlier don't have the `in` keyword. In those versions, you can test for text in a string by using the `find()` or `count()` method.

To test whether text is at the end of a string, use the `endswith()` method, as shown here. (The `startswith()` method works the same way but finds text at the beginning of a string.)

```
>>> mystring.endswith('fox')
True
```

Converting data to a string

To turn data other than a string into a string, use the built-in function `str()`, as in this example, which converts an integer to a string:

```
>>> str(2345)
'2345'
```

Sorting a list of strings

To sort a list of strings, use the `sort()` method of lists. Type the name of the list, a dot, and `sort()`, like this:

```
>>> mylist = ['whiskey', 'tango', 'foxtrot']
>>> mylist.sort()
>>> mylist
['foxtrot', 'tango', 'whiskey']
```

Because small letters are "bigger" than (come after) capital letters, if you need to alphabetize some text, you should convert it to all lowercase first. To convert a string to lowercase, type the name of the string, a dot, `lower`, and parentheses, as shown:

```
>>> x = "THIS IS A STRING"
>>> x.lower()
'this is a string'
```

Finding out more about string methods

For more information on string methods, type `help(str)` at the Python prompt.

The string methods work with both regular strings and Unicode strings (see the upcoming section, "Unraveling Unicode"). They include the following types of actions:

- Case manipulation (`capitalize`, `upper`, `lower`, `swapcase`, `title`)
- Counting (`count` — number of times substring is in string)
- Manipulating text encoding (`encode`, `decode`)
- Search and replace (`find`, `replace`, `rfind`, `index`, `rindex`, `translate`)
- Tests that return Boolean (`True` or `False`) values (`startswith`, `endswith`, `isalnum`, `isalpha`, `isdigit`, `islower`, `isspace`, `istitle`, `isupper`)
- Joining and splitting (`join`, `partition`, `rpartition`, `split`, `splitlines`)
- Formatting (`center`, `ljust`, `lstrip`, `rstring`, `rjust`, `strip`, `zfill`, `expandtabs`)

The Cheat Sheet attached to the front of this book briefly describes how most of the above methods work.

The string module versus the str type

Early versions of Python implemented string operations as functions in the `string` module. In Python 2.0, most of those functions were duplicated as methods of the `str` type. The `string` module still works, but use of the `string` module usually indicates an old program (except for `string.maketrans()`, for which there is no equivalent method).

Cat's Cradle: Indexing and Slicing

Strings (and other sequential data types) are divided into pieces called *elements* that are stored in order (in a sequence). In a string, each character is one element. You manipulate the individual elements by using operations called *indexing* and *slicing*.

An index number specifies the location of a particular element, and a range of index numbers specifies a *slice* of several elements.

This section describes the basics of indexing and slicing. You also find out some shortcuts and discover how to use slices to make copies of strings.

Strings can't be changed. But you can use slicing to make a new string based on part of an existing string.

Basic syntax

You use indexing to find an element of a sequence object (such as a character in a string) based on the element's index number. You use slicing to find a range of elements.

Indexing

To find an item corresponding to a particular index number, type the name of your string (or other sequence object) followed by an index number in brackets. Note that the first index number is 0. This example finds the third character, which has the index number 2:

```
>>> mystring = "truly, madly, deeply"
>>> mystring[2]
'u'
```

Slicing

To find items corresponding to a particular slice, you use the name of the string and brackets, as above. Inside the brackets, you enter a *slice* expression: the beginning of the slice, a colon, and the end of the slice. The end of the slice means "up to but not including" this element. In the example below, five elements are returned (index numbers 7, 8, 9, 10, and 11).

Here's an example:

```
>>> mystring[7:12]
'madly'
```

A step (sometimes called a *stride*) skips over some items in the sequence. To specify a step, type a second colon and the step number, like so:

```
>>> mystring = '123456789'
>>> mystring[0:9:2]
'13579'
```

Steps aren't supported in versions of Python earlier than 2.3.

Figuring out the tricks

Following are some shortcuts you can use with slicing and indexing syntax. The examples all use this string:

```
alpha = 'abcde'
```

✔ The beginnings and ends of slices are like notebook dividers — they sit *between* the elements.

✔ If you are counting from left to right when indexing or slicing, the first index number is 0, not 1, as shown:

```
>>> alpha = 'abcde'
>>> alpha[0]
'a'
>>> alpha[0:3]
'abc'
```

When slicing, the first index defaults to 0. If you leave out the first index, Python uses the first item in the sequence, like this:

```
>>> alpha[:2]
'ab'
```

✔ When slicing, the last index defaults to "the length of the sequence." You can access the last item when slicing by leaving out the number after the colon, like this:

```
>>> alpha[1:]
'bcde'
```

If you use a number larger than the size of the sequence,"the length of the sequence" replaces it.

```
>>> alpha[3:10]
'de'
```

However, this doesn't work with indexing. If you use a number larger than the size of the sequence, Python **raises an** IndexError.

```
>>> alpha[10]
Traceback (most recent call last):
  File "<stdin>", line 1, in <module>
IndexError: string index out of range
```

✔ If you are slicing, and the second index number is smaller than the first, you get an empty sequence (for example, an empty string).

```
>>> alpha[3:2]
''
```

✔ You can also count from right to left when indexing or slicing. (This is called *negative indexing*.) When indexing, the first index number, from the right, is -1, the next is -2, and so on — but the leftmost index is still 0.

```
>>> alpha[-1]
'e'
```

✔ If you are making a slice, however, -1 points *before* the last element. To get at the last element, you need to use ":]":

```
>>> alpha[-3:-1]
'cd'
>>> alpha[-3:]
'cde'
```

✔ To get the whole sequence as a slice, use [:] (which makes a copy).

```
>>> alpha[:]
'abcde'
```

✔ Specifying a negative step when slicing is one way to reverse a string.

```
>>> 'hello'[::-1]
'olleh'
```

Figure 6-1 shows the relationship of index numbers and elements in a string or other sequence object.

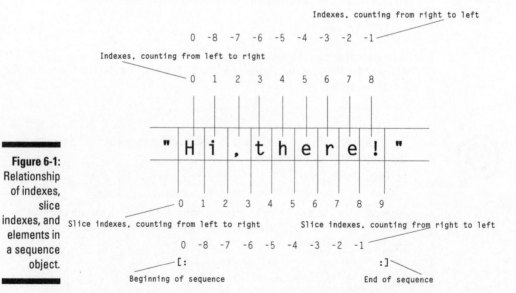

Figure 6-1: Relationship of indexes, slice indexes, and elements in a sequence object.

Changing the immutable string

Strings are immutable (cannot be changed). But you can use slicing and the + operator to make a new string, using some of the content from an existing string. To make a new string by slicing, follow this example, which uses slicing to take all but the first four characters of the candy string and concatenates it to the string 'milk':

```
>>> candy = 'dark chocolate bars'
>>> morecandy = 'milk' + candy[4:]
>>> print morecandy
milk chocolate bars
```

Interpolating Between the Lines

To format the output of strings, you can use the string methods mentioned in "Finding out more about string methods," earlier in this chapter. But there is another, more common way to format strings: the % operator. When used with strings, this operator is sometimes called the *interpolation operator*.

When we use the word *formatting*, we aren't referring to word processor–type formatting — changing fonts, colors, styles, and the like. We mean specifying what happens when a value is inserted into a string. For example, we might specify how many digits to display to the right of a decimal point.

The interpolation operator also lets you insert data in specific places in a string. This means you can calculate your data in one part of your program and print it or save it to a file in another part.

Using the interpolation operator

You can use the % operator in several ways:

- ✔ To include a single data item in a string
- ✔ To include multiple data items in a string by using a tuple
- ✔ To include multiple data items in a string by using a dictionary as a mapping key

Meanings of the formatting codes

A formatting code consists of the % character followed by a character called a *conversion type*. Each character stands for a particular type of data to be included in a string.

The `%s` formatting code (to indicate string data) is the most popular code, because it works on almost all types of data — if you use something other than a string as your data, Python converts it to a string automatically.

Here are some characters that stand for other kinds of data:

- ✔ `%c`: Single character (works with an integer or single-character string)
- ✔ `%d`, `%i`: Signed integer decimal
- ✔ `%f`, `%F`: Floating point decimal
- ✔ `%r`: A `repr()` representation of the data
- ✔ `%%`: Percent sign; used with other codes as an escape character for a real percent sign, as in the example below:

```
>>> "50%% of nothing is still %i" % 0
'50% of nothing is still 0'
```

Optional modifiers of the formatting code

You can add several optional modifiers to `%` codes. You must type the formatting modifiers and code without spaces and use this order:

1. The `%` operator

2. A *mapping key* in parentheses (described in "Formatting with a dictionary," later in this chapter).

3. Conversion flags, so-called because they affect how some kinds of data are converted when they're included in the string. They mostly specify how to handle + and – signs.

   To find out more, see the `FORMATTING` topic in Python's help utility by typing `help('FORMATTING')`.

4. The minimum amount of space to allow for the data (*minimum field width*) — a positive integer.

5. How many digits to include to the right of the decimal point of a decimal number (*precision*) — a dot (`.`) followed by the precision value.

6. The formatting code

The first and last of the preceding steps are required; the rest are optional.

This example prints pi to a precision of 10 decimal places:

```
>>> import math
>>> "The value of pi is about %.10f" % math.pi
'The value of pi is about 3.1415926536'
```

Formatting with one data item

If you have a single data item (for example, `mystring = 'swallow'`) and you want to include it in a string, follow these steps to write the code to do it:

1. **Type your string up to the point where you want your data to go, like this:**

   ```
   >>> "An African or European
   ```

2. **On the same line, type % followed by the formatting code; for example,**

   ```
   >>> "An African or European %s
   ```

   In the above example, `%s` indicates that you will insert string data.

3. **On the same line, type the rest of your string, a space, another %, a space, and the data item that you want to include.**

   Your final line might look something like this:

   ```
   >>> "An African or European %s?" % mystring
   'An African or European swallow?'
   ```

Formatting with multiple data items in a tuple

To include multiple pieces of data in a string, you use multiple formatting codes and pass the arguments in a tuple (that is, inside parentheses, with the values separated by commas; see Chapters 3 and 8 for a refresher on tuples).

This section works with line 4 of the following code, which calculates and prints a table of powers:

```
print "%2s %5s %12s" % ('x', 'x**2', 'x**x')
print "=" * 21
for x in range(1,6):
    print "%2d %5d %12d" % (x, x**2, x**x)
```

To insert multiple data items into a string, follow these steps:

1. **Type** `print`, **followed by a formatting code for each item you want to include, like so:**

   ```
   print "%2s %5s %12s"
   ```

   The numbers in this formatting code specify minimum field widths.

2. **On the same line, type a space, %, a space, and a tuple that includes one data item for each formatting code in the string, as shown here:**

   ```
   print "%2s %5s %12s" % ('x', 'x**2', 'x**x')
   ```

The code prints the following results:

```
x  x**2         x**x
=====================
1    1              1
2    4              4
3    9             27
4   16            256
5   25           3125
```

It's easy to forget to use tuples when formatting with multiple data items. If you remember to do this consistently, you'll be ahead in the debugging game. Even experienced Python programmers make this mistake, so if you see an error message like this, you're in good company:

```
>>> '%s %s' % 'the', 'larch'
Traceback (most recent call last):
  File "<stdin>", line 1, in <module>
TypeError: not enough arguments for format string
```

Here's the right way to do it:

```
>>> '%s %s' % ('the', 'larch')
'the larch'
```

Formatting with a dictionary

You can get data out of a dictionary and include it in your string by using the % operator. You use a *mapping key* to stand for the value to be used from the dictionary. Follow these steps to create a line of code that gets the value of the mathematical constant e from a dictionary and prints it as part of a string.

1. **Type your string up to the point where you want to include your data, like so:**

   ```
   "The value of e is approximately
   ```

2. **Type % and (in parentheses) the dictionary key for the value you want to include.**

   ```
   "The value of e is approximately %(e)
   ```

3. **Type the formatting code (so that the whole chunk of code looks something like this):**

   ```
   "The value of e is approximately %(e)f
   ```

4. **Type the rest of your string, a space, the % operator, a space, and the name of the dictionary.**

   ```
   "The value of e is approximately %(e)f" % mydict
   ```

Here's the line of code in context:

```
>>> math_const = {'pi': 3.141592, 'e': 2.718282}
>>> "The value of e is approximately %(e)f" % math_const
'The value of e is approximately 2.718282'
```

A formatting example using string methods

You can also use string methods to write code that prints a table of powers, similar to the one in the previous section, "Formatting with multiple data items in a tuple." The `rjust()` method right-justifies the string within an area the size of the number of spaces specified in its argument.

Note that this code has more lines than the code written with the % operator and tuples. If you're concerned about reducing the size of your programs, the % operator might be the way to go.

```
x = 'x'
y = 'x**2'
z = 'x**x'
print x, y.rjust(4), z.rjust(6)
print "=" * 14
for n in range(1,6):
    nn = str(n**2)
    nnn = str(n**n)
    print n, nn.rjust(4), nnn.rjust(6)
```

Here's what it prints:

```
x x**2   x**x
==============
1    1       1
2    4       4
3    9      27
4   16     256
5   25    3125
```

Unraveling Unicode

So far, you have been using strings that work with English text (and some Western languages, like French and German). But what if you need to use Russian or Japanese? Python 2.0 introduced a special string type called *Unicode strings* that let you manipulate strings in any language or alphabet.

Unicode strings work mostly the same way as regular strings. Here are a few of their unique features:

- ✔ Unicode strings in Python are specified with a lowercase u.
- ✔ In most installations of Python, a four-digit hexadecimal number represents each Unicode character.

  Regular (ASCII) characters use a two-digit hexadecimal number.

Creating a Unicode string

To create a Unicode string, precede the string with u, like so:

```
>>> z = u"Fruit bats pollinate the flowers of many fruits."
```

To create a Unicode string that uses a non-ASCII Unicode character, follow these steps:

1. **Type u to specify a Unicode string and then start typing the string.**

   ```
   u'Libert
   ```

2. **To specify a character that you want to represent by using Unicode, type \u and the character's hexadecimal value, like so:**

   ```
   u'Libert\u00e9
   ```

3. **Type the rest of the string and the ending quotation mark:**

   ```
   u'Libert\u00e9'
   ```

   The value 00e9 stands for the *é* character.

What is Unicode and why do we care about it?

When people started teaching computers how to talk, the computer geeks came up with a system called ASCII (American Standard Code for Information Interchange). ASCII characters are encoded by using 7 bits of information, which allows for only 128 (0–127) characters. That wasn't enough for non-English languages, accented characters, and other common symbols.

Enter Unicode. Unicode will eventually be able to encode every character set, including those for non-European languages, alphabets used by scholars, and mathematical and linguistic symbols. See www.unicode.org to find out more.

Location, location, location

How Python stores and displays your Unicode string depends on your *locale,* which is Python's idea of what language and character set you're using. The locale also determines the default character encoding that Python uses. The encoded string must match that encoding.

Here's how to see your default locale and encoding:

```
>>> import locale
>>> locale.getdefaultlocale()
['en_US', 'utf']
```

Locales are tricky because all (repeat, *all*) character input and output must go through the encode/decode process. When you print a Unicode string, Python automatically tries to do this conversion so that you see the characters you expect. Here's an example of this conversion in action:

```
>>> print u'Libert\u00e9'
Liberté
```

But you'll see an error if you try printing a Unicode string that contains characters that don't exist in your current locale. For example, if you try to print a Hebrew character with a locale that doesn't support any Hebrew encodings, you'll see this error:

```
>>> print u'\u05d0'  # Hebrew aleph character
Traceback (most recent call last):
File "<stdin>", line 1, in <module>
__builtin__.UnicodeEncodeError: 'ascii' codec can't encode character u'\u05d0' in
        position 0: ordinal not in range(128)
```

Note that many modern operating systems support multiple encodings, so you might not see this error if you try it yourself.

A twisty maze of codes

Unicode lets you process text by using only one code. But Unicode can't be used directly with character input and output, so you need to encode output and decode input.

Beginners tend to think of Unicode as another encoding of the character set they are used to using. Thus, they think that they need to encode "regular" text into Unicode and decode Unicode into regular text. That's backward. Here's the correct way to think about it:

When you start using Unicode, whatever regular character set you're using is a part of Unicode. Therefore, you need to *encode* Unicode characters into your regular character set, and *decode* your regular character set into Unicode.

Encoding, decoding, and other Unicode methods

All the regular string methods also work with Unicode strings. A couple of methods apply especially to Unicode: encode() and decode().

The list of standard encodings is available at www.python.org/dev/doc/devel/lib/standard-encodings.html.

Converting Unicode to an encoded string

To convert a Unicode string to an encoding, such as UTF-8 or Latin-1, you use the encode() method. Follow these steps:

1. **Create a Unicode string, like so:**

   ```
   y = u"Libert\u00e9, \u00e9galit\u00e9, fraternit\u00e9"
   ```

2. **Type the name of the string, a dot, encode, and (in parentheses) the encoding you want to convert to.**

   ```
   y.encode('utf-8')
   ```

This example shows the difference between the encoded and printed strings:

```
>>> q = y.encode('utf-8')
>>> q
'Libert\xc3\xa9, \xc3\xa9galit\xc3\xa9, fraternit\xc3\xa9'
>>> print q
Liberté, égalité, fraternité
```

Python's file objects and StringIO objects don't support raw Unicode; the usual workaround is to encode Unicode text as UTF-8 before saving it to a file or StringIO object.

Decoding a string into Unicode

The decode() method, new in Python 2.2, assumes that a string is in the specified encoding and turns it into Unicode. To decode a string into Unicode, follow these steps:

1. **Create an encoded string, like so (this string is encoded using UTF-8):**

   ```
   q = 'Libert\xc3\xa9'
   ```

2. **Type the name of the string, a dot, decode, and (in parentheses) the encoding that the string currently uses.**

   ```
   q.decode('utf-8')
   ```

The Midas touch — Unicode versus str

In Python, Unicode behaves a bit like Midas, the character in Greek legend who turned everything he touched (including his daughter) into gold. When you use a Unicode string and a regular string together, the results are always Unicode.

```
>>> myunicodestring = u"Midas is coming! "
>>> mystring = "Don't touch me, Midas!"
>>> myunicodestring + mystring
u"Midas is coming! Don't touch me,
        Midas!"
```

This example shows the difference between the encoded and decoded strings.

✔ Encoded string

```
>>> 'Libert\xc3\xa9'
```

✔ Decoded (Unicode) string

```
u'Libert\xe9'
```

\xe9 is Python's shorthand way of representing Unicode character \u00e9, which prints as é.

Both strings look the same when printed:

```
>>> print q
Liberté
>>> print q.decode('utf-8')
Liberté
```

Chapter 7

Counting Your Way
to Fun and Profit

*I*n Python, numbers come in several different data types. Chapter 3 introduces the number types and their operators. This chapter gives you more information on integers, binary floating point numbers, and complex numbers, and provides guidance for using Python's augmented assignment operators. It also introduces Python's built-in math modules, including the decimal module for doing true decimal arithmetic, and the random module for generating random numbers.

Integrating Integers

Integers are positive and negative whole numbers (numbers without a value to the right of the decimal point). We give you a brief overview of integers in Chapter 3; the following sections describe some finer points about Python's integers.

Why Python has two kinds of integers

Because of how computers store numbers in memory, Python uses two kinds of integers:

▶ Regular integers

▶ Long integers

In the recent past, most computers used 32 bits of memory to store an integer. But integers larger than a certain value (2,147,483,647, to be exact) take up more than 32 bits of memory. So Python uses a different mechanism to store them. Python represents long integers with the suffix L.

In future versions of Python, all integers will be handled the same way. For now, if you're writing programs that manipulate very large integers, each version of Python handles integers a bit differently. Your results may vary depending on the version. If you're using Python 2.2 or later, regular integers automatically convert to long integers, so you can mostly ignore the issue.

Avoiding unexpected results with integer division

If you enter only integers when you do arithmetic, Python returns the results in integers. This can give unexpected results if you're doing division with the / operator — you get only the integer part of the result.

In math terms, the / operator performs *floor division,* not true division.

For example, your math teacher would *not* let you get away with this result:

```
>>> 13 / 3
4
```

If you want true division, use one of the following solutions:

- ✔ Use the decimal module, like this:

```
>>> from decimal import Decimal
>>> Decimal(13) / Decimal(3)
Decimal("4.3333333333333333333333333333")
```

   The decimal module was introduced in Python 2.4. See the section, "Turning Python into a Calculator with decimal," later in this chapter, for details.

- ✔ Make sure that at least one of the numbers in a calculation is a *floating point* (decimal) number, like this:

```
>>> 13.0 / 3
4.333333333333333
```

- ✔ Use the division feature from the __future__ module, like this:

```
>>> from __future__ import division
>>> 13 / 3
4.333333333333333
```

> Using __future__ activates code that will become the default in
> Python 3.0; in this case, it activates true division for the / operator. For
> integer division, use the // operator.

Floating Along

The standard format for computers to store real numbers is called *binary
floating point,* which is different from the format most people are used to. For
example, if you type 0.1 into Python's interpreter, you see that Python's
internal representation of the number is different from what you typed:

```
>>> 0.1
0.10000000000000001
```

This happens because a computer can't accurately represent some decimal
numbers as floats. For more information than you really need to know about
why, see Appendix B of the Python Tutorial at www.python.org. (*For detail
nuts only:* The decimal numbers that can be represented accurately have a
fractional component containing only sums of powers of two.)

Automatic conversion

Python automatically converts different types of numbers so that you (usually) don't need to think about the compatibility of different number types.
For example, if you do a math operation with both integers and floats, Python
converts the integers to floats and gives the result as a float.

Formatting floats

If you don't want to look at weird numbers with 16 decimal places, use the
str() function to display the number as a string.

```
>>> 4.1
4.0999999999999996
>>> str(4.1)
'4.1'
```

You might be tempted to use the round() function to handle floating point
numbers. But round() requires you to specify a precision (the number of
digits to the right of the decimal point) and defaults to a precision of 0 (which
removes *all* the digits to the right of the decimal point). This probably isn't
what you want if you're working with decimal numbers!

Size limits on floats

Python's binary floating point numbers have a finite range. Python stores binary floats using at most 17 decimal digits of accuracy. In addition, the largest float you can store is 1.79769_10^{308} (which Python represents as 1.79769e+308). If you try to calculate or store a larger number, you may get a result such as this:

```
>>> x = 2.79769e+308
>>> x
inf
```

Long integers can be larger than floats, so you might get an "overflow error" or incorrect results when using large integers with binary floats or with the `float()` function (which converts numbers to binary floats). The following code attempts to convert $10^{1,000}$ to a float. Because the resulting number is too big for Python and the computer to handle, it raises an error:

```
>>> float(10**1000)
Traceback (most recent call last):
  File "<stdin>", line 1, in <module>
OverflowError: long int too large to convert to float
```

The following code also gives an incorrect result because of the 17-digit size limit on floats. (A number doesn't equal itself plus 1, no matter how big it is!)

```
>>> 10.0 ** 100 == (10.0 ** 100) + 1
True
```

Imagining Complex Numbers

Complex numbers have a real and imaginary part, both of which are floats.

A complex numeric literal is the sum of a real part and an imaginary part.

In Python, to specify an imaginary number, or the imaginary part of a complex number, append `j` to the number.

To separate the real or imaginary part of a complex number, type `x.real` for the real part or `x.imag` for the imaginary part, like this:

```
>>> x =(3+6j)
>>> x.real
3.0
>>> x.imag
6.0
```

Augmented assignment

Use *augmented assignment* operators to perform actions such as addition, concatenation, subtraction, and multiplication on an object and store the result using the same name. (An "augmented" assignment statement has an extra feature — an addition or concatenation operation — built in.) Here's why:

✔ Augmented assignment statements are easier to debug.

The statement `counter +=1` clearly uses only one object. If you use the statement `counter = counter + 1`, you must read the statement carefully to make sure the two objects are the same. If you're trying to debug someone else's thousand-line program, you'll appreciate the simplicity!

✔ Augmented assignment statements are more efficient.

These statements evaluate an object only once and change mutable objects in place; regular assignment evaluates an object twice and creates a new copy in the process. This can slow performance with large objects.

These are the most commonly used augmented assignment operators:

+= (addition or concatenation):

```
counter += 1
```
–= (subtraction):

```
counter -= 1
```
*= (multiplication):

```
counter *= 1
```

Using Math Modules

Along with the arithmetic operators (covered in Chapter 3) and the basic math functions of the __builtin__ module (introduced in Chapter 2) that's always available when you use Python, Python has several modules that provide math functions.

To import any of the math modules, type import followed by the name of the module. Use the following list to guide you to the module you need:

✔ **Real numbers:** The math module has most of the functions you need for real numbers. To see all the functions, type this into the interpreter:

```
>>> import math
>>> help(math)
```

✔ **Complex numbers:** The cmath module, for complex numbers, has most of the same functions as the math module but returns results as a complex number type (for example, 3+6j — see "Imagining Complex Numbers," earlier in this chapter).

The cmath module also returns values for calculations such as the square root of a negative number. (The math module treats such calculations as errors.)

If you're working with both complex and real numbers, use the module name (such as `cmath.sqrt()` or `math.sqrt()`) when calling a function. Many of the two modules' functions have the same names but work differently. The module name helps you keep track of which function you're using.

✔ **Decimal numbers:** The `decimal` module lets you work with decimal numbers rather than binary floating point numbers.

Decimal numbers give more accurate results for many calculations. See "Turning Python into a Calculator with decimal," later in this chapter.

✔ **Random numbers:** The `random` module includes tools for such tasks as generating random numbers and choosing randomly from several elements. For a fun introduction to the tricks up the sleeve of the random module, see Chapter 21.

Turning Python into a Calculator with decimal

The `decimal` module, new in Python 2.4, supports decimal floating point arithmetic.

If you're writing applications that require control over precision and rounding (such as financial software or statistics modules), this module is for you. Its results also match calculations done by hand (math educators take note!).

The `decimal` module gives more accurate results than binary floating point math for these types of calculations: *Calculating a percentage, modulo calculations* (which return the fractional result of division), and *equality tests.*

Like other numbers, decimal numbers are immutable.

To import the `decimal` module, use this statement:

```
from decimal import Decimal
```

Representing numbers by using the decimal module

To create a decimal number, type the following, substituting your number or object inside the parentheses:

```
Decimal(numerical_object)
```

The *numerical_object* can be any of these types of data:

✔ An integer

```
Decimal(3)
```

✔ A calculation

```
Decimal(3*5)
```

✔ A number represented as a string

```
Decimal("3.2")
```

✔ A float converted to a string with the `str()` function

```
>>> x = 3.2
>>> Decimal(str(x))
Decimal("3.2")
```

You can't use floating point numbers directly with the decimal module. They must be converted to strings first.

✔ A three-item tuple

```
>>> Decimal((0, (3, 1, 4), -2))
Decimal("3.14")
```

To create a decimal from a three-item tuple, use this format for the tuple:

1. The first item in the tuple is `0` (for positive) or `1` (for negative).

2. The second item is another (nested) tuple containing the digits of the number, one element for each digit.

3. The third item is a positive or negative integer specifying the exponent.

`Decimal` numbers work with Python's regular math functions. Give them names and use the names as arguments, or insert them directly as arguments:

```
>>> pow(Decimal(9), 2)
Decimal("81")
```

Viewing and changing parameters

The `decimal` module has parameters that control how it works with and displays numbers. To see the parameters, type the following:

```
>>> import decimal
>>> decimal.getcontext()
Context(prec=28, rounding=ROUND_HALF_EVEN, Emin=-999999999, Emax=999999999,
capitals=1, flags=[], traps=[DivisionByZero, InvalidOperation, Overflow])
```

One of the parameters is the maximum precision of decimal numbers (how many digits to the right of the decimal point you see). To change the precision parameter, type something like this:

```
>>> decimal.getcontext().prec = 7
```

If you want to change the precision of a specific number without changing the precision parameter for all the numbers, use the quantize() method. quantize() rounds the number to a specific number of decimal places. This example rounds to two decimal places:

```
>>> data = Decimal('7.324')
>>> data.quantize(Decimal('.01'))
Decimal("7.32")
```

Chapter 8

Processing Lists and Tuples

● ●

In This Chapter

▶ Discovering lists and tuples

▶ Deciding whether to use a list or a tuple

▶ Working with data in lists and tuples

▶ Using lists and tuples inside loops

▶ Avoiding common errors with compound data types

● ●

*L*ists and tuples are two of Python's *compound data types*, also called *container objects*. Compound data types group collections of data.

Python has several kinds of compound data types. Lists and tuples are *sequence* types because each element of data is numbered sequentially, starting with 0. Sequence types support operations called *indexing* and *slicing* for working with individual elements or subsets of elements. You can find out about indexing and slicing in Chapter 6.

A sequence data type is good when you want to operate on all the elements in a collection or when the order of elements in a collection is important. (In contrast, the dictionary data type — a *mapping* type — is for random access to elements, and a set is for comparing collections of objects. Dictionaries and sets are covered in Chapter 9.)

This chapter shows you the syntax for lists and tuples, when to use them, how to work with elements inside them, how to use them in loops, and how to avoid some of the common errors programmers make when working with them.

Introducing Lists and Tuples

The following sections describe the features and syntax of lists and tuples and explain when to use each.

What a list is

A list is a *mutable* data type, which means you can change the contents of a list without creating a new list. The elements of a list can be of different data types. A single list can contain numbers, strings, other lists, tuples — and even functions and classes.

In Python, a list *literal* (the actual data, not a name referring to the data) is defined by square brackets surrounding zero or more elements. Elements are separated by commas. Below are examples of lists:

```
a_list = ['this', 'is', 'a', 'list']
empty_list = []
another_list = [5]
```

Lists come with a variety of built-in methods that let you manipulate them. For example, to sort a list, you write code like this:

```
>>> mylist = [8, 33, 29, 4, 1, 5, 98]
>>> mylist.sort()
>>> mylist
[1, 4, 5, 8, 29, 33, 98]
```

What a tuple is

A tuple is a sequence data type that can contain elements of different data types. Tuples are different from lists because tuples are *immutable.* If you want to change the contents of a tuple, you must create a new tuple that has the new content you want.

If a tuple contains a mutable element (such as a list or dictionary), the mutable element *can* be modified. However, some of the obvious ways of changing the mutable element will cause errors because Python will attempt to modify the tuple. We recommend that you avoid changing mutable elements in tuples.

Tuples don't include a lot of special methods, the way strings and lists do. But tuples do include methods that support standard Python operators. For example, you can add tuples, check whether an item is inside a tuple, slice elements in a tuple, compare a tuple to other data, find a tuple's length, and so on.

Many Python functions, such as the `time` and `date` functions, return tuples.

Choosing between lists and tuples

Lists and tuples look similar at first glance, but they have intrinsic differences:

✔ A tuple is immutable, and a list is mutable.

✔ Tuples are more memory-efficient.

✔ Lists have several useful built-in methods.

Tuples are often better than lists for information that you don't want to change, for two reasons: They use less memory, and (because they're immutable) they won't change unexpectedly.

Lists are often better for information you want to change because there are more ways of manipulating them.

Guido (Python's creator) and the Python community promote the following conventions for choosing between lists and tuples:

✔ **Tuples for heterogeneous data, lists for homogeneous data:** Use a tuple if your data includes several different data types, such as names and addresses; use lists for elements that are all of the same type.

For example, if you're accessing a database, the fields of a record might be returned as a tuple, but the records themselves should be returned as a list. Therefore the overall database would be a list of tuples.

✔ **Tuples for sequence keys:** If you need to use a sequence as a dictionary key, you must use a tuple because dictionary keys are immutable.

✔ **Tuples for some functions:** Some functions require arguments to be passed in tuples.

✔ **Lists for mutable objects:** Avoid using mutable objects in immutable containers because errors and unexpected results can occur if you attempt to change the mutable objects.

A *tuple literal* is defined in one of three ways:

✔ A single element followed by a comma

✔ Multiple elements separated by commas

✔ An empty set of parentheses

When Python outputs a tuple, it encloses the elements in parentheses. You can (and usually should) use parentheses when creating a tuple, but you don't have to. Below are examples of tuples.

```
>>> a_tuple = ('this', 'is', 'a', 'tuple')
>>> tuple_2 = "this", "is", "another", "tuple"
>>> tuple_2
('this', 'is', 'another', 'tuple')
>>> empty_tuple = ()
```

A tuple (except for an empty tuple) must always use a comma, even if there is only one element, because the comma is the operator that defines a tuple.

Because the comma is *overloaded* (that is, it does more than one thing in Python) and because it has low precedence (that is, most other operations are evaluated before comma operations), it's usually a Good Idea to add parentheses to make it clear that you are using a tuple.

Below are the results of using the * operator on a single-element tuple and on an integer.

```
>>> another_tuple = (3,)
>>> another_tuple * 3
(3, 3, 3)
>>> not_a_tuple = (3)
>>> not_a_tuple * 3
9
```

Manipulating Sequence Objects

The following sections describe how to compare, combine, and search the contents of lists, tuples, and other sequence objects.

Comparing sequence objects

Sequence objects such as lists can be compared to other objects of the same data type. A comparison tells you whether the objects are equal or whether one is smaller than the other. Here's how it works:

- ✔ The first items of each sequence are compared, and then the second items, and so on.
- ✔ If an item inside a sequence is itself a sequence, then each of its items is compared against the item of the same number in the other sequence.
- ✔ If all items of two sequences are equal, the sequences are equal.
- ✔ If sequence 1 is the same as the beginning of sequence 2, sequence 1 is smaller (lesser).
- ✔ Strings are compared based on the ASCII order of their characters. Chapter 6 has more information about character order.

Table 8-1 shows the results of comparisons between sequences.

Table 8-1	Comparisons between Sequences
Comparison	*Reason*
`(1, 2, 3) < (1, 2, 4),` `[1, 2, 3] < [1, 2, 4]`	3 is less than 4
`'ABC' < 'C' < 'Pascal'` `< 'Python'`	ASCII order of characters
`(1, 2, 4) > (1, 2, 3, 4),` `(1, 2) < (1, 2, -1)`	First sequence is the same as the beginning of second sequence
`(1, 2, 3) == (1.0, 2.0, 3.0)`	Integers equal their float equivalents
`(1, 2, ('aa', 'ab')) <` `(1, 2, ('abc', 'a'), 4)`	Alphabetical order of characters in sub-sequence ('aa' is smaller than 'abc')

If you compare objects of different types, the types are ordered alphabetically by their names: Lists are smaller than strings, which are smaller than tuples. The rules for comparing objects of different types may change in future versions of Python.

Operating on sequence objects

The following operators work on lists and tuples. Most of these operators also work on other data types:

- ✔ **Addition** (+): Concatenates the contents of lists together to form a new list, or concatenates the contents of tuples together to form a new tuple. (You can't concatenate a list and a tuple.)

  ```
  >>> [1, 2, 3] + [2, 4]
  [1, 2, 3, 2, 4]
  ```

- ✔ **Sequence multiplication** (*): Repeats the contents of a list or a tuple.

- ✔ **Augmented assignment** (+= and *=): Simultaneously concatenates and assigns or repeats and assigns. The statement `mylist += newlist` is the same as `mylist = mylist + newlist`. The former works slightly faster and is easier to read.

- ✔ **Comparison** (< >, ==, !=): Tests whether the contents of two or more lists or two or more tuples are the same.

✔ **Contents test** (in): The keyword in determines whether a list or tuple contains the given element and returns True or False, as shown here:

```
>>> phone_sounds = ('beep', 'ring', 'flight of the bumblebee')
>>> y = 'beep' in phone_sounds
>>> y
True
```

Listcraft: Methods, Indexes, and Slices

In this section we describe important ways you can work with lists. You can turn other data into lists, count items in lists, sort lists in various orders, and use indexing and slicing to change, add, delete, and move individual list items.

Functions that work with or create lists

The list() function creates a copy of a list. It also turns any other sequence object or iterable into a list. (An *iterable* is an object whose elements can be retrieved one at a time.) This example turns a tuple into a list:

```
>>> mytuple = ('apple', 'orange', 'pear')
>>> mylist = list(mytuple)
>>> mylist
['apple', 'orange', 'pear']
```

If you feed a string to the list() function, it makes a separate list item out of each character, as in this example.

```
>>> mystring = "Boo!"
>>> list(mystring)
['B', 'o', 'o', '!']
```

To find out the number of elements in a list, use the len() function (it also works on other data types).

```
>>> len(mylist)
3
```

Methods of lists

A method is like a function except that it "belongs" with a particular object, and when you call it, you *qualify* it with the name of the object. The method names are *attributes* of the object.

List method syntax

To call a list method, type the list name, a dot, the method name, and parentheses. In the parentheses, pass any arguments the method needs. (Some methods don't require or use arguments.) Here's an example:

```
list_name.method_name(arguments)
```

The most popular list methods

The following are some of the most frequently used list methods:

✔ To add an item to the end of a list, use the `append()` method. This method changes the list in place. It returns `None`.

This example adds the string `'apple'` to a list:

```
basket = ['apple', 'banana', 'orange']
basket.append('apple')
```

✔ To find out the number of times a value occurs in a list, use the `count(value)` method.

This example counts the number of times the string `'apple'` appears.

```
>>> basket.count('apple')
2
```

✔ To add to a list the contents of another sequence object or iterable (an object whose elements can be retrieved one at a time), use the `extend()` method. If the iterable is a string, each character is added individually.

This example adds each character of the string `'pear'`.

```
>>> x = ['apple', 'apple', 'banana', 'orange']
>>> x.extend('pear')
>>> x
['apple', 'apple', 'banana', 'orange', 'p', 'e', 'a', 'r']
```

✔ To delete the first occurrence of an item in a list, use the `remove()` method. It raises a `ValueError` if the item isn't found.

This example removes the first `'apple'` string.

```
>>> x.remove('apple')
>>> x
['apple', 'banana', 'orange', 'p', 'e', 'a', 'r']
```

✔ The `sort()` and `reverse()` methods both change the list itself.

- The `sort()` method's default ordering is alphabetical for lists containing text, numerical for lists containing numbers, and so on.

- The `reverse()` method inverts the positions of items in a list.

✔ Python 2.4 and later also support these built-in functions:

- sorted(), which returns a sorted *copy* of the list (or other iterable).

- reversed(), which returns an iterator object that lets you use a loop to process the items in the list in reverse order.

The following examples show the use of the sort() and reverse() methods on a list of strings:

```
>>> x.sort()
>>> x
['a', 'apple', 'banana', 'e', 'orange', 'p', 'r']
>>> x.reverse()
>>> x
['r', 'p', 'orange', 'e', 'banana', 'apple', 'a']
```

List indexing and slicing

List and tuple elements have index numbers. Indexing and slicing operations on lists and tuples work mostly the same way that they do with strings. Here's a quick review of how index numbers work. For more about indexing and slicing, see Chapter 6.

✔ Working from left to right, the first element has the index 0, the next has the index 1, and so on.

This example shows the items at index 0 and 1 of the list x.

```
>>> x = ['apple', 'banana', 'pear']
>>> x[0]
'apple'
>>> x[1]
'banana'
```

✔ Working from right to left, the first element has the index -1, the next one -2, and so on — but the leftmost element is still 0.

This example shows the items at index -1 and -2.

```
>>> x[-1]
'pear'
>>> x[-2]
'banana'
```

✔ The beginnings and ends of slices sit *between* the elements, like notebook dividers.

This example shows that slice 0:1 contains just one element.

```
>>> x[0:1]
['apple']
```

How indexing and slicing are different with a list

Indexing and slicing work slightly differently with lists than they do with strings and tuples because lists are mutable. You can change a list by using indexing and slicing. With a tuple or a string, you need to give a new name to the changed object (or reassign the same name).

Retrieving items from a list with slicing

Following is a brief review of slicing syntax. You can find more information in Chapter 6.

The syntax for slicing is as follows:

```
sequence_object_name[firstindex:lastindex:step]
```

These are the rules for slicing:

- ✔ **You can leave out the first slice index (but not the colon following it).** It defaults to 0.
- ✔ **You can leave out the last slice index.** It defaults to the last item of the sequence.

  To access the last sequence item in a slice, if you don't know the length of the sequence, leave the index blank.

- ✔ **You can leave out the step and the colon preceding it.** The step defaults to 1.

- ✔ **When you specify a range, it begins with the first slice index specified and ends *before* the last slice index specified.** This is because slices point between elements. So [0:2] retrieves the first and second elements.

- ✔ **The notation [:] returns a shallow copy of the whole sequence.**

  The section, "List references that unexpectedly change," later in the chapter, has more on shallow copying.

The following example code creates a list of numbers and then, using slice syntax, selects and displays all the even-numbered items.

```
>>> mylist = range(0,10)
>>> mylist[::2]
[0, 2, 4, 6, 8]
```

Changing a list item by using its index number

One way to change the contents of a list is to assign a new item to a particular index number (also called an offset). This replaces whatever is already at that index number.

Gotcha! Assigning numbers and strings to slices

If you assign to a slice, you must assign an iterable. This means two things:

1. You can't assign a number to a slice.

```
>>> mylist = [1, 2, 3, 4, 5, 6]
>>> mylist [2:3] = 8
Traceback (most recent call last):
  File "<stdin>", line 1, in ?
TypeError: can only assign an iterable
```

2. If you assign a string to a slice, each letter becomes a separate list item.

```
>>> mylist[2:4] = 'three'
>>> mylist
[1, 2, 't', 'h', 'r', 'e', 'e', 5, 6]
```

One way around this second problem is to put the number or string into a list. The following example assumes you want to replace the numbers 3 and 4 with the strings 'three' and 'four':

```
>>> mylist = [1, 2, 3, 4, 5, 6]
>>> mylist[2:4] = ['three', 'four']
>>> mylist
[1, 2, 'three', 'four', 5, 6]
```

To assign a new item to a list by index number, follow these steps:

1. **Type the list name and then, in square brackets, type the index number, like this:**

```
mylist[1]
```

2. **On the same line, type = and the new list element, so your line looks something like this:**

```
mylist[1] = new_list_element
```

In the following example, the element at index 1 (the string `'eggs'`) is replaced with the string `'lovely spam'`.

```
>>> L = ['spam', 'eggs', 'ham']
>>> L[1] = 'lovely spam'
>>> L
['spam', 'lovely spam', 'ham']
```

You can't assign to an index number that doesn't exist. Python raises an `IndexError`, as shown here:

```
>>> L[3] = 'green eggs'
Traceback (most recent call last):
  File "<stdin>", line 1, in <module>
IndexError: list assignment index out of range
```

To add items to the end of a list, use the `append()` method:

```
>>> L.append('green eggs')
>>> L
['spam', 'lovely spam', 'ham', 'green eggs']
```

Assigning to a list with slicing

To assign several items in a row to a list, use a range of index numbers.

Assigning using a slice follows these rules:

- ✔ Python first deletes the items currently assigned to those index numbers and then inserts the new items.

- ✔ You don't have to assign the same number of items that you delete.

- ✔ You must assign an *iterable* (see the sidebar, "Gotcha! Assigning numbers and strings to slices").

To assign items to a list slice, follow these steps:

1. **Type the name of the list and, in brackets, type the slice notation, like this:**

   ```
   L[1:4]
   ```

2. **On the same line, type = and the items you want to assign.**

   If you assign items from another list, your whole line might look something like this:

   ```
   L[1:4] = ['spam', 'spam', 'spam']
   ```

   The resulting list now looks like this:

   ```
   ['spam', 'spam', 'spam', 'spam']
   ```

The following example manipulates a list of words by using slice assignment:

```
>>> L = ['spam', 'eggs', 'ham', 'green eggs']
>>> L[:2] = ("don't", "want")
>>> L
["don't", 'want', 'ham', 'green eggs']
>>> L[2:] = ("green eggs", "and", "ham")
>>> L
["don't", 'want', 'green eggs', 'and', 'ham']
```

List indexing and slicing operations

The following operations use the indexing and slicing features of lists:

- ✔ To return the index number of a list item, use the `index()` method.

  If the item isn't in the list, it raises a `ValueError`.

This example returns the index number of the second item in the list:

```
>>> mylist = [1, 'two', 3]
>>> mylist.index('two')
1
```

✔ To remove from a list the item(s) corresponding to the given index number or slice, use the keyword `del`.

This example deletes two items.

```
>>> mylist2 = ['busy signal', 'fast busy signal', 'no such number', 'at the
            tone, the time will be']
>>> del mylist2[1:3]
>>> mylist2
['busy signal', 'at the tone, the time will be']
```

✔ To insert an item *before* a particular index number, use the `insert()` method.

```
>>> basket.insert(0, 'peach')
>>> basket
['peach', 'apple', 'banana', 'orange']
```

✔ To remove and return an item at a particular index number, use the `pop()` method. The default index number for `pop()` is the last item in the list. This example removes and returns the item `'baked beans'` in the list `breakfast`:

```
>>> breakfast = ['spam', 'spam', 'spam', 'baked beans', 'spam', 'spam']
>>> breakfast.pop(3)
'baked beans'
>>> breakfast
['spam', 'spam', 'spam', 'spam', 'spam']
```

The following code uses a `while` loop to return and delete all the list elements one at a time:

```
>>> while breakfast:
...     breakfast.pop()
...
'spam'
'spam'
'spam'
'spam'
'spam'
>>> breakfast
[]
```

Steering Clear of List Gotcha's

This section describes how to avoid some common list errors.

Simultaneous test/add/delete

If you're testing a list condition in a `while` loop or iterating over a list in a `for` loop, avoid adding and deleting list elements at the same time. It's easy to lose track of how the list is changing. An exception is the use of `pop()` in a `while` loop to remove all list elements one by one.

List references that unexpectedly change

Because lists are mutable, you can change them without making a copy. But if you reference a single list from several places in your code, it might change when you aren't expecting it to.

Shallow copying

If a *container object* (an object — such as a list, tuple, or dictionary — that holds other objects) contains lists, then making a copy of the container object by using `newcontainer = oldcontainer` or `newcontainer = oldcontainer[:]` doesn't make a copy of the lists it contains. The new container continues to refer to the original lists. This is called *shallow copying*, and Python uses it because (among other reasons) it saves resources. The following example illustrates shallow copying. The `larder` list changes when one of the lists inside the `food` list is changed:

```
>>> breakfast = ['spam', 'baked beans']
>>> basket = ['peach', 'apple', 'gooseberries']
>>> food = [breakfast, basket]
>>> larder = food
>>> larder
[['spam', 'baked beans'], ['peach', 'apple', 'gooseberries']]
>>> del basket[0]
>>> larder
[['spam', 'baked beans'], ['apple', 'gooseberries']]
```

Deep copying

Sometimes you want to make a full, or *deep,* copy of a list (or any item that contains other items). To do so, import the `copy` module and use the `copy.deepcopy()` function. In this example, when you copy the `food` list to the `larder` list by using the `deepcopy()` function, changing the contents of one of the lists in `food` doesn't change the contents of `larder`.

```
>>> food
[['spam', 'baked beans'], ['apple', 'gooseberries']]
>>> import copy
>>> larder = copy.deepcopy(food)
>>> larder
```

```
[['spam', 'baked beans'], ['apple', 'gooseberries']]
>>> del basket[0]
>>> food
[['spam', 'baked beans'], ['gooseberries']]
>>> larder
[['spam', 'baked beans'], ['apple', 'gooseberries']]
```

Disappearing lists

The list methods append() and sort() change a list in place but don't
return the list. They return None. Don't use these methods in assignment
statements or else the list might disappear, as in this example:

```
>>> L = ["my", "list"]
>>> L = L.append('x')    # wrong!
>>> print L
None
```

To append to a list, just use the append() method by itself. Don't give the
result a name.

```
>>> L = ["my", "list"]
>>> L.append('x')
>>> print L
['my', 'list', 'x']
```

That tricky asterisk

If you repeat (*) a list, you get a list with multiple copies of its elements. But
if you repeat (*) a list *containing* a list, you get multiple shallow copies of the
contained list. The following examples demonstrate both repeating a list and
repeating a list that contains a list:

✔ A repeated list:

```
>>> mylist = [3, 'blind', 'mice']
>>> x = mylist * 2
>>> x
[3, 'blind', 'mice', 3, 'blind', 'mice']
```

✔ Repeating a list *containing* a list:

```
>>> y = [mylist] * 2
>>> y
[[3, 'blind', 'mice'], [3, 'blind', 'mice']]
```

In the preceding examples, if you change `mylist`, the value of `y` changes because `y` contains references to `mylist`. But the value of `x` doesn't change because `x` only contains copies of the *elements* of `mylist`. Here's what happens:

We change the first element of `mylist`:

```
>>> mylist[0] = 'two'
```

Here's the result:

✔ `y` reflects the new version of `mylist`:

```
>>> y
[['two', 'blind', 'mice'], ['two', 'blind', 'mice']]
```

✔ `x` doesn't change:

```
>>> x
[3, 'blind', 'mice', 3, 'blind', 'mice']
```

Performance problems

Manipulating large lists can cause performance problems. Here's how to avoid these problems:

✔ **Avoid copying long lists.**

For example, avoid using loops that delete elements from the beginning of a list (`del mylist[0]` or `mylist.pop(0)`) because doing so requires Python to make multiple copies of the list.

✔ **Avoid making multiple copies of the elements of a list.**

Copying the list itself doesn't take a lot of time, but copying the elements does.

✔ **Build lists when you need them.** Populating a list with elements before you need the list isn't necessary, and it might even waste memory.

Building Lists, Stacks, and Queues

This section describes two often-used list tasks: building a list one element at a time and building stacks and queues.

Building lists incrementally

Because lists are mutable, you can build them one element at a time. It is often useful to build lists from other iterable objects or to combine multiple lists. The easiest way of doing this is to write a `for` loop and build the new list with the `append()` method, as in the following example:

```
L1 = ['spam', 'spam', 'spam', 'baked beans', None, 'spam', 'spam']
L2 = []
for i in L1:
    if i is not None:
        L2.append(i)
```

After you run the above code, the value of L2 is `['spam', 'spam', 'spam', 'baked beans', 'spam', 'spam']`.

If you're iterating over a list in a `for` loop, it's best not to add elements to or delete elements from that list — doing so can introduce errors. It's safer to use code like the above example to build a *new* list and then change the elements of the new list.

Python provides several other tools for building lists:

✔ To convert or copy sequences (and other iterable objects) to a list, use the `list()` function (described earlier in this chapter).

✔ Another way to copy a whole list or other sequence and return a shallow copy is to use this slice notation: `mylist[:]`

✔ Python includes a feature called a *list comprehension,* which works in much the same way as a list-building `for` loop but is packaged more compactly. (See Chapter 16 to find out about this advanced feature.)

✔ To loop over two or more sequences at the same time, use the `zip()` function. It returns a list of tuples that associates the items in one sequence with the corresponding items in another sequence. It also truncates the resulting list to the length of the shortest sequence.

```
>>> a = [8, 3, 5, 11]
>>> b = ('eggs', 'spam')
>>> c = zip(a, b)
>>> print c
[(8, 'eggs'), (3, 'spam')]
```

If you use `zip()` again with the `*args` style parameter, you get a list of tuples that correspond to the original sequences you started with (but any items that were truncated are missing).

The `*args` style argument is explained in Chapter 11.

Here's what it could look like:

```
>>> zip(*c)
[(8, 3), ('eggs', 'spam')]
```

✔ To get tuples of list index numbers and their elements, use the
  enumerate() iterator.

```
>>> a = [8, 3, 5, 11]
>>> for I, item in enumerate(a):
...     print (I, item),
...
(0, 8) (1, 3) (2, 5) (3, 11)
```

Stacking and queuing with lists

Stacks and *queues* are concepts that describe how items get added to and
removed from lists. Stacks and queues are not Python objects, but you can
write code in which a list behaves like a stack or a queue.

A *stack* is like a spring-loaded plate dispenser where the last item on is the
first item off (this is also called "last in, first out" order, which is inscribed in
the Great Book of Geeky Acronyms as "LIFO"). A queue, as folks familiar with
British English know, is like a line at a store checkout counter: The first
person in is the first served (also called "first in, first out," or "FIFO").

Adding items to a stack

To add an item to the top of a stack, use append().

This example puts six plates on the pile:

```
>>> plates = []
>>> for p in range(6):
...     plates.append(p)
...
>>> plates
[0, 1, 2, 3, 4, 5]
```

Retrieving items from a stack

To retrieve an item from the top of a stack, use pop() without an argument
(so it defaults to the last item in the list).

To retrieve all the items, use pop() in a while loop. Get the plates off the
pile, last-on, first-off, like this:

```
>>> while plates:
...     plates.pop()
...
5
4
3
2
1
0
```

Queuing up

To use a list as a queue to process items "in the order in which they were received" (anyone who has tried to talk to a large company on the telephone will be familiar with that phrase), follow these steps:

1. **Use** `append()` **to add an item to the end of the queue.**

   In the following example, we create an empty list and then append six callers to it:

   ```
   >>> callers = []
   >>> for c in range(6):
   ...     callers.append(c)
   ...
   >>> callers
   [0, 1, 2, 3, 4, 5]
   ```

2. **Use** `pop(0)` **in a** `while` **loop to retrieve an item from the front of the queue, like this:**

   ```
   >>> while callers:
   ...     callers.pop(0)
   ...
   0
   1
   2
   3
   4
   5
   ```

To avoid performance problems, don't use `pop(0)` with a large list (more than about 100 elements).

Taking Tuples in Hand

This section describes some ways to work with tuples. We cover converting other objects to tuples, several ways of creating tuples, using tuples to swap values, and efficiently giving names to individual items in tuples.

Converting another object to a tuple

To convert another iterable object to a tuple, use the `tuple()` function:

```
>>> mylist = [1, 2, 3]
>>> tuple(mylist)
(1, 2, 3)
```

If you convert a list to a tuple, remember that the new tuple cannot be changed.

Tuple packing

If you type some names separated by commas, you create a tuple. This is called *tuple packing*. It works on either side of an assignment statement.

The following example creates a tuple containing two strings:

```
>>> q = 'blah, blah, blah'
>>> r = 'GINGER'
>>> what_they_hear = q, r
>>> print what_they_hear
('blah, blah, blah', 'GINGER')
```

To create a tuple containing more than two items, just use multiple comma operators. This example creates a tuple containing four strings.

```
>>> q, r, q, r
('blah, blah, blah', 'GINGER', 'blah, blah, blah', 'GINGER')
```

Tuple unpacking

Unpacking a tuple means giving a different name to each element of the tuple.

Tuple unpacking is useful because many functions in Python, such as the zip() function described in the previous "Building lists incrementally" section, return tuples. With tuple unpacking, you can easily get at the individual items in these tuples.

To *unpack* a tuple, just assign multiple names on a single line. Put the names you want to unpack into on the left side of the assignment statement and put the tuple on the right side. You need one name for each item in the tuple.

The following example unpacks a tuple consisting of three lists:

```
>>> x = [('rock crushes', 'scissors'), ('paper covers', 'rock'), ('scissors
            cut', 'paper')]
>>> rock, paper, scissors = x
>>> print rock
('rock crushes', 'scissors')
```

If you don't have the same number of names as tuple items, you get a `ValueError`, as shown here:

```
>>> rock, paper = x
Traceback (most recent call last):
  File "<stdin>", line 1, in <module>
ValueError: too many values to unpack
```

You can actually unpack any sequence object in this way. The following example unpacks a string:

```
>>> x = 'string'
>>> a, b, c, d, e, f = x
>>> a
's'
>>> print a, b, c, d, e, f
s t r i n g
```

However, unpacking is most commonly used with tuples because there are better ways to get elements out of strings and lists.

Using a tuple to swap values

Because of the special way assignments work with tuples, tuples are the *Pythonic* way of swapping values.

This example swaps the values associated with two names:

```
>>> q = 'blah, blah, blah'
>>> r = 'GINGER'
>>> q, r
('blah, blah, blah', 'GINGER')
>>> q, r = r, q
>>> q, r
('GINGER', 'blah, blah, blah')
```

Chapter 9

Diving into Dictionaries

● ●

● ●

In this chapter, we discuss dictionaries (dicts for short) and sets, two data types that store multiple data elements. Here are some of the things you can discover in this chapter:

✔ What dictionaries and sets are and how they differ from sequences

✔ Some of the most useful dictionary tools and set operations

✔ How to convert other types of data into dictionaries and sets

Dictionaries are useful in the following general and specific circumstances:

✔ When you need random access to elements.

✔ When you want to focus on uniqueness.

> But consider using sets if you are using Python 2.3 or later. See "Setting Them Up," later in this chapter.

✔ For mapping several spellings of a term to a preferred spelling.

✔ For using a key to find a function to call (known as a *dispatch table*).

✔ For looking up zip codes or bank account numbers.

✔ For working with numeric indexes with only a few noncontiguous keys, when you don't need to use slicing.

> Data that fits the preceding description is called *sparse* data. You can also use a list in this case, but a dict is more memory-efficient, which often makes things faster.

Defining the Dictionary

Here's how dictionaries (dicts) compare and contrast with other Python data types:

- ✔ **Dictionaries are a container type that stores data, like lists and tuples.**
- ✔ **Dictionaries are a *mapping data type* — indexed by keys.**

  A dictionary's elements (the items it contains) are key:value pairs. In contrast, lists and tuples store data by using numeric indexes (they are *sequence data types*) and support indexing and slicing.

- ✔ **Dictionaries are mutable.**

  That means a dictionary can be modified in place — you don't have to create a copy of it to modify it (as you do with strings and tuples).

- ✔ **However, a dict's *keys* must be immutable.**

Creating a dictionary

The simplest dictionary is a pair of braces ({ }), which defines an *empty* dict.

To create a dictionary with some data in it, follow these steps:

1. **Type a left brace, a key, a colon, and a value (the information you want to associate with the key), like this:**

   ```
   {"parrot": "Pining for fjords"
   ```

   The key can be any immutable data type, such as a string or integer. Most keys are strings. The value can be any data type.

2. **For each additional element in the dictionary, type a comma to separate it from the previous value and then type another key, a colon, and a value:**

   ```
   {"parrot": "Pining for fjords", "Polly": "Ex-parrot"
   ```

   Repeat Step 2 for each element you want to add.

3. **To end the dictionary, type a right brace: }**

   If you added two elements, your dictionary looks something like this:

   ```
   {"parrot": "Pining for fjords", "Polly": "Ex-parrot"}
   ```

Hash strings or hash browns?

Some other languages have dictionary structures; they are called things like *hashes, associative memories,* or *associative arrays.* We think *dictionary* is a friendlier term.

Dict keys must be immutable because Python associates them with a unique number called a *hash.* A hash value (or hash) is historically a number generated from a string of text. Because the number and string pair are unique, hashes prevent problems that might occur if two different objects have the same value.

Hashes are used for space-efficient storage, for security and cryptography, and so on. Another benefit of hashing is that after the hash is computed, keys can be looked up directly — there's no need for the computer to search through a whole list of keys. (In human terms, hashes help a computer be smart in the same way a human is smart when she knows to jump to the end of a physical dictionary to look up a term that starts with *Z.*) In Python, this feature makes dictionaries very fast.

In Python, most immutable objects have a hash, and the attributes of all namespace objects are stored in dictionaries.

Some details about dictionary keys:

- Keys must be an immutable data type — for example, a string, integer, or tuple.
- If you use a tuple as a key, the tuple cannot have any mutable elements.

  For example, you can't use a tuple that contains a list.
- You can type a key directly into the dictionary, or you can type the name of an object, like this:

```
>>> x = "mydictkey"
>>> mydict = {x: "mydictvalue"}
```

Order in the dict

Python doesn't store dictionary elements in any particular order. If you enter elements in one order, they may be stored in another (essentially random) order inside Python. Here's an example:

```
>>> lumberjack = {'sleep': "All night", 'work': "All day"}
>>> lumberjack
{'work': 'All day', 'sleep': 'All night'}
```

The steps to make a sorted list of dictionary keys depend on your Python version.

Python 2.4 and later

If you have Python 2.4 or later, follow these steps to get a sorted (usually alphanumeric) list of the keys of a dictionary:

1. **Type a list name and** = sorted, **followed by the name of your dict in parentheses, like this:**

   ```
   >>> sorted_keys = sorted(lumberjack)
   ```

2. **To see the sorted list of keys, type the name of the list.**

   ```
   >>> sorted_keys
   ['sleep', 'work']
   ```

Earlier versions

If you have Python 2.3 or earlier, follow these steps to get a sorted list of the keys of a dictionary:

1. **Type a name, an** = **sign, the name of your dict, and** .keys(), **like so:**

   ```
   >>> list_of_keys = lumberjack.keys()
   ```

2. **Use the** sort() **method to sort the list by typing this on the next line, substituting the name you created in Step 1 for** list_of_keys:

   ```
   >>> list_of_keys.sort()
   ```

3. **Type the list name again to see the sorted list of keys, like this:**

   ```
   >>> list_of_keys
   ['sleep', 'work']
   ```

Don't try to give a name to the result of list_of_keys.sort(). The sort() method changes the list in place but returns None, not a list (to find out more about list methods and what they return, see Chapter 8).

Doodling Around with Dicts

This section describes some of the common tasks you can do with dicts, such as storing, extracting, adding, deleting, and searching for keys and values.

Popular dict operations

The main operations for a dictionary are storing a key and its associated value and using the key to extract the value.

Storing a value

To store a key:value pair in an existing dictionary, follow these steps:

1. **Type the name of the dict and a key in square brackets, like this:**

   ```
   >>> mydict['dracula']
   ```

   The key can be new or it can be a key that's already in the dictionary. If you use an existing key, the new value replaces the old one.

2. **Type = and the value you want to store.**

   Your line of code might look like this:

   ```
   >>> mydict['dracula'] = 'stoker'
   ```

The following example code creates a dictionary and then creates a new key, 'dracula', and gives it the value 'stoker':

```
>>> mydict = {'jabberwocky': 'carroll', 'sherlock holmes': 'doyle'}
>>> mydict['dracula'] = 'stoker'
>>> mydict
{'jabberwocky': 'carroll', 'dracula': 'stoker', 'sherlock holmes': 'doyle'}
```

Here, the existing key 'dracula' is given a new value, 'oldman':

```
>>> mydict['dracula'] = 'oldman'
>>> mydict
{'jabberwocky': 'carroll', 'dracula': 'oldman', 'sherlock holmes': 'doyle'}
```

Extracting a value

There are two ways of extracting a value based on a dictionary key. The best option depends on a couple of factors:

- ✔ If you're certain the key is in the dictionary, or if you want to raise a KeyError exception when the key is not in the dictionary, use the square brackets syntax.

- ✔ If many of the keys you're searching for aren't in the dictionary, or if you want Python to return a value you specify rather than raise an exception when keys aren't found, use the get() method.

To raise an exception on failure

If you want to raise an exception if the key you're searching for doesn't exist, type the name of the dict followed by a key in square brackets, like this:

```
>>> mydict['jane eyre']
Traceback (most recent call last):
  File "<stdin>", line 1, in <module>
KeyError: 'jane eyre'
```

To return a value you specify on failure

To return a default value if the key doesn't exist, follow these steps:

1. **Type the name of the dict, a dot, `get(`, and a key.**

   Your code might look like this:

   ```
   >>> mydict.get('jane eyre'
   ```

2. **(Optional) Type a comma and a string you want to return if the key doesn't exist.**

   If you don't specify a string, the default value `None` is returned.

   ```
   >>> mydict.get('jane eyre', 'key not found'
   ```

3. **End the line by typing a right parenthesis:)**

   Your completed line of code will look something like this if the key doesn't exist:

   ```
   >>> mydict.get('jane eyre', 'key not found')
   'key not found'
   ```

Finding out about dict methods

Dictionaries come with built-in methods that allow you to perform the following tasks:

- Retrieve items from dicts by using `items()`, `keys()`, and `values()` methods.
- Use dicts in loops with `iterkeys()`, `itervalues()`, and `iteritems()` methods.
- Test whether a key is in a dict by using the `in` keyword.
- Delete items from dicts by using the `del` keyword and the `popitem()` and `pop()` methods.
- Make shallow copies of dicts by using the `copy()` method.
- Add items to dicts by using the `setdefault()` method.

Retrieving items from dicts

The `keys()`, `values()`, and `items()` methods are good for list-processing operations using the contents of dictionaries. The `pop()` and `popitem()` methods retrieve and delete things at the same time, so they're good for processing a temporary dictionary you don't need to keep or for processing items one at a time until there aren't any more.

items()

The `items()` method retrieves all the key:value pairs in a dictionary and returns them as a list of tuples. Each key:value pair is a tuple.

To retrieve all the items in a dictionary, type the name of the dictionary, a dot, and `items()`:

```
>>> mydict = {'bed price': '800 pounds', 'bed length': '2 feet long'}
>>> print mydict.items()
[('bed length', '2 feet long'), ('bed price', '800 pounds')]
```

keys()

The `keys()` method retrieves all the keys in the dictionary. It returns a list, as shown here:

```
>>> print mydict.keys()
['bed length', 'bed price']
```

values()

The `values()` method retrieves all the values in the dictionary. It returns a list, as shown here:

```
>>> print mydict.values()
['2 foot long', '800 pounds']
```

popitem()

To retrieve a single key:value pair and remove it from the dict, use the `popitem()` method, like this:

```
>>> mydict.popitem()
('bed length', '2 foot long')
```

You can't use `popitem()` to specify which key:value pair to retrieve. It's most often used in a `while` loop when you want to process items one at a time until there aren't any more but you don't care what order they're processed in.

The `popitem()` method was added in Python 2.1.

pop()

To remove a key:value pair and retrieve only the value, use the `pop()` method and pass the key in the parentheses, like this:

```
>>> mydict.pop('bed price')
'800 pounds'
```

Getting loopy with dicts

You can use a dict's keys, values, or key:value pairs in a loop. This is called *iterating over* the items.

The `keys()`, `values()`, and `items()` methods also work in loops, but the iterator methods are more efficient.

Here are several ways of looping with a dict.

Keys

To iterate over keys in Python 2.2 and later, create a `for` statement with the following syntax, substituting the name of your dictionary (you can also use a different name for the iterator, although `key` is standard for *keys*):

```
for key in mydict:
```

The preceding code works only in Python 2.2 and later. It is equivalent to the following in earlier versions:

```
for key in mydict.keys():
```

Values

To iterate over values, use this syntax in the `for` statement:

```
for value in mydict.itervalues():
```

Key:value pairs

To iterate over key:value pairs, use the following syntax:

```
for key, value in mydict.iteritems():
```

Testing a dict

How you test whether a single key appears in the dict depends on your version of Python. (You might want to do this if, for example, you wanted to see if a customer number was in your dictionary.)

Python 2.2 and newer

To check whether a single key is in the dictionary, use the keyword `in` within an `if` statement, like this:

```
if 'bed price' in mydict:
```

Older versions

If you are using Python 2.1 or earlier, use the `has_key()` method instead:

```
if mydict.has_key('bed price'):
```

Deleting items from a dict

You can delete a specific key:value pair from a dict by using the `del` keyword. If you're working with the dict in a loop and doing something with the dict data, using `pop()` or `popitem()` is more efficient; they return and delete elements at the same time.

Key:value

To delete a key:value pair from a dictionary, use the `del` keyword and give the key in square brackets. For example:

```
del mydict['bed price']
```

Individual elements

To delete elements from a dict one at a time in a loop, use either of these methods, depending on whether you want the key:value pair or just the value returned:

✔ `popitem()`: The `popitem()` method returns the *key:value pair* and deletes the pair from the dict.

```
while mydict:
    key, value = mydict.popitem()
```

✔ `pop()`: The `pop()` method returns the *value* and deletes the key:value pair from the dict.

```
for key in mylist:
    if key in mydict:
        value = mydict.pop(key)
```

All elements

To delete all the elements of a dict at once, use the `clear()` method. This removes all the elements at once (leaving an empty dict) and returns `None`:

```
mydict.clear()
```

Making a shallow copy of a dict

To make a shallow copy of a dict, use the `copy()` method.

```
mycopy = mydict.copy()
```

See the sidebar, "Understanding shallow copies," to find out more about shallow copies of dicts.

Get or set: Adding items to a dict

The `setdefault()` method (Pythonistas call it *get or set*) is like `get()`, which extracts a value by using a key. But `setdefault()` goes one step further: If the key is not found, it adds the key to the dict.

Understanding shallow copies

To understand shallow copies, you need to know something about how Python stores information. When you give a name to an object such as a list that stores some values, Python creates a reference (the name) to that object (the stored values).

```
>>> mylist = ['my', 'list']
```

Now, say you create a dictionary that contains this list:

```
>>> mydict = {'mynumber': 1, 'alist': mylist, 'mytuple': (1,2)}
```

If you look at the dict, it looks like the values stored in the list are stored in the dict, too:

```
>>> mydict
{'mytuple': (1, 2), 'alist': ['my', 'list'], 'mynumber': 1}
```

But in fact the dictionary is not storing the actual values stored in the list. It is only storing the reference to the list.

That means, if you change the list . . .

```
>>> mylist.append('changed')
```

. . . your dict also changes.

```
>>> mydict
{'mytuple': (1, 2), 'alist': ['my', 'list', 'changed'], 'mynumber': 1}
```

When you make a shallow copy of something, you copy only the references, not the actual values that the references point to. So if you make a copy of a dict by using the copy() method, the copy reflects any changes made to the list that the dictionary is referring to.

```
>>> mycopy = mydict.copy()
>>> mycopy
{'mytuple': (1, 2), 'alist': ['my', 'list', 'changed'], 'mynumber': 1}
```

To make a copy of the actual values so that these changes don't occur, import the copy module and use the deepcopy() function. See Chapter 8.

The standard use for setdefault() is for adding a list (or other mutable data type) to the dict and appending items to the list. Here's how the syntax looks:

```
mydict.setdefault(key, []).append(value)
```

Here's what happens:

1. If the key isn't in the dict, Python adds the key and uses an empty list as the value. Then it appends the value you specified to the list.

2. If the key is in the dict, Python tries to append your value to that key's value. (For this to work, the value must be a list because the append() method works only with lists.)

If you don't specify a value, the value None is used.

The following code creates a key, 13, and pairs it with a value of an empty list. Then it appends the string `'complaints'` to the list:

```
>>> rooms = {'12A': ['argument clinic'], 12: ['abuse']}
>>> rooms.setdefault(13, []).append('complaints')
>>> rooms
{'12A': ['argument clinic'], 12: ['abuse'], 13: ['complaints']}
```

The following code appends the string `"don't bother"` to the list that has the key 13.

```
>>> rooms.setdefault(13, []).append("don't bother")
>>> rooms
{'12A': ['argument clinic'], 12: ['abuse'], 13: ['complaints', "don't
bother"]}
```

The following syntax does the same thing with a set.

```
mydict.setdefault(key, sets.Set()).add(value)
```

Building Dictionaries

In Python, most compound data objects are created by processing data in a loop structure, so you'll often build lists, dictionaries, and so on by writing loops. Following are some loopy and non-loopy ways of building dicts.

Converting other data types into a dict

You have several ways to convert other data types into dicts. This section shows the dict() constructor, the fromkeys() method, and a for loop.

Converting a list of tuples

To convert a list of two-item tuples (or any iterable containing two-item iterables) to a dict, pass the list to the dict() method like this:

```
>>> list_of_tuples = [('spam', 1), ('eggs', 'green')]
>>> dict(list_of_tuples)
{'eggs': 'green', 'spam': 1}
```

Converting a sequence

To create a dict from a list or tuple and an optional mapping value, use the fromkeys() method. (This works in Python 2.3 or later.) The items in the sequence become the keys, and the mapping value (None by default) is used for the values. In this example, each item in the list is turned into a key and given the value 'breakfast':

```
>>> mylist = ['spam', 'eggs', 'orange juice']
>>> print dict.fromkeys(mylist, "breakfast")
{'eggs': 'breakfast', 'orange juice': 'breakfast', 'spam': 'breakfast'}
```

You can do the same thing by using the dict() constructor and a *list comprehension* (a line of code that creates a list from a range of items).

```
>>> dict([(i, 'breakfast') for i in mylist])
{'eggs': 'breakfast', 'orange juice': 'breakfast', 'spam': 'breakfast'}
```

 If you won't be working with values later, consider creating a set rather than a dict. A set has only keys, no values. To create a set from a list or tuple, just type set() and include the list or tuple in parentheses. For more information, see "Setting Them Up," later in this chapter.

To create a dict from a two-element iterable, you can also use a list comprehension. This code builds a dict of powers of 2:

```
>>> dict([(x, x**2) for x in (2, 4, 6)])
{2: 4, 4: 16, 6: 36}
```

You can get the lowdown on list comprehensions in Chapter 16.

Building a dict with keyword arguments

In Python 2.3 and later, you can pass keyword arguments (**kwargs) to the dict() method and build a dictionary, like this:

```
>>> sack = dict(cats=7, kits=7)
>>> sack
{'kits': 7, 'cats': 7}
```

For more about **kwargs, see Chapter 11.

Building a dict out of another dict by using a for loop

To go through a dict while building a second one, use a for loop and assign each pair in the old dict to the new dict, like this:

```
>>> mydict = {'bed price': '800 pounds', 'bed length': '2 foot long'}
>>> newdict = {}
>>> for key in mydict:
...     value = mydict[key]
...     newdict[key] = value
...
>>> newdict
{'bed length': '2 foot long', 'bed price': '800 pounds'}
```

In Python 2.1 and earlier, the in keyword doesn't work with a dictionary object; you need to use it with a dictionary method. So to write the above loop, you could use this syntax:

```
for key, value in mydict.items():
```

Updating a dictionary

To replace the values in a dictionary with new values, use the update() method. The new key:value pairs can come from either *another dictionary* (or other mapping object) or *an iterable of key:value pairs* (such as a list of two-item tuples).

The iterable (key:value) option requires Python 2.4 or later.

You can also replace values by using keyword arguments, as in this example:

```
>>> rooms = {'12A': 'argument clinic', 12: 'abuse'}
>>> rooms.update(A14='hit on the head lessons')
>>> rooms
{'12A': 'argument clinic', 12: 'abuse', 'A14': 'hit on the head lessons'}
```

Here's code that updates one dict by using key:value pairs from a second dict. If a key appears in both dicts, the second dict's values overwrite the first dict's values. The second dict is not modified.

```
>>> rooms2 = {'A14': 'canceled by Flying Fox'}
>>> rooms.update(rooms2)
>>> rooms
{'12A': 'argument clinic', 12: 'abuse', 'A14': 'canceled by Flying Fox'}
```

When Only a Dict Will Do

This section gives brief examples of some real-world uses for dicts, including a game that retrieves values associated with keys, a cache for storing frequently used items, and a way of finding duplicate keys.

Storing and retrieving values

A dict is useful for storing and retrieving immutable objects and corresponding values, like product prices, for example. Here's a small game that uses a dict for this purpose:

```
choice = raw_input("Choose scissors, rock, or paper: ")
results = {"scissors": "cut paper", "rock": "crushes scissors", "paper": "covers
           rock"}
print choice, results[choice]
```

Here's one round of the game:

```
Choose scissors, rock, or paper: paper
paper covers rock
```

You can also use `if/elif/else` statements for this purpose (see Chapter 10), but a dictionary is often better because it's built when a program first runs (which is more efficient) and it's easier to read if a lot of key:value pairs are involved. It's also easier to maintain and modify.

Using a dict as a cache

If you're using a `for` loop to process some items, a dict can store the results for reuse. This type of storage is called a *cache*. There are two ways to write caching code. The one you use depends on whether you're processing a lot of different items or mostly multiple copies of similar items.

The following examples refer to a function called `getValue()`. This isn't a function built in to Python; you'll have to write it yourself.

Different items

If many unique items probably won't be in the dict, write code like this:

```
result = []
cache = {}
for key in mylist:
    if key in cache:
        result.append(cache[key])
    else:
        value = getValue(key)
        cache[key] = value
        result.append(value)
```

We use a cache because the `getValue()` function is expensive (that is, it takes a lot of time). However, you should avoid optimizing code when you don't need to — it makes code harder to read.

Similar items

The following code is efficient if you're processing many similar items, but it's harder to read:

```
result = []
cache = {}
for key in mylist:
    if key in cache:
        result.append(cache[key])
    else:
        # Add to cache and append to result
        result.append(cache.setdefault(key, getValue(key)))
```

If you think that the keys will almost always be in the dict, the following is even more efficient. That's because `try` blocks take very little time if an exception isn't raised, but exceptions take a lot of time to process:

```
result = []
cache = {}
for key in mylist:
    try:
        result.append(cache[key])
    except KeyError:
      # Add to cache and append to result
      result.append(cache.setdefault(key, getValue(key)))
```

Dealing with duplicate keys

Because `setdefault()` returns the value for a key, it's easy and efficient to write a loop that converts a list of key:value tuples into a dict in which each key contains a list of values. This is handy when you expect key duplications.

This code processes a list of tuples and finds that two values share a key:

```
>>> L = [(1, 'pear tree'), (5, 'golden rings'), (1, 'partridge')]
>>> d = {}
>>> for key,value in L:
...     d.setdefault(key, []).append(value)
...
>>> d
{1: ['pear tree', 'partridge'], 5: ['golden rings']}
```

Setting Them Up

Sets are a data type that supports mathematical operations like union, intersection, difference, and symmetric difference.

What sets are and aren't

Here's how sets fit in with the rest of Python's data types:

- ✔ The set() type is built into Python 2.4 and later. If you're using Python 2.3, you must import the sets module before using sets. The data type in the sets module is called Set() (with a capital *S*), not set().

- ✔ Like a dict, a set is an unordered collection of elements.

- ✔ Unlike a dict, a set contains only keys (that is, unique, immutable objects). A set does not have values, and it is not a mapping type.

- ✔ Unlike a sequence, the elements in sets aren't stored in any particular order, so sets don't support indexing or slicing.

- ✔ In sequences, an element can occur multiple times, but a set contains only unique elements, no duplicates.

- ✔ Regular sets are mutable, and you can't use one as an element of another set or as a dictionary key. (But see the section, "Immutable or frozen sets," later in this chapter.)

Here's an example of a set based on a list that contains some duplicate elements. The set contains no duplicates.

```
>>> basket = ['apple', 'orange', 'apple', 'pear', 'orange', 'banana']
>>> fruits = set(basket)
>>> fruits
set(['orange', 'pear', 'apple', 'banana'])
```

Membership testing with sets

A set is useful for comparing individual items against a group of elements. For example, if you have a set that contains all states on the Atlantic coast, you can check whether a user-entered state is on the Atlantic.

Checking elements

To test whether an element is in a set, use the `in` keyword, like this:

```
>>> 'Maine' in atlantic_states
True
>>> 'Oregon' in atlantic_states
False
```

Checking subsets and supersets

To test whether one set is a subset or superset of another, use the appropriate method listed below. Both return `True` or `False`.

> ✔ `a.issubset(b)`: Tests whether all the elements of set a are also in set b.
>
> ✔ `a.issuperset(b)`: Tests whether set a contains all the elements in set b.

Finding set elements

Set *operators* and *methods* can be used to combine sets and find their intersections and their unique elements.

Set operations have corresponding methods. In some cases, using the method syntax rather than the operator creates easier-to-read code.

The following operations are the most commonly used.

Difference

The difference operation compares two sets and returns a set containing the elements that are in the first set but not in the second set. The difference operator – uses this syntax:

```
a - b
```

The difference method uses this syntax:

```
a.difference(b)
```

The following example finds the set of round things that aren't pink:

```
>>> roundthings = ['orange', 'gumball', 'egg', 'tire']
>>> pinkthings = ['lipstick', 'gumball', 'baby blanket']
>>> a = set(roundthings)
>>> q = set(pinkthings)
>>> a - q
set(['orange', 'egg', 'tire'])
```

Union

The | operator returns the *union* of the sets (all the elements from both sets). The union method uses this syntax:

```
a.union(b)
```

This example finds the set of all round things and all pink things:

```
>>> a | q
set(['lipstick', 'tire', 'orange', 'gumball', 'egg', 'baby blanket'])
```

Intersection

The & operator returns the *intersection* of the sets (the elements that are present in *both* sets). The intersection method uses this syntax:

```
a.intersection(b)
```

This example finds all the round pink things:

```
>>> a & q
set(['gumball'])
```

Symmetric difference

The ^ operator returns the *symmetric difference* of the sets — elements in

✔ Exactly one set

✔ *Not* both sets

The symmetric difference method uses this syntax:

```
a.symmetric_difference(b)
```

This example finds all the things that are either round or pink but not both:

```
>>> a ^ q
set(['orange', 'egg', 'lipstick', 'tire', 'baby blanket'])
```

Immutable or frozen sets

Python 2.4 has a built-in data type called frozenset. It's similar to set, but it's *immutable* (that is, after you've created one, you can't change it). Because a frozenset is immutable, it can be used as a dict key or as an element in a set.

In the following example, a `frozenset` instance is used to associate a three-item set key with the value `None`:

```
>>> mylist = ['foo', 'bar', 'spam']
>>> s = frozenset(mylist)
>>> s
frozenset(['foo', 'bar', 'spam'])
>>> d = {s: None}
>>> d
{frozenset(['foo', 'bar', 'spam']): None}
```

If you try to use a regular set as a dict key, Python builds an immutable set from your set and uses that set as the dict key instead.

Python 2.3 has a similar subclass of sets called `ImmutableSet`. It is available if you import the `sets` module.

Part III
Structures

The 5th Wave   By Rich Tennant

"We're here to clean the code."

In this part . . .

This part covers Python's code blocks, the chunks of code that manipulate data and return results.

If you've ever seen a flow chart, you'll be comfortable with Chapter 10, which describes `if` statements and loops . . . loops . . . loops. . . .

Chapter 11 takes you inside the magic boxes called *functions*. You'll discover how to put stuff into them and how to get stuff out of them.

Modules and packages are the Lego blocks of Python programs. Chapter 12 shows you how to build and work with both module files, which store chunks of code that work together, and packages, which are directories that contain related modules.

Lucky Chapter 13 inducts you into the temple of object-oriented programming. Classes, like factories or templates, create other objects that do the actual work. After you read this chapter, you'll understand what it's like to be a capitalist baron who controls the means of production.

Classes are such an important concept that we couldn't get away with just one chapter about them. Python 2.5 introduced *new-style classes*. You don't have to use them, but if you want to, Chapter 14 is where they are.

What do you do when something weird happens in your Python program? Chapter 15 offers advice. Here, you find out how to anticipate and handle exceptions in your programs.

If you've devoured the rest of the chapters in this part and you're still hungry, turn to Chapter 16. Here, we introduce some advanced features of Python programming. Even if you don't want to use these features yourself yet, you'll appreciate being able to recognize them in other people's programs.

Chapter 10

Staying in Control

· ·

In This Chapter

▶ Getting a handle on conditions and comparisons

▶ Finding out about `if` statements

▶ Learning to love loops

· ·

*W*ith Python, you use *control structures* to determine whether a chunk of code runs or how many times to run that code.

This kind of code is also called a *compound statement.* A compound statement is a kind of *code block* (lines of code that perform an action).

In this chapter, we show you

✔ The condition and comparison operators that control structures use

✔ Tests you can do on data to decide whether and how code should run

✔ How to use `if` blocks to test several specific conditions

✔ When and how to use `for` and `while` loops to execute code repeatedly

Things to Know about Control Structures

This section describes some general things you need to know about how control structures work. It applies to all the structures in this chapter.

✔ A control structure starts with a keyword — `if`, `for`, `try`, `while`, or `with`. The first line also contains an expression and ends with a colon.

✔ You can nest control structures. So an `if` statement can be nested inside a `for` loop, and vice versa. (You can also nest `for` in `for` and `if` in `if`.)

✔ Python uses indentation to group statements together.

Each line within a code block must be indented by the same amount — the convention is four spaces for the first block, eight spaces for any block nested in the first block, and so on.

✔ When you enter a compound statement (a statement with more than one line) in interactive mode (see Chapter 2 for instructions), you need to end it with a blank line (a Return). This tells the parser that you have typed the last line of the block.

All about Conditions and Comparisons

Control structures use conditions and comparisons to tell Python when to carry out actions. A *condition* tests whether some expression is true or false. A *comparison* tests whether one value is larger than, equal to, or smaller than another. This section covers the truth values of objects and the operators that you use for conditions and comparisons.

The value of truth

In Python, every object has a *truth value* — a Boolean value of *true* or *false*.

In Python, true and false don't work quite the same way they do in the rest of life. For example, any string except an empty string evaluates as true. So you could tell Python `'I am a billionaire'`, and it would be true!

True and False aren't true and false

Python 2.2.1 and later have built-in Boolean data types `True` and `False`, which are associated with the `bool()` built-in function. (Other functions and methods also return Boolean results, such as `isdigit()`.) Comparison expressions, such as `x < y`, also return `True` and `False`.

History geeks may be interested to know that previous versions of Python used 1 and 0 rather than `True` and `False` because that's how it works in the C programming language. The odd result of this is that the `True` and `False` data types are integers:

```
>>> 1 + True
2
```

It's important to remember that the Boolean *data types* are not the same thing as the truth values of objects returned by Boolean *operators*. When you check the truth value of objects by using Boolean operators (for example, by using `x and y`), you are checking whether the objects are empty. The Boolean operators return a Python object (for example, in `x and y`, the object `x` or the object `y` is returned); they don't necessarily return `True` or `False`.

False objects

All Python objects evaluate as true except for *null, empty,* and *zero* objects.
The following objects evaluate as false:

✔ `False` (one of the two Boolean objects)

✔ Zero (0) (for any numerical data type)

✔ Empty string `' '`

✔ Empty list `[]`

✔ Empty tuple `()`

✔ Empty dictionary `{}`

✔ Empty set `set()`

✔ None (a special Python object that stands for "no value")

Testing an object for truth

Testing whether an object is true or false is simple. Just use an `if` block:

1. **Type** `if` **followed by a literal or the name of an object. Then type a colon and press Return:**

   ```
   >>> if "a":
   ```

2. **Type four spaces, and then type something for Python to do. Press Return twice when you're finished.**

   ```
   >>> if "a":
   ...     print "yes!"
   ...
   yes!
   ```

Python performs the action only when the object evaluates as true. This test does not assume that the object is any particular data type. Because you're not comparing the object against anything else, you can think of it as "letting the object evaluate itself."

`if name_of_object:` is short for `if bool(name_of_object) == True`.

Testing the elements of a sequence object

In Python 2.5, new built-in functions allow you to test the truth values of multiple elements of a sequence object (such as a list) or other iterables at once.

all ( )

The all() function returns True if all the elements are true. It also returns True if the sequence object is empty. For example:

```
>>> mylist = [1, 2, 3]
>>> all(mylist)
True
>>> myotherlist = [0, 2, 3]
>>> all(myotherlist)
False
>>> myemptylist = []
>>> all(myemptylist)
True
```

any ( )

The any() function returns True if at least one element is true (the object must not be empty). For example:

```
>>> any(mylist)
True
>>> any(myotherlist)
True
>>> any(myemptylist)
False
```

Boolean operators

You use Boolean operators to test the truth values of objects (to test whether objects are empty). You can test more than one object at once, and you can set up conditions that depend on the truth value of one object or the truth value of all the objects you're testing.

The Boolean operators are evaluated in this priority order:

1. not

2. and

3. or

The operators and and or are *short-circuit operators*. Python evaluates expressions with these operators from left to right and stops as soon as the outcome is determined. Python returns the object it evaluated last and skips the rest of the expression.

All about or

The or operator stops evaluating as soon as it finds something that's true. In the following example, the first item is true, so processing stops there and Python returns the first value.

```
>>> 3 or 4 or 5
3
```

In the next example, the first item is false, but the second item is true, so processing stops and Python returns the second value:

```
>>> 0 or 1 or 2
1
```

If no item evaluates as true, the last (false) item is returned.

```
>>> 0 or [] or ''
''
```

Embrace the power of and

The and operator requires *all* the conditions to be met for the expression to be true. Evaluation stops either when an object tests false or when all items have been tested.

The following examples show the results of two expressions using and:

✔ This example tests all the items and returns the last value:

```
>>> 3 and 4 and 5
5
```

✔ This example stops after testing the second item (0) because it tests false:

```
>>> 3 and 0 and 5
0
```

Comparison operators

Comparison operators test whether something is equal to and/or greater than or less than something else. Table 10-1 lists the comparison operators.

Table 10-1	Python's Comparison Operators	
Operator	*Usage*	*Meaning*
<	x < y	x is less than y
<=	x <= y	x is less than or equal to y
>	x > y	x is greater than y
>=	x >= y	x is greater than or equal to y
!=, <>	x != y, x <> y	x is not equal to y
==	x == y	x is equal to y

All comparison operators have the same priority. Statements with multiple comparison operators are evaluated from left to right.

The difference between equals and equals equals

In Python, = (the assignment operator) gives a name to an object. The = operator is part of a statement. If you want to test whether something is equal to something else, you must use the == operator.

Is you is or is you ain't my baby?

There are two special comparisons: is and is not. These don't test the values of x and y; they test the *identities* of x and y — that is, whether x and y are bound to the same object.

To avoid problems, make a habit of using == and != to compare objects' values rather than using is and is not to compare their identities. Usually, you use is and is not only when you want to test whether something has the special value None. (There is only one None.)

Get in!

The comparison operators in and not in check whether a value occurs in a sequence data type (a list, tuple, or string), a dict, or a set.

The following example checks for the text "fox" in a set:

```
>>> data = set(["the", "quick", "brown", "fox"])
>>> if "fox" in data:
...     print "Call out the hounds!"
...
Call out the hounds!
```

If your program works with lots of data, it's a Good Idea to use dicts or sets to store the data. Searching dicts and sets is faster than searching sequences.

Comparatively speaking

Comparisons can be linked in a chain. The follow example tests three values. Both tests must be true for the comparison to be true.

```
>>> if 1 < 2 < 3:
...     print "yes!"
...
yes!
```

Linked comparisons can be hard to read. In some cases, combining comparisons with Boolean operators (and, or, not) and parentheses will improve readability of your code. Compare these pairs of expressions and decide which are easier to read:

```
if a < b and b < c:
if a < b < c:
```

```
if a < b > c < d:
if (a < b) and (b > c) and (c < d):
```

The Boolean operators have lower priorities than comparison operators — that is, they are evaluated after comparison operators. You can use parentheses to make sure comparisons are evaluated in the order you want.

Feeling Iffy

An if statement is an instruction that Python carries out only if a condition is true. You often use a *comparison operator* to test the condition in an if statement. The condition must be either true or false (no gray areas here!). This is referred to as *Boolean* comparison.

You can translate an if statement into English as follows: "If this is true, then carry out the instructions below."

Writing an if statement

To write an if statement, follow these steps:

1. Type if, a condition, and a colon, like so:

```
if weather == "raining":
```

2. **On the next line, type an instruction about what to do if the condition is true.**

```
if weather == "raining":
    bring_umbrella = "yes"
```

Be sure to indent this line (and any other lines of the block) four spaces.

You might see single-line code blocks combined on one line like this:

```
if weather == "raining": bring_umbrella = "yes"
```

We don't recommend using this style in your own code. It's harder to read, and probably won't be allowed in Python 3.0 and later.

Adding another condition to an if block

If you want to test several conditions, you can include additional code blocks to an `if` statement. These blocks begin with the keyword `elif` (which is short for "else if"). The `elif` statement says, essentially, "Otherwise, if this other thing is true, then carry out this other instruction."

Crucial code that always has to run doesn't belong in `if` or `elif` code. Python reads `if` blocks (`if` and `elif` statements) in order. As soon as it finds a true condition, it stops evaluating. The rest of the block is not executed.

To write an `if` block that includes an `elif` statement, follow these steps:

1. **Write an `if` statement.**

   Use the instructions in the "Writing an if statement" section, earlier in this chapter. Your code might look something like this:

   ```
   if weather == "raining":
       bring_umbrella = "yes"
   ```

2. ***Without indenting,* on the next line, type `elif`, a condition, and a colon (`:`).**

   ```
   if weather == "raining":
       bring_umbrella = "yes"
   elif weather == "windy":
   ```

If you are typing in a program that automatically formats Python code, you might have to press Backspace or Delete one or more times to make sure that this line is not indented. This is called *dedenting*.

3. **On the next line, indent four spaces and type an instruction, like so:**

```
if weather == "raining":
    bring_umbrella = "yes"
elif weather == "windy":
    bring_jacket = "yes"
```

You can type more instructions. Be sure to indent any additional instruction lines four spaces.

Adding an else statement to an if block

An `else` statement always comes last in an `if` block. It means "If none of the preceding statements was true, then carry out this final instruction."

Don't put critical code in an `else` statement. The `else` code gets executed only if *none* of the other statements in the `if` block is true.

To write an `if` block that includes an `else` statement, follow these steps:

1. **Write an** `if` **statement.**

   If you have only one condition to test, skip to Step 3.

2. **If you have additional conditions to test, write one or more** `elif` **statements.** Use the instructions in the section "Adding another condition to an if block," earlier in this chapter.

3. **On the next line, type** `else:`.

   This text should line up with `if`. You might have to dedent if you're typing in a program that formats Python code automatically.

4. **Go to the next line, indent four spaces, and type at least one instruction.**

```
go_out = "now! what are you waiting for?"
```

Be sure to indent any additional instruction lines four spaces.

Your completed code block might look like this:

```
if weather == "raining":
    bring_umbrella = "yes"
elif weather == "windy":
    bring_jacket = "yes"
else:
    go_out = "now! what are you waiting for?"
```

Combining tests

You don't always have to write `elif` statements when you want to test multiple conditions. If you want to perform the same action in more than one condition, you can combine the conditions in a single `if` or `elif` statement.

The code snippets in Listings 10-1 and 10-2 both test for the same conditions, but the example combining multiple conditions in the `if` statement is easier to read:

Listing 10-1: `elif` **block**

```
if age < 18:
    print "Discount rate"
elif age > 65:
    print "Discount rate"
else:
    print "Adult rate"
```

Listing 10-2: **Two conditions in an** `if` **statement**

```
if (age < 18) or (age > 65):
    print "Discount rate"
else:
    print "Adult rate"
```

Staying in the Loop

Computers are good at doing things over and over again. Humans tend to find repetitive tasks boring. That's why we program with *loops*. Loops are code blocks that tirelessly repeat until the task is finished. Python has `for` loops and `while` loops. Both kinds of loops have these things in common:

✔ They start with a keyword (`for` or `while`), followed by an expression and ending with a colon.

✔ They are code blocks, and the code inside them is indented.

The right loop for your task depends on several factors. See the section "Choosing Your Loop" later in this chapter.

For a Good Time . . .

A `for` loop is a way to repeat some instructions (a *code block*) a number of times. In this section, we explain the workings of the `for` loop and discuss iterables, which are objects you can use to generate a `for` loop.

How for works

Here's a basic `for` loop:

```
for mychar in "hello!":
    print "the ascii value of", mychar, "is", ord(mychar)
```

The preceding example shows all the important features of a `for` loop:

- ✔ The keyword `for`
- ✔ A name that holds a value each time through the loop (this name is sometimes called the *loop target*)
- ✔ The keyword `in`

  Note that `in` used in a `for` loop works differently from the Boolean operator `in` (see the "Get in!" section earlier in this chapter). Here, `in` is used to separate the loop target from the iterable.

- ✔ An iterable (a sequence or iterator object) — in this case, the string `"hello!"`
- ✔ A colon
- ✔ An indented statement

In a `for` block, Python gives the name to each element in the iterable, one at a time, in order. It reuses the name each time through the loop. After Python gives the name to a new element, it executes the instructions in the code block.

The example at the beginning of this section computes and prints the ASCII value of each character in a string (using the `ord()` function):

```
the ascii value of h is 104
the ascii value of e is 101
the ascii value of l is 108
the ascii value of l is 108
the ascii value of o is 111
the ascii value of ! is 33
```

Iterables, getcher iterables!

A `for` loop works only with objects that have, or can generate, multiple elements. Such objects are called *iterables* (because a `for` loop generates multiple iterations, or repeats, using the elements in the object).

Manipulating an object with a `for` loop is also called *iterating over a sequence* or *looping through a sequence*.

Here are some of Python's objects that can be used with a `for` loop:

```
for element in range(1,4):        # range
    print element
for element in [1, 2, 3]:          # list
    print element
for key in {'one':1, 'two':2}:     # dictionary
    print key
for line in open("myfile.txt"):    # text file
    print line
for value in mydict.itervalues():  # iterator object
    print value
for key, value in mydict.iteritems():   # tuple unpacking
    print key, value
```

Home on the range

It's common to use a `for` loop to iterate over a sequence of numbers by using the function `range()`, which generates lists of arithmetic progressions.

To use the `range()` function, feed it the following arguments:

✔ Required: An integer specifying the end of the range

The `range()` function generates a list of numbers *up to* but *not including* the end-of-range number. For example, if you want a list of all the single digits, you would use 10, not 9, as the end of the range:

```
>>> range(10)
[0, 1, 2, 3, 4, 5, 6, 7, 8, 9]
```

✔ Optional: An integer specifying the start of the range. It goes before the integer that specifies the end of the range. If left out, it defaults to 0.

This example shows a `range()` function with a starting number of 2.

```
>>> range(2, 10)
[2, 3, 4, 5, 6, 7, 8, 9]
```

✔ Optional: An integer to add to the current number to generate the next number. (This is called a step.) If left out, it defaults to 1.

If you include the step, you must include the start-of-range number.

This example shows a `range()` function with a step of 3.

```
>>> range(0, 10, 3)
[0, 3, 6, 9]
```

You can use `range()` with negative numbers, too, as shown here:

```
>>> range(-10, -100, -30)
[-10, -40, -70]
```

Howdy, xrange-r!

The xrange() function is similar to range(), but instead of returning a list, it returns an iterator object that generates the numbers in the range.

Loops using xrange() are a bit faster and use less memory.

You can see Python's internal difference between range() and xrange() by comparing the following. Note that Python converts the xrange() object to an internal "equivalent":

```
>>> range(0, 10, 3)
[0, 3, 6, 9]
>>> xrange(0, 10, 3)
xrange(0, 12, 3)
```

Using the range() function with a list

To iterate over the index numbers of a sequence (such as a list), use a for statement with range() and len() (which finds the number of elements in a sequence), like this:

```
for i in range(len(list_name)):
```

The enumerate() function, new in Python 2.3, works similarly. See the "Numbered and approved" section, later in this chapter, to find out more.

It isn't safe to modify the list you're iterating over! To duplicate selected items or otherwise modify items in a list you're using in a loop, either

✔ Use a while loop (see the next section).

✔ Create a new list to store the modifications, as shown in this example:

```
>>> man_from_st_ives = ['wives', 'sacks', 'cats', 'kits']
>>> newlist = []
>>> for i in man_from_st_ives:
...     newlist += ['7', i]
...
>>> newlist
['7', 'wives', '7', 'sacks', '7', 'cats', '7', 'kits']
```

Whiling Away

A while loop performs an action an indefinite number of times, as long as a condition is true.

If the condition is always true, the while loop never stops (unless a return or break statement is encountered, or an exception is raised).

To write a `while` loop, follow these steps:

1. **Type** `while`, **a Boolean expression, and a colon (:).**

   Here's an example:

   ```
   while number_of_bottles > 0:
   ```

2. **On the next line, type four spaces and then type the action you want repeated, like this:**

   ```
   while number_of_bottles > 0:
       print number_of_bottles, "bottles of beer on the wall"
   ```

   If you add more lines, be sure to indent them.

A `while` loop is useful in a program that waits for user input. The program in Listing 10-3 reports on the results of several "coin tosses." The `while` loop checks whether the user has asked to quit the program.

Listing 10-3:   Coin toss program

```
import random
headcount = tailcount = 0
userinput = ''
print "Now tossing a coin..."
while userinput.lower() != "q":
    flip = random.choice(['heads', 'tails'])
    if flip == 'heads':
        headcount += 1
        print "heads! the number of heads is now %d" % headcount
    else:
        tailcount += 1
        print "tails! the number of tails is now %d" % tailcount
    print "Press 'q' to quit",
    userinput = raw_input("or another key to toss again:")
print "the total number of heads:", headcount
print "the total number of tails:", tailcount
```

Choosing Your Loop

Python has two kinds of loops: *while* loops and *for* loops. In general you should use a `for` loop, but there are a few specific situations where a `while` loop is better. This section explains when each type works best.

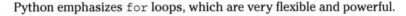

What for's for

Python emphasizes `for` loops, which are very flexible and powerful.

Most of the time, when you want to repeat a block of code more than once, you should use a `for` loop. Use `for` loops in the following situations:

- ✔ **When you want to iterate through a sequence one item at a time**
- ✔ **When you want to repeat a loop a certain number of times**
- ✔ **When you're reading a text file**

A `for` statement has two parts:

- ✔ An iterable, which provides elements one at a time

  In this `for` statement, the iterable is `range(10)`:

  ```
  >>> for i in range(10):
  ```

- ✔ A loop target (a name), which is given to each value that the iterator generates

  In the above `for` statement, the loop target is `i`.

The `for` loop is so flexible because there are many ways to use the loop target name in the body of the loop. For example, you can give a new value to the name inside the loop (as long as you don't mind if that value goes away when the loop restarts). This code gives a new value to `i`:

```
>>> for i in range(5):
...     if i < 3:
...         i = "more spam!"
...     else:
...         i = "bleargh!"
...     print i,
...
more spam! more spam! more spam! bleargh! bleargh!
```

The other side of the coin is that if you give a new value to the loop target, you can't expect the value to stick. This code doesn't print what you might expect, because `i` gets reassigned to a number when the loop restarts:

```
>>> for i in range(5):
...     print i,
...     if i < 3:
...         i = "more spam!"
...     else:
...         i = "bleargh!"
...
0 1 2 3 4
```

Why to while

The while loop is useful for these situations:

✔ **Event-driven programs:** Many programs wait for a user to take an action (such as clicking a mouse button), and then respond to the action. Often, a main while loop collects user actions (*events*) and sends them to chunks of code that act on particular events (*event handlers*).

✔ **Loops that need to run an undetermined number of times:** If you don't know how much data you need to process — for example, when you're reading a binary file — you might use a while loop that repeats its action until it detects that there is no more data.

✔ **Processing a container object while modifying it:** The spider.py program in Chapter 4 includes this kind of while block. The block uses the pop() list method to removes items from the links_to_process list. A while loop is used because no matter how long links_to_process is, it will run as long as there are items left in the list. However, it's important that the while block removes items from the list. If it didn't, the code would run forever.

```
while self._links_to_process:
    url = self._links_to_process.pop()
    self.log("Retrieving: " + url)
    self.process_page(url)
```

The while loop, because it includes a Boolean expression, can stop unexpectedly if it encounters data (such as None) that evaluates as false. This while loop stops in the middle of processing the list because data is given the value None, which evaluates as false:

```
>>> def process(a):
...     print a,
...
>>> mylist = [1, 2, None, 4, 5]
>>> data = mylist.pop()
>>> while data:
...     process(data)
...     data = mylist.pop()
...
5 4
```

The correct way to process items from a list in a while loop is as follows:

```
>>> mylist = [1, 2, None, 4, 5]
>>> while mylist:
...     process(mylist.pop())
...
5 4 None 2 1
```

Loopy Statements and Functions

This section describes some special statements that work with loops. It also details several useful functions that work with loops. Some of these statements and functions also work with other code blocks.

Useful looping statements

Several statements help you get the most out of loops. Each of the following statements works as part of a loop code block and goes on a line by itself.

Take a break — or else!

The keyword break stops the processing of a loop and exits the loop. Any code in the block that comes after the break statement is ignored (any else clause is also skipped). If the loop is nested inside another code block, the program goes back to the block that the loop was nested in.

In a loop, the break is usually part of a nested if statement. In the following example, break exits the if loop when the element has the value 'n'.

```
>>> y = "astring"
>>> for i in y:
...     if i == 'n':
...         print "broke!"
...         break
...     print i,
...     print "*",
...
a * s * t * r * i * broke!
```

You and who else?

Loops, like if statements, can have an else clause that executes when the condition in the loop evaluates as false. One way to use the else clause is with a nested if sub-block that has a break statement in it. It works like this:

1. Each time around the loop, the condition in the if statement is tested.

2. If the condition is true, the break statement causes everything else in the loop (including the else block) to be skipped. Control exits the loop.

3. If the condition is false, the loop starts over again.

4. If the loop iterator runs out before the if condition evaluates as true, the for loop's else clause gets executed.

The following code determines whether a string (in this case, `"larch"`) contains any lowercase vowels:

```
mystring = "larch"
vowels = set('aeiou')
for a in mystring:
    if a in vowels:
        print mystring, "has a vowel"
        break
else:
    print mystring, "does not have a vowel"
```

The result is:

```
larch has a vowel
```

Let's continue

When Python sees a `continue` statement in the middle of a loop code block, it skips the rest of the code in the block and goes back to the top of the loop. Here's how it works. This code block prints both "5" and "five" because the `print n,` statement is executed each time through the loop.

```
>>> for n in range(10):
...     if n == 5:
...         print "five",
...     print n,
...
0 1 2 3 4 five 5 6 7 8 9
```

When we add `continue` to the `if` block, Python skips the last `print n,` statement when the loop condition evaluates as true; therefore, it prints only "five":

```
>>> for n in range(10):
...     if n == 5:
...         print "five",
...         continue
...     print n,
...
0 1 2 3 4 five 6 7 8 9
```

Use `continue` statements sparingly because they can make your code hard to read, especially if they are nested in complex structures.

Thanks, but I'll pass

The `pass` keyword tells the Python interpreter to do nothing. It is usually used in `class` statements, but you'll also find it useful in `while` or `for` loops when the program requires no action. In this example, the `argument_clinic()` function does nothing if its argument is greater than or equal to 5:

```
>>> def argument_clinic(minutes):
...     if minutes >= 5:
...         pass
...     else:
...         print "No it isn't!"
...
>>> minutes = 4
>>> argument_clinic(minutes)
No it isn't!
>>> minutes = 5
>>> argument_clinic(minutes)        # nothing happens
>>>
```

The `pass` statement is also useful when you are starting to build a program. You can create the skeleton of the program's code blocks by using `pass` and then fill in what the blocks do later. (But don't forget to take out `pass`!)

This example code will eventually solve all the world's problems, but for now it's just a placeholder:

```
def grand_solution(problems):
    """ solve all the world's problems here """
    # We will figure this out someday
    pass
```

Loopy functions

This section describes some functions that are especially useful when working with loops.

All the functions described in this section work with iterables in general, not just with sequences.

Numbered and approved

In Python 2.3 and later, use the `enumerate()` function in a loop to return the index (position) and value of each element. Follow these steps:

1. **Type the following, substituting your own iterable for the example list:**

   ```
   for i, v in enumerate(['tic', 'tac', 'toe']):
   ```

2. **On the next line, indent four spaces and type some code that you want Python to execute.**

   ```
   for i, v in enumerate(['tic', 'tac', 'toe']):
       print i, v
   ```

Here's the result of the code:

```
0 tic
1 tac
2 toe
```

Technically speaking, `enumerate()` returns an iterator that creates an (index, value) tuple for each data item. The tuples generated by the preceding code are `(0, 'tic')`, `(1, 'tac')`, `(2, 'toe')`.

The two-loop tango

The `zip()` function, new in Python 2.0, loops over two or more sequences at the same time. It returns a list of tuples in which an item in each sequence is paired with the corresponding items in the other sequences.

Think of a zipper zipping together two sets of teeth!

To write a `for` statement that zips two sequences, type the following (substituting your own sequence names):

```
for a, b in zip(sequence_one, sequence_two):
```

The following example uses the `zip()` function in a `for` statement to explain the rules of the game "rock, paper, scissors":

```
>>> mylist1 = ['rock', 'paper', 'scissors']
>>> mylist2 = ['scissors', 'rock', 'paper']
>>> mylist3 = ['paper', 'scissors', 'rock']
>>> for a, b, c in zip(mylist1, mylist2, mylist3):
...     print "%s beats %s but not %s" % (a,b,c)
...
rock beats scissors but not paper
paper beats rock but not scissors
scissors beats paper but not rock
```

Gentlemen and ladies, unpack your tuples

A `for` loop is a convenient way to *unpack* the values in a tuple. A canonical example of tuple unpacking uses the `iteritems()` method of dictionaries, which first turns each key:value pair into a two-item tuple.

We use `items()` in this example to show how the transformation to a list of two-item tuples takes place. In actual code you should use the `iteritems()` method instead. The result is the same, but it's more efficient.

This example shows how unpacking works:

```
>>> cheese_inventory = {'Red Windsor': 'the van broke down',
'Caerphilly': 'on order', 'Red Leicester': 'fresh out'}
>>> cheese_inventory.items()
[('Red Windsor', 'the van broke down'), ('Caerphilly', 'on
order'), ('Red Leicester', 'fresh out')]
```

You can use the following `for` loop with the `iteritems()` method to unpack the tuple elements:

```
>>> for key, value in cheese_inventory.iteritems():
...     print key, ":", value
...
Red Windsor : the van broke down
Caerphilly : on order
Red Leicester : fresh out
```

Going backward

The `reversed()` function returns an iterator that goes through the sequence items backward. The `reversed()` function is new in Python 2.4.

The following example uses `reversed()` with the `range()` function as its argument to count down through the sequence:

```
for f in reversed(range(1, 11)):
    print f,
print "blastoff!"
```

Here's what it prints:

```
10 9 8 7 6 5 4 3 2 1 blastoff!
```

Out of sorts

The `sorted()` function returns a new sorted list while leaving the source list unchanged. It works with both lists and immutable sequence objects. This function is new in Python 2.4.

```
>>> mylist = [1, 10, 2, 9, 3, 8, 4, 7, 5, 6]
>>> mynewlist = sorted(mylist)
>>> mynewlist
[1, 2, 3, 4, 5, 6, 7, 8, 9, 10]
>>> mylist                        # original list is unchanged
[1, 10, 2, 9, 3, 8, 4, 7, 5, 6]
```

In contrast, the list method `sort()` changes the original list in place.

```
>>> mylist.sort()
>>> mylist
[1, 2, 3, 4, 5, 6, 7, 8, 9, 10]
```

To use the `sorted()` function in a `for` statement, type the following (substituting the name of your sequence object):

```
>>> mytuple = ("an", "african", "or", "european", "swallow", "?")
>>> for f in sorted(mytuple):
...     print f,
...
? african an european or swallow
```

Chapter 11

Fun with Functions

. . . .

. . . .

A *function* is a block of code that performs a specific action and returns a result.

In this chapter, you find out about calling functions, writing functions and their docstrings, and passing arguments to functions. You're also inducted into the arcane mysteries of the namespace.

1 Love Chunky Code

Here's how functions make your life easier as a programmer and make things easier on people who read and use your code, too:

✔ **Functions let you write code only once.**

When you create code that you want to reuse, be sure to define it as a function. This saves you from typing the same code over again when you want to use it in another program.

✔ **Functions hide unnecessary complexity from the user.**

No one ever has to care what this function does unless it's included in your program. And even if someone does use the function, they don't have to care *how* it works, as long as it performs the way its documentation says it will.

✔ **Functions make your code easier to understand.**

If you name a function according to what its code does, then someone reading the program just has to look at the name to get an understanding of what the program is doing at that point. (Of course, you should also include comments in your program and comments and docstrings in your function to further explain what's happening.)

✔ **Functions help you organize your program logically.**

Writing most of your code chunks in functions helps you organize your program's structure logically, and that can make your programs easier to understand.

Calling a function

Using a function is known as *calling* the function. When you call a function, the function's code runs and returns a result.

To call a function, follow these steps:

1. **Type a name to hold the result of the function followed by an equals sign (=).**

   You don't have to do this, but usually you want to do something with the function result, and it's easier if a name has been given to the result.

2. **Type the name of the function.**

3. **In parentheses, give the function information about what you want it to act on.**

   Giving a function information is called *passing arguments*. Some functions don't take any arguments, but most do.

   You can pass the function a value or a name.

In the following example, the sum() function is given one argument: the name of a list (purchases). The name total is given to the result:

Parameters versus arguments

In this chapter, we use the terms *parameter* and *argument* when discussing the data that a function needs to do its work. Here's a way to understand the difference:

A *parameter* is a placeholder for the data. When you are writing a function, you use parameters to tell the function to expect data to be passed. Then you use the parameter name inside the function to stand for that data.

An *argument* is the actual data that's passed when you call the function. Here's an example:

```
>>> def a_function(a_param):
...     print "my parameter is a_param
            and my argument is",
            repr(a_param)
...
>>> a_function("my arg")
my parameter is a_param and my argument
            is 'my arg'
```

TECHNICAL STUFF

Functions versus methods

What's the difference between a function and a method? Not much. A method is a kind of function — both perform a specific action on some information you give them. However, a method is associated with a particular object and performs its action on that object. Often, that object is a data type. For example, a list comes with the `append()` method, which lets you add items to the end of the list. Whenever you create a new list object by using a statement such as `my_list = [1,2,3]`, the object `my_list` has access to all the methods for list objects.

Functions, on the other hand, stand on their own. You don't have to create an object in order to use one.

You call functions and methods using different syntax:

✔ To use a function, type the function name:

```
my_function(x)
```

✔ To use a method, append it to the name of the object, separating the name and the method with a dot, like this:

```
my_list.append(x)
```

```
>>> purchases = [13.02, 2.99, 4.45]
>>> total = sum(purchases)
>>> print total
20.46
```

Defining a Function

Unless you're using a built-in function, you need to define the function before you can call it. These are the basic steps for writing a function:

1. **On the first line, write the** `def` **statement for the function.**

    Follow these steps:

    a. *Write* `def` *and the function name.*

    b. *In parentheses, add the names of parameters that the function will act on. Separate parameters with commas.*

        If your function doesn't have parameters, it still needs the parentheses.

    c. *Type a colon at the end of the statement.*

    Your `def` statement might look something like this:

```
def my_function(arg1, arg2):
```

2. (Optional, but very important) On the next lines, write the docstring for the function.

Follow these steps:

   a. *On a new line, indent four spaces and type three quotation marks (a triple quote).*

   b. *Type an explanation of what the function does and how to use it.*

   See the sidebar "What's up, Doc?" to find out what to include.

   c. *On the next line, indent four spaces and type a triple quote.*

Your function and its docstring might look something like this:

```
def my_function(arg1, arg2):
    """
    Perform my function on arg1 using arg2. Return a list.
    """
```

3. Write the function's code.

Indent each line of code four spaces. (If your function contains another subordinate or nested code block, such as an `if` statement, that block's code must be indented an additional four spaces, and so on.)

When you're finished, the function might look like this (but containing Python code, of course!):

```
def my_function(arg1, arg2):
    """
    my function does this
    """
    do something
    if this:
        do that
    return something else
```

Giving another name to a function

After you import a function, you can give it a new name. The additional name refers to the same object at the same location as the old name, as this example shows:

```
>>> tinyfunction
<function tinyfunction at 0x61430>
>>> myfunc = tinyfunction
>>> myfunc
<function tinyfunction at 0x61430>
```

It's important to remember the difference between *giving a new name to a function* and *calling a function while giving a name to the result.* When you call a function, you add parentheses at the end of the function name. These examples show the difference:

What's up, Doc?

If the first code in a function is a string, it becomes the docstring for the function. The docstring defines what the function does and works with Python's `help()` utility. We recommend writing docstrings for all your functions.

A docstring usually spans multiple lines, so it begins and ends with triple quotes.

By convention among Python programmers, a basic docstring for a function looks like this:

1. The first line (the only line for a simple function) is a description of what the function does, or a summary if the function does several things or has several options.

   For example, take this function that prints something:

   ```
   def printme(me):
       print me
   ```

   This function does only one thing, so the docstring might look like this:

   ```
   """Print the argument"""
   ```

2. If the function needs more than one line of documentation, the second line should be blank.

3. The third and subsequent lines explain options, defaults for optional arguments, and other usage notes.

   Say we change the `printme()` function so it takes an optional argument — a list of words not to print:

   ```
   def printme(me, bad_word_list=None):
       if bad_word_list and me in bad_word_list:
           print "How dare you!"
       else:
           print me
   ```

We might give it the following docstring:

```
"""

Print argument. Optionally check against list of words not to print.

Keyword argument:
bad_word_list -- list of words not to print (default None)
"""
```

You can find out more about Python's docstring conventions by reading Python Enhancement Proposal (PEP) 257 at:

www.python.org/dev/peps/pep-0257

```
>>> myfunction = tinymodule.tinyfunction  # giving a new name to a function
>>> myresult = tinymodule.tinyfunction(2) # calling a function
```

Returning values from a function

Names you define inside a function disappear after the function exits. To get values out of a function, you must do two things:

- ✔ **Include a** `return` **statement in the function with a name or value, like this:**

```
def my_function(b):
    a = b + 42
    return a
```

- ✔ **Use the function in an expression or in an assignment statement:**

```
my_value = my_function(3)
```
The name on the left side of the equals sign in the assignment statement now stores the value that the function returned, as shown:

```
>>> my_value = my_function(3)
>>> print my_value
45
```

If a function has no `return` statement, or if the `return` statement doesn't specify what to return, the function returns `None` (a built-in name). Here's a function without a `return` statement.

```
>>> def no_return_function(b):
...     print b
...
>>> my_value = no_return_function(3)
3
>>> print my_value
None
```

So why would you ever want a function without a `return` statement? Some functions manipulate an item in place instead of returning a new item. Some functions perform an action that doesn't need to return a result (for example, saving a message to a log). Such a function might not need a `return` statement.

The `return` statement not only passes a value out of the function, it also stops Python from running the rest of the code in the function. So `return` either should be the last statement in the function or should be used in conditional code, such as an `if` block, to jump out of the function when a certain condition is met.

Argument Clinic: Passing Data

Parameters are placeholders for information that you give to a function so it can carry out an action.

There are many ways to specify a function's parameters. This section introduces specifying positional parameters, default-value parameters, and arbitrary numbers of parameters. It also describes how to avoid the quirks of default-value parameters and mutable objects.

Introducing parameters and arguments

Here are a few things to know about function parameters:

- ✔ **A function can have any number of parameters (or no parameters).**
- ✔ **When you define a function, you specify how many parameters it has.**

  It can have a specific number of parameters or an indefinite number of parameters.
- ✔ **You can define default values for any or all of the parameters.**

When you call a function, you need to give it a value corresponding to each parameter. (This actual value is called an *argument*.) Here are a few things to know about arguments:

- ✔ **Arguments are passed when you call the function.**
- ✔ **If the parameter has a default value, you don't have to pass an argument.**
- ✔ **You can pass an argument as a literal or as a name.**

  If you pass an argument as a name, the function acts on the object the name refers to.

Specifying arguments when you call a function

The basic way of specifying arguments is to *pass* them when you call the function.

To pass an argument, type it between the parentheses of a function when you call the function, like this:

```
>>> a_function(myarg)
```

The following example creates a function that prints the value of its argument, gives a name to a tuple, and passes the name to the function:

```
>>> def a_function(x):
...     print "you passed me the argument", repr(x)
...
>>> myarg = (1,2,3)
>>> a_function(myarg)
you passed me the argument (1, 2, 3)
```

The following example passes the same function a string literal without defining a name:

```
>>> a_function("hello")
you passed me the argument 'hello'
```

Specifying arguments with keywords and default values

A function can have default values for some of the parameters. (Such default-value parameters are sometimes called *keyword arguments*.) Here are some circumstances in which default-value parameters are useful:

✔ **A particular value will be used more often than others.**

For example, Python's round() function takes a required number argument and an optional precision argument. The precision parameter defaults to 0 because, most of the time, when you round a number, you want the integer closest to the number rather than a decimal.

✔ **The function is designed to work in more than one way, depending on which arguments are passed.**

For example, the open() function opens a file for reading by default. If you want to open a file for writing, you need to specify a mode argument, 'w'.

When adding default-value parameters to function definitions, follow these rules:

1. **Type any parameters that won't have keywords first.**

   Parameters without keywords are called *positional*.

2. **Type keyword arguments in the form** *keyword=value*.

The following function definition has one required (positional) parameter (ingredient) and two default-value parameters:

```
def recipes(ingredient, servings=4, mode="Vegetarian"):
```

When calling a function that includes default-value parameters, follow these rules:

1. **Pass values for all positional parameters first.**

   Use the same order in which the function's parameters are defined.

2. **Pass values or names for any default-value parameters whose default values you want to override.**

Here are some additional guidelines for default-value parameters:

- Don't pass information for default-value parameters whose default values you want to use. For example, this function call uses both defaults:

```
>>> recipes('shiitake mushrooms')
```

- If you include default-value parameters in the order in which they were defined, you can just pass their values, like this:

```
>>> recipes('arugula', 8, "Carnivore")
```

- If you are including default-value parameters in a different order or skipping some parameters, use the *keyword=value* format, as shown here:

```
>>> recipes('arugula', mode="No peanuts")
```

Avoiding the quirks of default values

Default values are useful as function parameters, but you need to be aware of their quirks.

Immutable default values stay the same

Python evaluates default values in function definitions only once — when the function is defined, that is, when the `def` statement first runs. (Another way to say this is that Python *binds the default to the parameter*.) `def` is an executable statement; this is why you have to define a function before you can call it. After that, if you change the value of a name you used as a default in the function definition, the function will continue to use the original value when the value is an immutable data type. In the example below, the `def` is passed the value of the integer `mynum`. When `mynum` is changed later, the function still uses the old value:

```
>>> mynum = 8            # Integers are immutable.
>>> def f(arg=mynum):
...     return arg
...
>>> f()
8
>>> mynum = 10           # We're changing mynum here...
>>> f()                  # ...but the function still uses 8.
8
```

Mutable default values can change

When you use a mutable object (such as a list, dictionary, or class instance) as a default and change the object inside the function, then the next time you call the function, the function uses the changed object. For example, the following function creates a list that accumulates the arguments passed to it.

```
>>> def f(q, mylist=[]):
...     mylist.append(q)
...     return mylist
...
>>> print f('a')
['a']
>>> print f('b')
['a', 'b']
>>> print f('c')
['a', 'b', 'c']
```

Here's what's going on:

1. When the function is defined, it creates an empty list object named `mylist`.

2. Inside the function, the `append()` method adds an item to the list.

   The `append()` method changes the contents of the list *in place* — that is, `mylist` still refers to the same object after being changed.

3. When the function is called again, it grabs the same list from the same place and uses the new contents.

Assignment (=) always changes

Assignment always causes a name to refer to a different object (that is, it *rebinds*), even if the object is mutable. So if you use assignment (=) inside the function rather than the `append()` method, `mylist` doesn't accumulate arguments.

```
>>> def f(q, mylist=[]):
...     mylist = mylist + q
...     return mylist
...
>>> a = [1]
>>> f(a)
[1]
>>> a = [2]
>>> f(a)
[2]
```

Augmented assignment (+=) doesn't rebind mutable data types

Augmented assignment operators (+= and *=) rebind when used with an immutable data type, but don't rebind when used with a mutable data type, such as a list. When used with a list, += is the equivalent of the extend() method; it adds items to the end of a list. So if we rewrite the function to use augmented assignment, the function extends mylist (which is mutable) by adding the argument to the end of the list:

```
>>> def f(q, mylist=[]):
...     mylist += q
...     return mylist
...
>>> a = [1]
>>> f(a)
[1]
>>> a = [2]
>>> f(a)
[1, 2]
```

Working on a copy of a mutable object

Because using mutable objects as arguments can have unexpected results, you're better off operating on a copy of the object. This function creates a new copy of its list and then adds a value to each list element:

```
def f(mylist, data):
    newlist = mylist[:]              # make a copy of mylist
    for i in range(len(mylist)):
        newlist[i] = mylist[i] + data
    return newlist
```

Calling the above function doesn't change the original list:

```
>>> alist = [1, 2, 3]

>>> x = f(alist, 5)
>>> print x
[6, 7, 8]
>>> print alist
[1, 2, 3]
```

Using a default value of None to redefine a mutable object

If you want a function to redefine a list as empty each time you call it, use a default parameter of mylist=None. None is immutable, so the function won't be referring to a list object that might change.

The following code gives the parameter mylist a default value of None in its def statement and then redefines mylist as an empty list inside the function:

```
def f(a, mylist=None):
    if mylist is None:
        mylist = []
    mylist.append(a)
    return mylist
```

When you call the above function several times, it doesn't accumulate arguments:

```
>>> a = 1
>>> f(a)
[1]
>>> a = 2
>>> f(a)
[2]
```

Specifying a function with an arbitrary number of arguments

To pass an arbitrary number of arguments to a function, use the parameter *args in the def statement for the function. Here are tips and rules for using *args:

- ✔ The parameter *args stands for a set of positional arguments that aren't explicitly named in the function definition.

- ✔ When you call the function and pass it arguments, *args automatically creates a tuple out of the arguments.

- ✔ The parameter *args must come last in the function definition (or next-to-last if there is also a **kwargs parameter).

To pass an arbitrary number of *keyword=value* pairs to a function, use the parameter **kwargs in the function's def statement. Here's how it works:

- ✔ When you call the function and pass the keyword=value pairs, **kwargs automatically creates a dictionary from them.

- ✔ The parameter **kwargs must come last in the function definition.

The names don't have to be *args or **kwargs; Python cares only that the * or ** operator comes first in the name. But Pythonistas always use *args and **kwargs. This consistency makes programs easier to read by humans.

This example program shows how *args and **kwargs work in a function that also has two positional parameters:

```
def a_function(a, b, *args, **kwargs):
    print "a is", a
    print "b is", b
    print "*args is this tuple:", args
    print "**kwargs is this dictionary:", kwargs
```

It produces the following result:

```
>>> a_function(1, '2', 'three', 'blind', 'mice', see="how", they="run")
a is 1
b is 2
*args is this tuple: ('three', 'blind', 'mice')
**kwargs is this dictionary: {'see': 'how', 'they': 'run'}
```

Unpacking arguments

To pass the elements of a list, tuple, or dictionary as arguments in a function, use the * operator (for lists and tuples) or the ** operator (for dictionaries) when calling the function to *unpack* the elements.

To unpack, you need these things:

✔ **A function**

   The function can have any kind of parameters — positional or default, *args, or **kwargs ... or even no parameters at all.

✔ **A list, tuple, or dictionary with the *same* number of elements as the number of parameters in the function**

Unpacking lists or tuples

To pass the elements of a list or tuple as arguments in a function, use this line of code (substituting your function name and list or tuple name):

```
myfunction(*my_list_or_tuple)
```

The following code defines and calls a function, passing a list as its argument, using the * operator:

```
>>> def func_with_three_args(a, b, c):
...     print "the arguments are:", a, b, c
...
>>> weapons = ['fear', 'surprise', 'ruthless efficiency']
>>> func_with_three_args(*weapons)
the arguments are: fear surprise ruthless efficiency
```

Unpacking dictionaries

To pass the key:value pairs of a dictionary to a function, use this line of code (substituting your function name and dict name):

```
myfunction(**mydict)
```

The dictionary keys must have the same names as the function's parameters. The following code passes a dictionary to func_with_three_args() using the ** operator. The dictionary's keys match the argument names:

```
>>> not_in_stock = {"a":"Red Leicester", "b":"Jarlsberg", "c":"Camembert"}
>>> func_with_three_args(**not_in_stock)
the arguments are: Red Leicester Jarlsberg Camembert
```

What's in a Namespace

A *namespace,* also called a *symbol table* or *scope,* is storage for the names of objects Python knows about.

The most important thing to remember about *function namespaces* is this: When you give a name to a value, you are always assigning within the function's local namespace unless

- You explicitly say that the name is global
- You specify that the name is an attribute of a particular object

Discovering where Python looks for names

Python has three basic layers of namespaces, listed here in order of most specific to most general. Python looks for names in this order and stops looking as soon as it finds the name:

1. Local (names defined inside a class, function, or method)

2. Global (names defined inside a module — often function names and class names, but can be other names, too)

3. Built-in (names that are always available)

If Python can't find a name in any of those places, it raises a NameError exception. If you get an AttributeError, that means that Python found the leftmost (first) name but didn't find the name after the dot. Each object has its own namespace that Python searches. For more information about object namespaces, see Chapters 12 and 13.

Understanding function namespaces

When Python encounters a function definition in a chunk of code, it *executes* the definition. That prepares the function for being called later. When Python executes the definition, the following things happen:

✔ The function's name is stored in the current namespace.

If the function is part of a module, this is the module's namespace. If the function was imported directly, it might be the main namespace in interactive mode.

✔ Python creates a new namespace for storing any local names defined within the function.

Python searches from local to global for names, but it doesn't search from global to local. That means global namespaces don't know about the names inside local namespaces.

This behavior of Python's is useful for hiding complexity. It also prevents bugs that might occur if all names were automatically global — if that were true, it would be easy to use a name twice without realizing it, and unexpected things might happen. When names are automatically local, they are less likely to conflict.

How local and global names work with assignment

Names are automatically local (unless you tell Python to treat them as global). This means that if you give a name to a value (using an equals sign) inside a function, when you exit the function, Python will forget about the name. Here's a program that demonstrates this feature of namespaces using Groucho's famous saying. You could type it into a text file and save it with the name groucho.py:

```
# groucho.py
a_book = "man's best friend"
print "outside of a dog, a book is", a_book

def a_dog():
    a_book = "too dark to read"
    print "inside of a dog, it's", a_book

a_dog()
print "we're back outside of the dog again"
print "and a book is again", a_book
```

Figure 11-1 illustrates global and local names.

If we run the program from the command line, it has this output:

```
% python groucho.py
outside of a dog, a book is man's best friend
inside of a dog, it's too dark to read
we're back outside of the dog again
and a book is again man's best friend
```

Global name assignment

a_book="man's best friend"

Local name assignment

a_dog

a_book="too dark to read"

Figure 11-1:
A global and
a local
name
assignment.

How local and global names work with references

Because Python searches for names first locally and then globally, you can *reference* a global name inside the function — assuming the function doesn't contain a local name that's the same as the global name. This example program (we call it `brightdog.py`) and Figure 11-2 show that a function can access the name `a_book` defined outside the function:

```
# brightdog.py
a_book = "man's best friend"
print "outside of a dog, a book is", a_book
def a_bright_dog():
    print "inside of THIS dog, a book is still", a_book
a_bright_dog()
```

This code, run on the command line, produces the following result:

```
% python brightdog.py
outside of a dog, a book is man's best friend
inside of THIS dog, a book is still man's best friend
```

You can also define a function inside another function. This creates a new local namespace for the nested function. This namespace is called a *nested scope*. Nested scopes are mostly useful for functional programming. (Chapter 16 has some information on functional programming.) Nested scopes work differently in Python 2.1 and later than they work in earlier versions. We don't cover them in this book.

Global name assignment

a_book="man's best friend"

Global name referenced locally

a_dog

print "inside of THIS dog.
a book is still", a_book

Figure 11-2:
A global
name
referenced
locally.

Think globally, act locally

It's easy to explicitly tell a function that a name is global: You just use the key-word `global` with the name. In the example program below, which we call `colors.py`, defining the name `eggcolor` as global allows the function to change the value of that name, and the changed value remains in effect after Python exits the function. In contrast, the name `meat`, which isn't declared global, is changed only inside the function.

```
# colors.py
eggcolor = "green"
meat = "ham"
print eggcolor, "eggs and", meat
def breakfast():
    global eggcolor
    eggcolor = "red"
    meat = "bacon"
    print eggcolor, "eggs and", meat
breakfast()
print eggcolor, "eggs and", meat
```

If you run this code on the command line, you get the following result:

```
% python colors.py
green eggs and ham
red eggs and bacon
red eggs and ham
```

It's usually a Bad Idea to use global names because they are more likely to cause name conflicts in complex programs.

Sorting out module namespaces

Each module (a file with Python code, ending in .py) has its own namespace. All the functions defined in the module use the module's namespace as their global namespace. The functions won't look elsewhere (except for the built-in namespace) for names that are referenced within them. This means that the author of a module can use global names in a module without worrying about their conflicting with global names used elsewhere. In other words, whenever you see "global" used in Python, think "module global."

For more about modules, see Chapter 12.

When a module imports another module, the imported module's name becomes part of the importing module's namespace. You can then access its functions and other information by using the module name, a dot, and the function name, the same way you can when you import a module into interactive mode.

Imagine you have a module called mymod.py that does nothing but import another module:

```
# module 'mymod'
import math
```

If you import this module into interactive mode, you can print the math.pi constant by typing this code:

```
>>> import mymod
>>> mymod.math.pi
3.14159265359
```

But the name math and its constant pi are known only inside the module. The surrounding namespace of interactive mode still doesn't know about the math module:

```
>>> print math.pi
Traceback (most recent call last):
  File "<stdin>", line 1, in <module>
NameError: name 'math' is not defined
```

It's possible to manipulate a module's global names by using the same notation used to refer to its functions, *modulename.itemname*. You should do this *only* if you know what you're doing. (It's an advanced feature we don't cover in this book.)

Chapter 12

Building Applications with Modules and Packages

In This Chapter
▶ Working with module files
▶ Building big programs with packages

Python provides ways to organize code into files and directories:

- ✔ *Modules* are the files that contain the building blocks and glue of your program, including functions, `import` statements, classes, and so on.
- ✔ *Packages* organize modules in directory hierarchies that help users understand how everything works together.

This chapter shows you how you can use modules and packages to organize your projects and take advantage of all the tools available for Python.

Modular Living: Storing Your Code in Files

Python strongly encourages you to organize function definitions and other statements in separate files. These files are called *modules.* A module is a text file containing Python definitions and statements. The filename is the module name with the suffix `.py` appended.

Some Python modules are written in languages other than Python, most commonly C or C++. Such a module is called an *extension module.*

In the following sections, we give you the lowdown on creating your own modules, getting access to the modules that come with Python, and using modules in your programs.

> ## Better coding through modularity
>
> Modules have several benefits that let you code more efficiently and spend less time stomping bugs:
>
> ✔ **Modules save time.**
>
>   You can write code once and use it in many programs.
>
> ✔ **Modules hide complexity.**
>
> Each module creates its own namespace, so its names won't conflict with names defined elsewhere.
>
> ✔ **Modules make debugging easier.**
>
>   Storing chunks of code in modules makes it possible to write shorter programs. Python's debugging tools specify which module an error is found in.

Importing a module or its contents

To access a module's code, you import the module into either

✔ **Interactive mode**

  Importing a module in interactive mode is covered in Chapter 2.

✔ **Another Python program**

  Both these ways of importing are similar. The only difference is where you type the `import` statement.

The following sections cover how to import a module, what Python does when you import a module, and ways of accessing the goodies in a module.

Importing a module

To import a module in interactive mode, or in another Python program, type `import` followed by the name of the module without the `.py` suffix, like so:

```
import modulename
```

Initializing a module

Importing a module for the first time in a particular program, or in interactive mode, causes Python to perform a series of actions called *initializing the module*. Here's how initializing works:

1. Python creates a module namespace that stores the names defined in the module.

2. Python runs the code in the module.

3. Python stores the name of the module in the local namespace.

Initializing happens only the first time the module is imported. If you import the module again, the module code doesn't run, but the import updates the current namespace.

Accessing functions and other items inside a module

When you import a module, all the functions and other information in the module (collectively called the module's *attributes*) are available to you.

To access a module attribute, type the module name, a dot, and the attribute name. If you are calling one of the module's functions (see Chapter 11) or creating a class instance (see Chapter 13), also pass any arguments that are required. For example:

```
mymodule.myfunction(x)
```

Other ways of accessing module attributes

You can import attributes from a module into the local namespace directly by using one of the following lines of code:

✔ To import a specific item directly, type `from`, the module name, `import`, and the item name, as shown:

```
from mymodule import myfunction
```

✔ To import all of a module's functions directly, type `from`, the module name, `import`, and an asterisk (*), a wildcard character that stands for "all." For example:

```
from mymodule import *
```

Warning! Most of the time it's a Bad Idea to use the `import *` syntax because

✔ You can't control what you're importing.

✔ You risk polluting the local namespace with all the names from the imported modules, which makes debugging much more difficult.

When you access module attributes through the module name, you're less likely to run into conflicts between the names inside one module and the names inside another module. And your code will be easier to read.

For example, you might have two modules that each have a function to combine two values in some way. If each module's function were named `combine()`, then if you tried to access each of these functions directly, you might accidentally use the wrong one, or readers of your code might not know which function you were using at any particular time. But if you always use `modulename.combine()`, then which function you're using is clear.

There's one situation, however, when it's appropriate to import an item from a module directly. That's when a module is a wrapper around a single class or function. For example, the module `cStringIO` contains a single function called `StringIO()`. (See Chapter 19 for details.) The simplest way to use `StringIO()` is to import it with this line of code:

```
from cStringIO import StringIO
```

If you don't remember the names of the functions inside a module, use the `dir()` command in interactive mode to list them, like this:

```
>>> dir(mymodule)
```

Giving a local name to a module

In this section, you find out two ways to give a local name to a module or a module's functions: You can give an extra name to a module or function, or you can give a module a different name when you import it.

This section also explains the difference between giving an extra name to a function and calling the function while giving a name to its result.

Giving an extra name to a module or function

To give an extra name to a function or module (so that both names refer to the same thing), first make sure the object has been imported; then type the new name, =, and the name of the function or module, like this:

```
myfunction = tinymodule.tinyfunction
```

Importing a module using a different name

To import a module (but not a function) using a different name, type `import`, the module name, `as`, and the name you want to use. For example:

```
import tinymodule as mymod
```

Although it's not common, you can also combine the `from import` and `import as` syntax, as follows:

```
from tinymodule import myfunction as a_function
```

If you import a module using a different name, the local namespace won't know the real module name; it will know the module only by the name you used to import it.

The syntax for giving a local name to a function is different from the syntax for calling a function and giving a name to the result. When you call a function, you add parentheses at the end of the function name:

```
myresult = tinymodule.tinyfunction(2)
```

Rules for writing and naming modules

The same rules apply to naming modules that apply to naming other Python objects: Hyphens and spaces aren't allowed, and you can't use a Python keyword as the name. If you do any of these things, you'll get errors.

The Python community uses the following conventions for writing modules. The conventions make Python code more standard and easier to read:

- ✔ **Modules have short, lowercase names.**
- ✔ **Modules that exist mostly to export a single class are named after the class.**

  In this case, the module and class have the same name, but the module name is lowercase and the class name is capitalized.

- ✔ **All `import` statements come at the beginning of a module.**
- ✔ **The name of a non-public module (or function, class, method, name, or attribute) should begin with a single leading underscore.**

  For example:

  ```
  _myNonPublicModule
  ```

  A non-public name is not imported when you type `from modulename import *`, although you can still import it explicitly. See Chapter 13 for more about non-public names.

Avoid giving your module file the same name as a standard Python module. Otherwise, the wrong module might be imported.

Module, module, where is the module?

Python keeps track of module files and other files it needs in several ways.

On most operating systems, the `PYTHONPATH` environment variable lists the paths (directories or folders) where Python's modules are stored. `PYTHONPATH` uses the same format as the shell variable `PATH`. The format depends on the operating system you are using. For example, on UNIX or Mac OS, Python might be installed in `/usr/lib/python/` or `/usr/local/lib/python/`. On Windows it might be installed in `C:\Program Files\Python25`.

When you import a module, Python searches possible module locations in the following sequence until Python finds a file with that name and the suffix `.py`:

1. The current directory
2. The directories listed in `PYTHONPATH`

3. The directories in the PATH environment variable (which depends on your operating system and account setup)

All the search paths that Python knows are stored in the list `sys.path`, which is part of the `sys` module. This list stores these path names:

✔ The directory containing the input script (or the current directory)

✔ The contents of the `PYTHONPATH` variable

✔ The default search path

To modify `sys.path`, you use list methods. You need to import the `sys` module first. The following example appends a path to `sys.path`:

```
>>> import sys
>>> sys.path.append('/ufs/guido/lib/python')
```

Be careful not to remove important directories (such as the directory in which Python is installed, or any subordinate directories) from the search path, or Python may lose track of its modules.

Finding what's in standard modules

Python comes with a library of standard modules. Many of these modules are covered in Part IV and elsewhere in this book.

If you want to find out the gory details about any of the standard modules that we don't cover, see the Python Library Reference at www.python.org (it's usually also included when you install Python; instructions for installing Python documentation are in Appendix A).

The built-in function `dir()` returns a sorted list of the names a module defines. To use it, type `dir` followed by the module name in parentheses, like this:

```
>>> dir(modulename)
```

To get help on a named item in a module, type `help`; then type (in parentheses) the module name, a dot, and the item name. For example:

```
>>> help(modulename.functionname)
```

Wrapping It Up in a Package

A package is a collection of related modules stored in a directory and subdirectories. This section explains why packages are useful, the requirements for setting up packages, and the ways to import packages.

A __name__ is a __name__, except when it's __main__

Within a module, the module's name (as a string) is stored in the global name __name__. But there's an exception to this: If the module file is run as a program from the command line, Python sets the module's __name__ to '__main__'.

This feature is useful for including code (usually test code) in a module file that runs only when you start the module from the command line (by typing `python modulename.py`). The code looks like this:

```
if __name__ == '__main__':
    do something
```

When you include code that runs only under these circumstances, you don't have to remove the code when you import the module. That's because when a module is imported, __name__ is the module's name, not '__main__'.

This code goes outside any function definitions or import statements in the module, usually at the very end of the module.

Here's an example of a small function and some test code for it.

```
def f(x):
    y = x**x
    return y

if __name__ == "__main__":
    print "testing..."
    print "passing the value 2"
    z = f(2)
    print "the function returns", z
```

The purposes of packages

Packages are another way of taking advantage of Python's ability to hide complexity.

Packages have some useful features:

- **A package has its own namespace.**

  Names defined within a package — including module names — won't conflict with names defined elsewhere.

- **Packages can contain modules.**

- **Packages can contain subpackages.**

  Packages are ideal for storing and organizing a lot of related features.

Requirements for packages

These are the requirements and guidelines for packages:

- ✔ **A package lives inside a directory, and its subpackages live inside subdirectories of that directory (generally speaking).**

- ✔ **Store the package's main directory in either**

    - • One of the two special package directories on your computer

    - • The directory of your application

    See "About special package directories," later in this section.

- ✔ **Just as a module file names the module, a package directory names the package.**

    That allows you to import items in the package by using the import *packagename.modulename* format.

- ✔ **A package directory must contain a file called __init__.py.**

    In the simplest case, __init__.py is just an empty file. But it often contains code that initializes the package. For example, the best way to import specific submodules with a particular package or subpackage is to load them in the __init__.py file.

    The __init__.py file sometimes contains the __all__ list (see next item).

- ✔ **Include an index of your package's contents in a list named __all__.**

    This list helps Python code run on different operating systems. When you include module names in __all__, the command from *packagename* import * imports only those modules.

    If no one will ever import * from your package, you don't need the list.

About special package directories

When Python is installed, it sets up specific directories for packages. If you store packages in one of these special package directories, you're less likely to run into trouble if your package names are the same as module names elsewhere on the Python path.

There are two special directories for packages:

- ✔ lib/site-python/

    This directory is for packages that work the same way with all Python versions.

✔ `lib/python`*XX*`/site-packages/`

This directory is for packages that depend on the Python version. *XX* changes to represent the Python version number.

Example package structure

Here's an example structure for a package that handles graphics. More package help is available at `www.python.org/doc/essays/packages.html`.

```
graphics/                       Top-level package
    __init__.py                 Initialize the graphics package
    formats/                    Subpackage for file format conversions
            __init__.py
            gifread.py
            gifwrite.py
            ...
    effects/                    Subpackage for graphics effects
            __init__.py
            speckle.py
            swirl.py
            invert.py
            ...
    filters/                    Subpackage for filters
            __init__.py
            noise.py
            mask.py
...
```

Importing items from packages

You can import items from packages in several ways.

Importing with packages works in much the same way as importing with modules, except that you sometimes have to include more levels of names.

Individual modules and packages

You can import individual modules and packages in a couple of ways, depending on how they will be used in your program.

Importing by full name

If you'll be using many parts of a complex package, use the following format to import an individual item by its full name:

```
import graphics.effects.invert
```

This type of package import statement has a couple of rules:

✔ Each name except for the last must be a package.

✔ The last name must be a module or a package; it can't be a class, function, or named object (attribute).

To call a function from a module imported by its full name, type the full name of the module and then the function name, like this:

```
graphics.filters.noise.edges(args)
```

Import by using from

If you'll be using only a few parts of a package, use the following format to import an individual item by its full name:

```
from graphics.filters.noise import edges
```

This format works for importing any of the following objects defined in the package: *submodule, subpackage, function, class,* and *named object.*

Here are a couple of examples of importing an individual item:

✔ The following example imports the `noise` module:

```
from graphics.filters import noise
```

If you import `noise` this way, you use this code to call its function:

```
noise.edges(args)
```

✔ The following example imports the `edges()` function:

```
from graphics.filters.noise import edges
```

If you import `edges()` this way, you use this code to call it:

```
edges(args)
```

Import all items from a package

If you're sure that it won't cause namespace conflicts (for example, if you're using one small package in your program and not importing other modules or packages), use the following format to import all the items from a package:

```
from graphics import *
```

Using `import *` imports the items in the `__all__` list.

If no `__all__` list is defined, the `import *` statement imports these names from the package:

✔ The package name

✔ Names found in import statements in the file

✔ Names of modules and subpackages (but not submodules)

✔ Names defined in __init__.py files

The import * statement does not import any names with a single under-score prefix (for example, _mymodule).

When packages contain subpackages, there's no shortcut to refer to submod-ules of sibling packages (packages defined at the same level). You need to use the full name of the subpackage (*packagename.subpackagename*). Python 2.5 has a shortcut for importing from sibling modules. The shortcut is part of the absolute importing feature, which is covered in the following section.

Absolute imports in Python 2.5

In Python 2.4 and earlier, type the whole package and subpackage hierarchy when you import from a package (for example, from graphics.filters import noise). If you don't, someone reading your import statement has no way of knowing whether it imports another module from the package or a top-level package that's part of the Python distribution.

Although it's possible to use relative imports in Python 2.4 and earlier, the rules are too complicated to document in this book.

Absolute importing, new in Python 2.5, addresses this problem. There's no ambiguity about which module is being imported because Python searches for imported modules or packages on sys.path only. To import sibling mod-ules in a package, use relative imports (see the following section). To access absolute importing, type this code into your module or into interactive mode:

```
from __future__ import absolute_import
```

Relative imports in Python 2.5

When you turn on absolute importing in Python 2.5 (by using from __future__ import absolute_import), new syntax is available for importing other modules in the package directory your module is in. Follow these rules:

✔ Use the from...import syntax.

✔ Type one or more dots in front of the name of the package or module you're importing from:

• The first dot stands for the current module's package.

- The second dot stands for the package containing the current module's package (the parent package).

- The third dot stands for the parent of the parent, and so on.

Here are some relative import statements. If you write the `swirl.py` module in the package hierarchy (described in "Example package structure," in this chapter), you import other modules in the package as follows:

✔ This statement imports `swirl.py`'s sibling module, `speckle.py`:

```
from . import speckle
```

✔ This statement imports the `gifread` module:

```
from .formats import gifread
```

✔ This statement imports the `edges()` function from the `noise` module in the `filters` package:

```
from .filters.noise import edges
```

Chapter 13

Getting Classy

. . . .

In This Chapter

▶ Getting a taste of object-oriented programming

▶ Finding out about classes and their instances

▶ Getting the scoop on inheritance

▶ Meeting more namespaces

▶ Avoiding class quagmires

. . . .

This chapter is about *classes,* a tool for creating new types of objects in Python. When you create a class, you put data (also called *state*) and behavior in one suitcase. Programs based on these suitcases of data-plus-behavior are easily customized.

Python also uses classes to organize many of its own features. For example, Python's built-in data types, such as strings and lists, are classes. The use of classes hides complexity from users who don't care about it. You can use a list without worrying about how lists work, and you can perform an action such as sorting a list without worrying about how sorting works. (And if you ever had to write a sort function, you know that's a good thing.)

In this chapter, you find out how to create and use these Python objects:

✔ Classes, subclasses, and superclasses

✔ Class methods

✔ Class instances

✔ Class and instance attributes

You also find out why classes are important to Python's modular design.

Alley-OOP! Some Object-Oriented Programming Concepts

Python is a language that supports *object-oriented programming* (*OOP* for short). In OOP parlance, *objects* are bundles of data and actions (*methods*) that operate on the data. OOP programs are built around such bundles.

In contrast, languages such as C focus on *procedural programming,* and the Scheme/Haskell languages focus on *functional programming.* Python is a balanced language with good support for both procedural and OOP styles and some support for functional programming.

Objects and functions aren't mutually exclusive — in Python, methods are just functions attached to objects. But considering a program in terms of data/action bundles is a different approach than creating data objects and then using separate actions on them.

We don't describe object-oriented programming in detail in this book, but the following concepts are important for understanding Python classes.

Objects

In object-oriented programming, an *object* is a thing that bundles data and behavior.

To use a real-world example, imagine you have a dog (you might not have to imagine).

✔ The dog belongs to a breed.

  If the dog were a Python object, the breed would be its *type* or *class*. As shown in "Using multiple inheritance," later in this chapter, you can even create "mutt" types.

✔ The dog has characteristics associated with it: its name, age, and so on.

  If the dog were a Python object, these characteristics would be its *data attributes*.

✔ The dog can do actions — run, sit, bark, mutilate shoes, and so on.

  If your dog were a Python object, these would be its *method attributes*. All of the attributes "go with" the dog wherever it goes.

Likewise in Python, if you have an object — say, a list — you use the name of the specific list object to access both

✔ Its data (the items in the list)

✔ The actions that list objects can do (slice, append, and so on)

Inheriting, overriding, and extending

Subclasses *inherit* behaviors, abilities, and properties from the general (*parent*) classes they are based on. For example, Labrador Retrievers are a subclass of all dogs and inherit the properties and abilities of dogs.

When a subclass changes the way a parent class works or changes its data attributes, the subclass is *overriding* the properties of the parent class. The Lab is gentler than some other kinds of dogs, so a Lab class might be said to *override* the gentleness quality of dogs in general.

When your subclass includes new data or methods, it is *extending* the properties of the parent class. A Lab has the built-in skill of retrieving. A Lab class might be said to *extend* the abilities of dogs to include retrieving.

One way to think of inheritance is to use the phrase *is a*. A Lab *is a* dog; that means a Lab inherits properties and abilities of dogs.

Polymorphism and duck-typing

In some languages, a single function or method works only with specific types of objects. In Python, many tools work with more than one type of object. For example, the `in` keyword (which calls the special method `__contains__()`) acts on lists, tuples, and dictionaries — objects of different types. This feature is called *polymorphism*.

Mirror, mirror on the wall, what's the object of this all?

Python terminology gets a little confusing at times, especially with all the different things that the word *object* can stand for. In Python, the word *object* refers to any item in a Python program that has its own storage space — from a simple name to a multi-megabyte dictionary (or any of its elements) to a function, module, class, or instance. But in object-oriented programming, the word *object* refers to any item that combines data and behavior. These items (along with other items) are also objects in Python. Specifically, they are called *classes* (or *class objects*) and *instances* (or *instance objects*). Any objections?

Python's polymorphism is based on names. For example, `file` objects have three basic methods named `read()`, `write()`, and `close()`. If you create a class that has those three methods, then even though your class isn't officially a `file` object, you can use instances of your class in many of the places that Python expects a file object. Pythonistas often call this feature *duck-typing* because it's like the saying, "If it looks like a duck and quacks like a duck, it must be a duck." In programming terms: If this object has the attributes of a file and the `read()`, `write()`, and `close()` methods of a file, the program accepts it in cases where the data type `file` is called for.

Now Class, for Instance . . .

In this section, we explain how classes fit in with other Python objects and, in general terms, how classes and class instances work together. These are the most important things to remember:

- ✔ A *class* is a general description of something.
- ✔ A *class instance* is a specific example of what the class describes.
- ✔ In order to do things with a class, you usually need to create an instance.

Classes, modules, and functions

Python classes are similar to Python modules and functions in these ways:

- ✔ Classes, modules, and functions all contain assignments and statements.
- ✔ Both classes and modules usually include function definitions — code blocks that begin with a `def` statement and perform some action. (In classes, these are called *methods* rather than functions.)
- ✔ Classes, modules, and functions all have their own namespaces.
- ✔ You call classes and functions by using the name followed by parentheses. Calling a class does one thing: It creates an instance of the class.

A class is like a template

A class is a template for data and behavior. You use the template to make specific objects called *instances*. The instances share the attributes of the class.

Say you have a copy of the American Kennel Club breed standard for a Labrador Retriever. The AKC document is like a class because it describes the qualities and abilities a Lab has. The data attributes for the Lab breed — its coat quality, size, eye color, and so on — are described in the class, and so are the method attributes — its ability to retrieve, to swim, and so on.

A Python class defining a Labrador Retriever might include this code:

```
class Lab:
    weight = 60                    # data attribute
    def retrieve(self, thing):  # method attribute
        return(thing)
```

Note that the AKC breed standard isn't a dog, it is just a description of the dog. Likewise, in Python, the class isn't the actual object you manipulate. To work with the class, you first tell the class to create an *instance*. (This is where our example breaks down — you can't use the AKC breed standard document to create a dog; you need a couple of other dogs for that!)

Telling the difference between a class object and a function object

The way you create a class instance looks superficially similar to the way you name the result of a function. In fact, if you don't know whether the object is a class or a function, you might not be able to tell which is being used by looking at the assignment. (Classes frequently do not take arguments, and functions usually do, but this isn't universally true.)

```
>>> fido = Lab()           # creating a class instance
>>> y = len('mystring')    # calling a function
```

To determine what kind of object is associated with a name, use the type() function, like this:

```
>>> type(fido)
<type 'instance'>
>>> type(y)
<type 'int'>
>>> type (Lab)
<type 'classobj'>
>>> type(len)
<type 'builtin_function_or_method'>
```

Note that a function can return an instance.

```
>>> def foo():
...     return Lab()
...
>>> type(foo())
<type 'instance'>
```

An instance is a copy made from the template

An instance is a specific object, with its own name, that has the same attributes as the class you use to create it.

If you get a Lab from the animal shelter and name her Pilot, then your dog is like an *instance* of the Labrador Retriever class. She has her own name, but she shares the attributes of Labrador Retrievers in general.

So if you were to describe Pilot in Python code, you would type this, which creates an instance (`pilot`) of the `Lab()` class:

```
>>> pilot = Lab()
```

All about class and instance attributes

Each thing that you name inside a class, whether it's a method, data, or some other kind of code, is an *attribute* of the class.

When you create an instance of the class, it starts with the same attributes as the class. You can add or alter instance attributes after that.

To see the value of a class or instance data attribute, type the class or instance name followed by a dot and the attribute name, like this:

```
>>> Lab.weight
60
>>> pilot.weight
60
```

Use the same code to see how Python internally identifies a method attribute:

```
>>> Lab.retrieve
<unbound method Lab.retrieve>
>>> pilot.retrieve
<bound method Lab.retrieve of <__main__.Lab instance at 0x62300>>
```

Object-oriented programmers say that `Lab` *has a* weight and *has a* `retrieve()` method. See the sidebar, "When Not to Use Inheritance," later in this chapter.

Making and Calling Classes

The following sections cover the syntax of writing a class, calling a class to create an instance, and using a method via an instance. These, along with assigning and changing attributes (discussed in the previous section), are the most common class and instance tasks.

In this section, we use the following example class:

```
class NameTag:
    def __init__(self, myname):
        self.myname = myname

    def say(self):
        print "Hello, my name is", self.myname
```

Creating a class

To write the first line of a class definition, type `class`, the name of the class, and a colon, like this:

```
class NameTag:
```

By convention, class names are capitalized and have embedded caps. By contrast, function and method names are usually all lowercase. This makes it easier to tell at a glance which object is being used at a particular point in a program.

Writing an __init__ ( ) method

Most classes have an __init__ () method. This method runs when you make an instance of a class. It specifies how many arguments the instance needs and puts the instance into a known initial state.

Rules

A few key things to know about __init__ () methods:

- ✔ **The** __init__ () **method is a special method called an** *initializer.*

  In Python, special methods begin and end with two underscore characters.

- ✔ **It's conventional for the** __init__ () **method to come first in the class definition.**

- ✔ **The** __init__ () **method, like other methods, needs a** `self` **parameter (which stands for the instance), plus any other parameters that the class needs to create an instance.**

Basic syntax

To write a basic __init__() method that includes only the self parameter, follow these steps:

1. **On the line beneath your class definition header, indent four spaces.**

2. **Type** def __init__(self):

Arguments

Many classes require you to pass arguments when you make instances from them. Creating attributes for these parameters in the __init__() method lets other methods access them easily.

To write an __init__() method that includes parameter attributes, follow these steps:

1. **On the line beneath your class definition header, indent four spaces and type this:**

   ```
   def __init__(self
   ```

2. **On the same line, type a comma and the name of a parameter, like this:**

   ```
   def __init__(self, myname
   ```

3. **Repeat Step 2 for each parameter you want to include.**

4. **Type an end parenthesis and a colon:**) :

   Your def statement might look like this:

   ```
   def __init__(self, myname):
   ```

5. **Go to the next line and indent four spaces past the** def **statement.**

6. **Create an attribute for the first parameter by typing** self, **a dot, the name of the attribute, an equals sign, and the name of the parameter, like so:**

   ```
   def __init__(self, myname):
       self.myname = myname
   ```

7. **Repeat Step 6 for each parameter in the** def **statement.**

Writing more methods

The __init__() method usually gives the class only some initial information. Most classes also include methods that perform actions. You create methods by using the def statement, exactly the way you write a function.

To write a method, follow these steps:

1. **Making sure to indent 4 spaces, type** def, **the name of the method, and** (self, **like this:**

   ```
   def say(self
   ```

2. **(Optional) Type any additional parameters the method requires. Separate parameters with commas.**

   Don't use attributes as parameters — you access them through `self`.

3. **End the line by typing) :.**

4. **On the next line, indent four more spaces and type the code for the function.**

   If your code references class or instance attributes, be sure to use the `self.name` syntax.

   This example code includes only the `self` parameter.

```
def say(self):
    print "Hello, my name is", self.myname
```

Pure selfishness

When you work with Python classes, you encounter the name `self` a lot.

The easiest way to understand `self` is this: `self` stands for the instance that you create from a class. For example, if you create an instance named `pilot` from the class named `Lab()`, `self` stands for `pilot`.

When you are writing a class and you define a method in that class, you need to explicitly include the `self` parameter in the method definition, as in the example below. Otherwise the method wouldn't have any way of knowing which instance to use.

```
class NameTag:
    def __init__(self, myname):
        self.myname = myname
```

When you give a name to a value in a method definition, you use `self.` in front of the name. The line `self.myname = myname` makes the `myname` parameter automatically available to other instance methods. That means you can call those methods without passing `myname` as an argument. Note the following code:

```
def say(self):
    print "Hello, my name is", self.myname
```

If this were a function, you would have to pass `myname` as an argument or else Python would complain that `myname` isn't defined. But because it's a method and you've already defined `self.myname` in the `__init__` statement, the method can figure out the value of `myname` by using the `self` object.

The `self` parameter also makes life easier when you create an instance. Python automatically passes the `self` argument for you. For example, if you create an instance of `NameTag()`, you only have to give it the value of `myname`. It automatically uses the name of the instance as the value for `self`.

Static and class methods of new-style classes work differently. See the Chapter 14 for the lowdown on new-style classes.

Creating other class attributes

You can put any kind of code or assignment into a class. Anything inside a class that you give a name to becomes an attribute of the class.

For example, we could add a `favorite_color` attribute to our NameTag class:

```
class NameTag:
    favorite_color = "Blue"
```

Then if we create an instance of the class, the instance also has this attribute:

```
>>> grail_seeker = NameTag('lancelot')
>>> grail_seeker.favorite_color
'Blue'
```

Creating an instance

To create an instance of a class (which is also known as *calling a class*), you give it a name, and then type the class name, parentheses, and any parameters. Follow these steps:

1. **Type a name for the instance, followed by an equals sign, like this:**

   ```
   hello =
   ```

2. **Type the class name and (as shown:**

   ```
   hello = NameTag(
   ```

3. **If your class requires parameters, include values or names for them. Separate parameters with commas.**

   If you call the `NameTag` class created in the previous section, you need to pass a value for one parameter, `myname`.

   ```
   hello = NameTag('Arthur'
   ```

4. **Type).**

   The completed code looks like this. The instance name is `hello`.

   ```
   hello = NameTag('Arthur')
   ```

Calling a method via an instance

After you have created an instance (by using code like `instance_name = ClassName()`), you can perform the actions defined by the class's methods.

To call a method via an instance, type this on one line:

- ✔ The name of the instance
- ✔ A dot

> ✔ The name of the method
>
> ✔ A pair of parentheses
>
> Pass any needed arguments inside the parentheses.

For example, to call the `retrieve()` method of the `pilot` instance, type this code:

```
>>> pilot.retrieve("ball")
'ball'
```

You can't use this code to call the method by using the name of the class because the class is only a template for the instance object. An AKC breed standard document can't retrieve a ball — only the actual dog can. Here's what happens if you try to call the method by using the name of the class:

```
>>> Lab.retrieve("ball")
Traceback (most recent call last):
  File "<stdin>", line 1, in ?
TypeError: unbound method retrieve() must be called with Lab instance as first
            argument (got str instance instead)
```

There is actually a way to call a method by using the name of a class. This is known as *calling an unbound method*. It's mostly an advanced programming technique, but it's also used to extend methods in subclasses (see "Extending superclass methods," later in this chapter). Briefly, you create an unbound method by using the name of the class instead of the name of the instance (for example, `Lab.retrieve` rather than `pilot.retrieve`). To call it, you pass it an instance name along with any other arguments the method requires — for example, `Lab.retrieve(pilot, "ball")`.

Where did self go?

Does something seem to be missing in the code for calling a class? The `__init__()` method in the class `NameTag` has two parameters — `self` and `myname`. Why do you need to pass only one parameter when you create a class instance?

The answer is that `self` is a special parameter that essentially passes itself "behind the scenes" when you use the class instance. So you don't have to pass `self` in this statement (although there are some cases in which you do). In fact, if you do pass it in this statement, you get an error:

```
>>> hello = NameTag(self, 'Arthur')
Traceback (most recent call last):
  File "<stdin>", line 1, in ?
NameError: name 'self' is not defined
```

Getting Inside the Factory: How Class and Instance Namespaces Interact

A class and an instance each have a namespace, which is storage for the names of objects that Python knows about. When you create an instance of a class, the instance has its own namespace, but it also shares the class's namespace.

Whenever Python encounters a name that's part of an instance, it looks for the value first in the instance's namespace. If it can't find the value there, it looks in the class's namespace.

Function namespaces and global namespaces interact in similar ways. See Chapter 11.

So anything that you do to the class namespace (such as changing an attribute of the class) is also reflected in the instance — except when the instance has already overridden that value from the class namespace. The next section shows how it works.

Changing the values of class and instance attributes

You can change the values of a class's attributes. When you create an instance of your class, you can also change (or *override*) the values of any class attributes it inherits. The effect these changes have depends on what data types the attributes are, how you change the values, and in what order you change the values.

When we first define our Lab instance, pilot, it has the same value for weight that the Lab class defines:

```
>>> Lab.weight
60
>>> pilot.weight
60
```

Changing the value of the class attribute

To change the value of the class attribute, type the class name, a dot, the attribute name, =, and a new value, like this:

```
>>> Lab.weight = 50
```

Changing a class's attributes in code outside the class (and especially outside the class's module) makes your code hard to read and to debug.

Changing the value of the instance attribute

To change the value of the instance attribute, type the instance name, a dot, the attribute name, =, and a new value, like this:

```
>>> pilot.weight = 45
```

Effects of changing attribute values

The effects of changing attribute values are as follows:

- ✔ If you change the class attribute first, the instance value also changes:

```
>>> Lab.weight = 50
>>> pilot.weight
50
```

- ✔ If you change the instance attribute first, the class value does not change:

```
>>> pilot.weight = 45
>>> Lab.weight
60
```

If the attribute is a mutable data type, such as a list, and you use a method that changes the attribute in place (such as the `append()` method of lists — see Chapter 8), then changing the instance attribute *does* change the class attribute. Be sure to operate only on copies of mutable instance attributes or avoid using change-in-place methods on them.

- ✔ Giving a new value to the instance attribute *overrides* the value it originally gets from the class. So if you change the class attribute *after* you change the instance attribute, the instance attribute does not change.

```
>>> pilot.weight
45
>>> Lab.weight = 100
>>> pilot.weight
45
```

Adding an attribute to an instance

In "Making and Calling Classes," earlier in this chapter, we describe how to add an attribute to a class, and the preceding section describes how to change the value of a class or instance attribute. You can also add a data attribute (and value) to an instance that you've created. Just write code like this:

```
>>> pilot.coat_color = "yellow"
```

This attribute is stored in the instance's namespace, so the class won't know about this attribute, as illustrated here:

```
>>> Lab.coat_color
Traceback (most recent call last):
  File "<stdin>", line 1, in ?
AttributeError: class Lab has no attribute 'coat_color'
```

Class and Instance Conventions

Python programmers use some important conventions when writing and implementing classes. Python will understand your code if you don't use them, but humans who have to read your code and figure out what it does will appreciate your using them. Some conventions are as follows:

✔ Modules that exist mostly to export a single class should be named after the class.

✔ Class names begin with an uppercase letter. Attribute and method names begin with lowercase letters.

✔ The name self is used to refer to the name of a class instance.

A brief privacy note

When you're writing a class attribute, you specify that it is *private* by naming it with a single leading underscore. Unlike private attributes in modules and packages, however, Python doesn't treat private attributes in classes in any special way. The single leading underscore is just a convention that says to people reading your code, "don't touch this!" (That is, don't try to rewrite it, change it, or use it in any way, or else you might break something.)

Private attributes are most often used in large class hierarchies (but you should use them any time you want to inform users of your class that this is *not* part of the public interface).

If you name a class attribute with *two* leading underscores, that tells Python to use *name mangling* so that base classes and subclasses can't see the attribute (unless they manually do

the name mangling themselves). This is an advanced programming tool because it's hard to use with inheritance.

Attributes with two leading *and* two trailing underscores (like __getattr__) aren't private. They are special methods (discussed earlier in this chapter).

Some OOP purists denigrate Python's privacy mechanisms because the privacy mechanisms don't *enforce* privacy. Pythonistas counter that anyone who really wants to break privacy can do it, and it's more important to document things — and then get on with your work. (In general, Pythonistas say, "Python is a language for consenting adults." That is, Python usually won't prevent you from doing something stupid or complex if you really want to.)

Inheriting the Farm: Overriding and Extending Classes

You can change the features of a class or create new features by creating a *subclass* (or *child class*) that inherits attributes from its parent class and then changes some of the attributes inherited from the parent class.

Classes that subclasses inherit from are called *parent classes, superclasses*, or *base classes.*

Creating a subclass

To create a class that inherits from another class, you type class, the name of the subclass, and then, in parentheses, the name of the superclass the subclass inherits from. To create a subclass of the NameTag class we work with earlier, you use a class statement like this:

```
class GeekNameTag(NameTag):
```

Python 2.5 adds a new feature: classes without base classes can use empty parentheses (the same way functions can have no arguments). That is, you don't have to specify a superclass in the parentheses. For example, you could just type class C():

In general, when you create a subclass, you create only what you want to override or extend about the superclass's behavior. So you don't need to write an __init__() statement unless you want to make changes to the superclass's __init__() statement.

Overriding superclass methods

To create a subclass that overrides a method of a superclass, you write a method with the same name as the superclass method you want to override, and you give this method different behavior.

In the following example, the subclass defines a say() method that behaves differently from the superclass's say() method.

```
class GeekNameTag(NameTag):
    def say(self):
        print "The current value of my name is", self.myname
```

When not to use inheritance

In some cases, writing a subclass that inherits from a superclass isn't the best solution. Suppose you are planning a conference, and you created a `Registration` class. You might think of making `Registration` inherit from `NameTag` so you can use the `say()` method. But it's better to make a nametag *attribute* for the registration class that uses `NameTag` as a value, like this:

```
class Registration:
    def __init__(self, name):
        self.name = name
        self.nametag = NameTag(name)
```

Using an attribute that refers to an instance of a different class is called *object composition*. One way to describe what's going on in the above example is to say that an instance of the `Registration` class *has an* attribute that is an instance of the `NameTag` class. To put it in material-world terms, if you produce a bunch of registration packets for a conference, each packet is like an instance of the `Registration` class, and each package *has a* name tag in it, which is an instance of the `NameTag` class.

Here's what happens when you create an instance of the class and the subclass and call each instance's `say()` method:

```
>>> superclass_inst = NameTag('Lucy')
>>> subclass_inst = GeekNameTag('Linus')
>>> superclass_inst.say()
Hello, my name is Lucy
>>> subclass_inst.say()
The current value of my name is Linus
```

Extending superclass methods

There are two basic ways to extend superclass methods. You can

- Extend a method that already exists in the superclass
- Write a new method that uses data from a superclass method

Extending an existing superclass method

Extending an existing method of a superclass is similar to overriding, except that you *also* call the superclass method in the extended code. You extend a superclass method if you want the method to perform as written and you also want to manipulate its result in some way.

To create a subclass that extends the methods of a superclass, follow these steps:

1. **Define a method with the same name as the superclass method you're extending.**

```
class WeirdGreeting(NameTag):
    def say(self):
```

2. **In that method's code, call the superclass method by typing the superclass name, a dot, the superclass method name, and its argument in parentheses.**

```
class WeirdGreeting(NameTag):
    def say(self):
        NameTag.say(self)
```

3. **Perform some additional manipulations, either on the value returned by the superclass method or on the subclass's instance data.**

The following subclass extends the `say()` method of `NameTag`:

```
class WeirdGreeting(NameTag):
    def say(self):
        NameTag.say(self)
        print self.myname.swapcase()
```

You might call it like this:

```
>>> greet = WeirdGreeting('Totoro')
>>> greet.say()
Hello, my name is Totoro
tOTORO
```

Adding a new method

You write a new subclass method if you want the subclass to add some completely new behavior to a parent class. The following example creates a new subclass of `NameTag` and also creates a method on the subclass that extends the parent class by saving the `NameTag` data in a database. (**Note:** This code is incomplete; it works only if a database file has been created and opened.)

```
class PersistentNameTag(NameTag):
    def save(self):
        db.write(pickle.dumps(self))
```

Using multiple inheritance

A class with more than one superclass inherits its attributes from all its superclasses. Such a class uses *multiple inheritance*.

To write a subclass that uses multiple inheritance, type the names of more than one superclass in a `class` statement. For example:

```
class SubClassName(SuperClass1, SuperClass2):
```

And here's how you would create a "mutt" type of dog (this dog is probably easier to create as a Python class than in real life):

```
class Heinz57Dog(Chihuahua, Greyhound, Mastiff, Dalmatian):
```

Namespace searching in classes and superclasses

Subclasses have access to the namespaces of all the classes they inherit from. When a subclass inherits from parent classes, a namespace hierarchy is created. When other classes (not direct parents of the subclass) get into the act, the namespace structure is called a *framework*.

When you are working with classes, Python searches for names in the following order and stops searching as soon as it finds the name:

1. Instance

2. Class

3. Superclasses that the class inherits from

This is similar to how function and module namespaces work — Python searches the function's local namespace first, and then the module's global namespace, and then the main or built-in namespace.

This gives rise to the following behaviors:

Inheriting from a single superclass

The names and definitions in a subclass or its instance override the same names and definitions in the superclass.

Inheriting from multiple superclasses

When a class has more than one superclass, Python searches first the instance, and then the subclass, as usual. When Python starts searching the superclasses, it uses a method called *depth-first, left-to-right searching*, which searches in the following order:

1. Leftmost superclass in the class statement

   For example, in the class statement
   `TotallyBizarreGreeeting(WeirdGreeting, NameTag)`, searching
   would begin with `WeirdGreeting`, the leftmost superclass named.

2. Subclasses of the leftmost class

3. Next class to the right in the class statement

4. Subclasses of this class

5. And so on . . .

Here is a simple example:

```
class A:
    def foo(self):
        print "foo called in A"

class B:
    def foo(self):
        print "foo called in B"

    def bar(self):
        print "bar called in B"

class C(A,B):
    pass
```

If you import the preceding example into interactive mode, here's what you
get when you create an instance of C and use it.

1. The instance of C looks in class A first and finds the `foo()` method
   there.

   It executes that and never sees B's `foo()` method.

2. When you call the `bar()` method, the instance of C doesn't find it in
   class A, so it looks in class B.

This example shows the result:

```
>>> x = C()         # Create an instance of C
>>> x.foo()         # Call the foo() method
foo called in A
>>> x.bar()         # Call the bar() method
bar called in B
```

Operator interception and overloading

You can change the way Python operators work in your classes. This applies both to expression operators (such as x * 3) and operations on objects (printing, calling a function, and so on). Inheritance is one trick that makes this possible, but Python also has some special tools to help:

Hooking into the power of special methods

Methods with names that begin and end with two underscores — special methods — are also called *hooks*. They have special behaviors. When you use an operator such as +, Python calls the special method __add__ behind the scenes. If you implement the __add__() method for your class, Python will call it each time you use the + operator with instances of your class.

These methods are provided so you can make your own class instances work the same way Python's built-in types do. It's good practice not to change the behavior of the operators in ways users and readers of your program don't expect (such as changing __add__ so that it subtracts!).

Table 13-1 lists some of the operator overloading methods. To see them in the documentation for most of Python's built-in data types, type help(*data_type*), substituting the name of the data type you need help with — for example, help(list).

For a complete list of special methods, see "Special method names" in the Python Language Reference: http://docs.python.org/ref/special names.html.

Table 13-1	Some Commonly Used Special Methods	
Method	*Used For*	*Syntax*
__add__()	+	X + Y
__eq__(), __neq__() and others	Comparing	X == Y, X != Y, and so on
__getattr__()	Looking up	X.attribute
__getitem__()	Retrieving an index or key	X[key], X[index], X in Y, used in loops and tests

Method	Used For	Syntax
__init__()	Initializing objects	MyClass()
__iter__()	Creates iterables	iter(X),for i in X:
__repr__()	Printing, converting	print X,X
__setattr__()	Assigning a value to an attribute	X.attr_name = value
__setitem__()	Assigning an index or key	X[key] = value X[index] = value
__str__()	Converting objects to strings	str(X)

Super strings

The following example class includes a method that overrides Python's built-in __str__() method. It checks whether one or two names were passed and returns the names in first name–last name order:

```
class Employee:
    def __init__(self, lastname, firstname=None):
        self.lastname = lastname
        self.firstname = firstname

    def __str__(self):
        if self.firstname:
            return "%s %s" % (self.firstname, self.lastname)
        else:
            return self.lastname
```

When you create instances of this class and print them, the behavior of str() changes. (The print command calls str(*object*).)

```
>>> a = Employee('Aahz')
>>> b = Employee('Maruch', 'Stef')
>>> c = 'Maruch, Stef'
>>> print a
Aahz
>>> print b
Stef Maruch
>>> print c
Maruch, Stef
```

When to Go to Class

You might benefit from creating classes in your program in the following situations:

- **Several functions use the same parameters.**

    If your program's functions pass a lot of arguments back and forth, consider creating a class and making the functions into methods. Methods can access their data through the instance (`self`), so you don't have to pass the data.

    You could do this by using globals, but there's more of a danger that things would get changed when you don't want them to. Furthermore, globals don't allow you to create multiple instances.

- **Your program carries out the same operation multiple times.**

    Classes are ideal for this purpose because each instance you create is separate from the others, and you don't have to reset everything to perform the operations again.

- **Your program is event-driven.**

    An event-driven program often has a function that collects events (user actions) and sends them to other functions to be processed. If this event function is a method of an `Application` class, application information doesn't have to be passed as arguments.

- **Your program uses a persistent database.**

    Class instances can be stored on disk by using the `pickle` or `shelve` modules. (See Chapter 19.) The `pickle` feature creates an external file and saves an object in it. `pickle` can also create a string suitable for storing in a database. The `shelve` feature "pickles" objects by using a database that you access with keys.

- **You want a data type that bundles several items.**

    An empty class definition can store data attributes. For more information, see Chapter 21.

Chapter 14

Introducing New-Style Classes

In This Chapter

▶ New-style classes and their features

▶ Method resolution order

▶ Mind-boggling metaclasses

*I*f you're new to Python and you have read Chapter 13 on classes, you might be groaning at the prospect of yet another chapter on classes. Actually, almost everything in Chapter 13 also applies to the new-style classes we discuss in this chapter. New-style classes simplify Python's object hierarchy in ways that save you effort if you want to make changes to a built-in data type. They come with some new features that are of interest mostly in advanced programming. We discuss them here so you'll recognize them in programs.

This chapter provides an introduction to new-style classes and their features. You also find out about method resolution order and two features you *shouldn't* use — static methods and the __slots__ class attribute.

An Object's Object: Intro to New-Style Classes

The primary difference between a *classic* (or *old-style*) class and a *new-style* class is that a new-style class always inherits from object, either directly (class myclass(object):) or indirectly by inheriting from one of Python's built-in types (class myclass(dict):), which inherits from object.

The original purpose of new-style classes was to allow subclasses based on built-in Python data types, such as dict and list. They also fix some problems with classic classes and add a bunch of new features (such as properties).

New-style classes were introduced in Python 2.2; however, they were somewhat experimental in 2.2, and subtle but significant changes were made in Python 2.3. (In case you're curious, most of the changes involved multiple inheritance features.) If you're using Python 2.2, stick with classic classes.

Classic Coke or New Coke?

There is a controversy in the Python community about new-style classes. Some people say you should use them for all the classes in your code. Others say you should use them only where a regular class won't do. The controversy is based on the following facts:

✔ **Regular classes will go away in Python 3.0.**

Not to worry — the vast majority of Python code written with regular classes will still work because classic class code isn't *that* different from new-style class code.

✔ **Python 2.1 and earlier don't support new-style classes at all, and new-style classes work differently in 2.2 than in 2.3 and later.**

So if you use new-style classes, your code might have problems running in Python 2.2 and earlier.

We focus on classic classes in this book because they're still the default and will remain the default until Python 3.0; in addition, the vast majority of code in existence (including the Python library) still uses classic classes.

Before Python 2.2, data types could be created only by using the C programming language, and classes couldn't inherit from built-in or third-party data types. If you wanted a new object that worked kind of like a Python dict, for example, you had to write the whole thing from scratch. You couldn't write a subclass based on dict because C types were very different from Python classes (specifically, classes were all of the class type, and class instances were all of the instance type). Python 2.2 introduced the *type/class unification* in the form of new-style classes.

In the new-style class tutorial found at www.python.org, Guido Van Rossum (Python's creator) provides an example of a new-style class that extends the dict type by providing a default value when a key is missing:

```
class defaultdict(dict):
    def __init__(self, default=None):
        dict.__init__(self)
        self.default = default

    def __getitem__(self, key):
        try:
            return dict.__getitem__(self, key)
        except KeyError:
            return self.default
```

The documentation for new-style classes hasn't yet been integrated with the rest of the official Python documentation at http://python.org. Here's where to find information about new-style classes:

```
www.python.org/doc/newstyle/
```

Everything comes from object

The basic rule for a new-style class is that it has to inherit from `object`. (We know what you're thinking: "Oh no, another use of the term *object*!") In this case, `object` is a built-in type. All the Python built-in data types are really subclasses of `object`. If you type `help(__builtin__)` into the Python interpreter, part of what you see is a hierarchy of classes, starting with `object`:

```
Help on built-in module __builtin__:
NAME
    __builtin__ - Built-in functions, exceptions, and other objects.
[....]
CLASSES
    object
        basestring
            str
            unicode
        buffer
        [...]
```

Methods of inheritance

There are two ways to set up inheritance for a new-style class. You can inherit directly from object, or you can inherit from a built-in data type.

Inheriting from object

To write a class that inherits directly from `object`, start with this line:

```
class MyClass(object):
```

To make all classes in a single module new-style classes, put this statement at the top of the module:

```
__metaclass__ = type
```

Inheriting from a built-in data type

Your class can inherit from a built-in data type (which inherits from `object`).

Use the following method if you want something that works a lot like a built-in data type but has a few differences (like Guido's `defaultdict` example).

Some functions return a specific data type. If you pass an instance of your subclass to a function that returns a specific data type, it may return an instance of a built-in type rather than an instance of your subclass.

In this example, we create a subclass of `list` and an instance of that subclass. When we use the `append()` method on the instance, the changed instance still belongs to the subclass we created. But when we use the `list()` function with the instance, it returns an object of the `list` type.

```
>>> class MyList(list): pass
...
>>> ell = MyList()
>>> ell.append(1)
>>> ell
[1]
>>> type(ell)
<class '__main__.MyList'>
>>> ell2 = list(ell)
>>> ell2
[1]
>>> type(ell2)
<type 'list'>
```

New Improved Class Features

New-style classes provide several enhancements over old-style classes:

✔ **The** `__getattribute__()` **method**

✔ **A new return value for** `type()`

✔ **The** `super()` **function**

✔ **The** `property` **type**

✔ **Class methods, including the** `__new__()` **class method**

✔ **Static methods**

✔ **The** `__slots__` **class attribute**

Getcher attributes!

With classic classes, one of the tools of subclassing is the special method `__getattr__()`, which returns an attribute of an object. New-style classes add the special method `__getattribute__()`. The difference between `__getattr__()` and `__getattribute__()` is that `__getattr__()` is called only if an attribute isn't found, but `__getattribute__()` is called for all attributes.

Hey, baby, what's your type?

New-style classes give you more specific information about the instances you create from a class:

- ✔ If you create an instance of an old-style class, the value returned by `type(myinst)` is `<type 'instance'>`.

- ✔ If you create an instance of a new-style class, the value returned by `type(myinst)` is the same as the instance attribute `myinst.__class__`.

Calling the right superclass method

The `super()` function provides a way to get at a subclass's superclasses when you are using multiple inheritance. You usually use it in a method to call a method in the superclass. To use it, type `super(classname, objectname)`. It returns a bound superclass object.

Here's how to use the `super()` function to re-create the example `NameTag` class code in Chapter 13. (Note that you must convert `NameTag` to a new-style class first.) The only difference is that you use `super()` instead of explicitly using the `NameTag` class. Notice that when you use `super()`, the class name argument must be the current class.

Using `super()` makes it easier to change the name of a parent class. You only need to change the class definition, not all the superclass calls in the methods.

Extended method using (classic) `NameTag` superclass:

```
class WeirdGreeting(NameTag):
    def say(self):
        NameTag.say(self)
        print self.myname.swapcase()
```

Extended method using the new-style `NameTag` class and `super()` function:

```
class WeirdGreeting(NameTag):
    def say(self):
        super(WeirdGreeting, self).say()
        print self.myname.swapcase()
```

The super() function has some limitations:

✔ **It is a _cooperative_ function:** Each parent class that defines the method must also call super().

✔ **It works simply only when all methods have the same _signature:_** That is, they must have the same parameter lists. (It is possible to use super() when methods have different signatures, but difficult.)

The traditional way of calling a superclass's method is to use the name of the superclass you want when calling the method:

```
x = MySuperclass.its_method()
```

That's my property!

Properties are attributes that you manage by using various get and set methods, so they are also called _managed attributes._ Before new-style classes came along, the only way to customize attribute management was to override __getattr__ and __setattr__. This was tricky and caused performance problems.

Set up properties

To set up properties in your class, follow these steps:

1. **Define a new-style class and an __init__() method.**

   Usually, you set up a private attribute (self._x in this example) because it's only used behind the scenes by the methods. See Chapter 13 for more on private attributes.

   ```
   class MyClass(object):
       def __init__(self):
           self._x = 0
   ```

2. **Define class methods that get, set, or delete an attribute.**

   It's a good idea for the names of these methods to include the words get, set, and del so it's clear what's going on. For example:

   ```
   def getx(self):
       print "Getting _x"
       return self._x

   def setx(self, x):
       if x < 0:
           raise ValueError("Negative values prohibited: %r" % x)
       self._x = x
       print "Setting _x"
   ```

3. **Define a property and, in parentheses, pass the names of the methods you defined, as in the following example.**

   Note that you do not call the methods (don't include parentheses after the method names).

   To include a doc attribute for a property (which shows up when you ask for help on the property), type doc= and a string inside the parentheses.

   ```
   x = property(getx, setx, doc="no negative x")
   ```

Use properties

To use a property, create an instance of the class. To assign and retrieve values, pretend that the property is a regular attribute — Python automatically calls the methods for you. These examples show how:

```
>>> my_inst = MyClass()
>>> my_inst.x
Getting _x
0
>>> my_inst.x = 10
Setting _x
>>> foo = my_inst.x
Getting _x
>>> foo
10
>>> print MyClass.x.__doc__
no negative x
>>> my_inst.x = -10
Traceback (most recent call last):
  File "<stdin>", line 1, in ?
  File "a.py", line 11, in setx
    raise ValueError("Negative values prohibited: %r" % x)
ValueError: Negative values prohibited: -10
```

When only class matters

Class methods are passed the class of the object but not the object itself. They're useful when

- ✔ A method needs to know only the class name and doesn't care about any underlying data.

- ✔ You call methods directly on the class and you want to return an instance (for example, the dict.fromkeys() method).

The following sections describe creating and calling class methods. You also find out about the special __new__() method.

Creating class methods

You put class methods in your classes by defining a method (call it g()) and then typing the code g = classmethod(g).

In this example, the g() class method returns the name of the class and a value x that it's passed:

```
class E(object):
    def g(cls, x):
        return cls.__name__, x
    g = classmethod(g)
```

Another way to create class methods is to use *decorator syntax*, like this:

```
@classmethod
def g(cls, x):
```

We tell you more about decorators in Chapter 16.

Python programmers conventionally use the name cls (or occasionally klass) to refer to the name of the class that gets passed to a class method. (These weird names are used because class itself is a keyword and can't be used as the name of an object.) This is similar to the convention of using self to refer to the instance that a class creates.

Calling class methods

To call a class method, use the class name, a dot, and the method name.

This example calls the class method g() from class E created by the preceding class definition.

```
>>> print E.g(3)
('E', 3)
```

You can also call a class method on an instance, like this:

```
>>> print E().g(3)
('E', 3)
```

What's new in class methods

The __new__() class method deserves special mention.

When you create an instance with an old-style class, Python first creates the instance and then calls the __init__() method to initialize it. But this doesn't work well for immutable instances or with metaclasses. So new-style classes have a class method, __new__(), that returns the instance. You can define both __new__() and __init__() in a class. If you define both, __init__() is called after __new__().

Classes that use __new__() are different in several ways from classes that only use __init__():

- ✔ The __new__() method creates a new instance, so it takes a cls parameter.

  An __init__() method takes a self parameter because it is called after the instance is created.

- ✔ The __new__() method must call its base class's __new__() method to create the instance.

  With an __init__() method, you can either call the base class's __init__() or override it.

- ✔ The __new__() method must explicitly return the created instance via a return statement.

  An __init__() method doesn't return anything.

Here's a trivial example of a __new__() method:

```
class derived_from(str):
    def __new__(cls, *args, **kwargs):
        instance = str.__new__(derived_from, *args, **kwargs)
        return instance
```

Unless you need to have a __new__() method in your class, it's conventional to use __init__() to process the passed-in arguments and then raise an exception if they are incorrect. It's a Bad Idea to use __new__() to return an error value rather than a correctly created instance. (It's okay for __new__ to raise an exception, though.)

Cutting through the static about methods

Static methods are basically functions attached to a class rather than to a module. The difference between a static method and a class method is that a static method has no cls parameter. When a static method is called in a program, it looks just like a function call.

A static method begins with a def statement, has no self or cls parameter, and ends with *name_of_method* = staticmethod(*name_of_method*). The line @staticmethod before the def statement is decorator syntax that also indicates a static method. See Chapter 16 for more information about decorators.

Don't use static methods; they add unnecessary complexity to your programs. Use functions if you want to do things with classes that don't require a class instance.

Don't use the slots machine

The `__slots__` class attribute provides a way of restricting the attributes of class instances. It's intended as an advanced memory-saving technique for classes that will have millions (yes, millions) of instances. It doesn't work well with inheritance.

Simple rule: If you don't understand metaclasses, don't use `__slots__`.

If our warning isn't enough, take Guido's word for it:

> `__slots__` *is a terrible hack with nasty, hard-to-fathom side effects that should only be used by programmers at grandmaster and wizard levels. Unfortunately it has gained an enormous undeserved popularity amongst the novices and apprentices, who should know better than to use this magic incantation casually.*

Island of Dr. MRO

In Python, MRO doesn't stand for *Meals Ready to Open;* it stands for *Method Resolution Order.*

The important thing to remember about MRO is this: If you use new-style classes, you don't have to worry about method resolution order, because Python handles it automatically.

MRO matters when you write a class that inherits from more than one parent class. For example, assume your class inherits from two parent classes, and each parent class has a `write()` method. If your class calls a `write()` method, Python looks for it first in the class itself and then in the parent classes. But how will Python know which `write()` method to use? And more important, how will you know which one gets used? If you guess wrong, you might get the dreaded Unexpected Results.

With classic classes (see Chapter 13), Python looks for the method in this way:

1. It looks in the parent class listed first (leftmost) in the class definition.

2. It looks at that class's parent classes, and so on until there are no more parent classes.

3. It goes to the next class listed in the class definition, and all of its parent classes, and so on.

    This is called *depth first and then left to right* order.

Unfortunately, this order doesn't work with new-style classes, because they all inherit from `object`. If this order were used, the same parent class would be examined multiple times, and you'd still be in the position of not knowing which class's method was discovered first. Even worse, sometimes a parent class is supposed to be overridden by a subclass, but the parent class's method gets called instead!

So the way MRO works in new-style classes is this:

A new-style class has an `__mro__` attribute that prescribes the order for searching parent classes. It is created by a complicated algorithm that guarantees that each parent class exists only once in the `__mro__`.

Best of all, Python generates a class's `__mro__` attribute automatically, so you don't have to worry about the "complicated algorithm!" Just examine the `__mro__` attribute to see in what order the superclasses are searched.

The algorithm does still work left-to-right, so if you want a particular superclass to get its method called first, make sure that it's listed first in the classes you inherit from.

Exploding Your Head with Metaclasses

Python 2.2 and later have a functionality called *metaclasses*. Just as you use a class to create instances, you use a metaclass to create classes.

Roles

A metaclass is just a class — but it creates classes rather than class instances. In other words, it really is turtles all the way down.

A metaclass doesn't really create the class. Instead, Python executes the class code (just like initializing a module) and then passes the class to the metaclass. The metaclass can do whatever it likes, and the class name is given to what it returns.

The Python community's wisdom about metaclasses is summed up by Python guru Tim Peters: "Metaclasses are deeper magic than 99% of users should ever worry about. If you wonder whether you need them, you don't." Therefore, read this section to find out what a metaclass is and how to recognize one when you see it, but don't worry about how to put one into your own program.

In a metaclass, the first argument for a method is conventionally called `cls` rather than `self`. Metaclass methods operate on the class that the metaclass creates. A metaclass doesn't create instances, and if you try to create an instance of a metaclass, you get an error that looks like this:

```
Traceback (most recent call last):
TypeError:  unbound method [...]
```

The default metaclass for all new-style classes is `type()`. (Surprise! `type` is really a metaclass instead of the function we've been calling it all along. It just does a good job of disguising itself until you need to use its other capabilities.)

Applications

To use a metaclass, use the __metaclass__ name either

- ✔ In the body of a class
- ✔ At the top of a module (if you want all the classes in that module to use that metaclass).

Here's an example that sets up a class to use a metaclass. Notice that you only *refer* to `MyMetaClass`; you don't call it (there are no parentheses).

```
class MyClass:
    __metaclass__ = MyMetaClass
```

Even if you want to write code that creates multiple classes, you rarely need to use metaclasses. A function can return a class. A function that returns a class is called a *class factory*. An example of a class factory called `class_with_method()` can be found in this article on metaclass programming in Python:

```
www-128.ibm.com/developerworks/linux/library/l-pymeta.html
```

The `classobj()` function of the `new` module also acts as a class factory.

Chapter 15

Feeling Exceptional

*P*eople who use your Python programs don't always do exactly what you want them to do, and sometimes a program gets input it doesn't expect. Python has built-in tools for handling these situations.

This chapter describes some of Python's error-handling features, including exceptions and code blocks you write to capture exceptions. We also introduce you to writing your own exception handlers and discuss two ways of approaching error handling.

All about Special Handling

In Python, as in English, an *exception* is a special case — something that needs special handling. When the Python interpreter encounters something unexpected, it generates an internal message, or *raises an exception*. You write code to tell Python what to do when an exception occurs. Python's built-in exception code usually displays an on-screen error message containing information about what kind of problem occurred and where.

Python also uses exceptions for control flow in non-error conditions, especially in `for` loops, which we discuss in Chapter 10.

"I didn't think they would do that!"

When you write programs for other people to use, especially programs that ask users to provide input of some kind, users may give your program input it doesn't expect.

For example, if your program asks the user to input a number, she might accidentally type a letter instead. If your code is set up to work only with a number, this input would cause your code to fail. Proper exception handling catches input of the wrong type, prints a friendly reminder about what input to use, and lets the user try again. That way, the user can correct the problem easily instead of having to restart the program or look at a confusing error message such as this:

```
TypeError: cannot concatenate 'str' and
                'int' objects
```

Here's an example of Python's error handling. If you forget a colon when writing a `for` statement, Python prints an error message called `SyntaxError`:

```
>>> for x in range(5)
  File "<stdin>", line 1
    for x in range(5)
                    ^
SyntaxError: invalid syntax
```

This *exception handling* functionality makes debugging and using programs easier. Without it, a program would just mysteriously quit whenever it encountered a bug. You've probably used programs that do that and know how frustrating it can be!

But Python takes exception handling even further: You can write your own exception handlers based on Python's built-in ones. For example, if you don't want an error message displayed to the screen, you can design your program to catch specific errors your users might make and then write exceptions that give users hints about how to use your program correctly.

Trying Things Out

Python programmers handle exceptions in a code block that begins with the word `try`. Blocks that use `try` are often nested inside each other to provide complete error handling. There are two kinds of `try` blocks:

✔ `try/except`: If exceptions occur in the `try` code, the `except` clause captures and handles the exceptions.

✔ `try/finally`: The try code and the `finally` code always run. If exceptions occur in the `try` code, the `finally` clause re-raises the exceptions for handling elsewhere in your program.

In Python 2.5, these two types can be combined into one block: `try/except/else/finally`. See "try/except/else/finally: Together at last," later in this chapter.

The following sections describe the inner workings of `try` blocks.

Using try/except statements

You use a `try/except` block if you want the `except` code to run *only* if there is an exception. It looks like this:

```
try:
    some code
except SomeException:
    exception-handling code
```

Tracking down tracebacks

Python keeps track of what your program does. Each time you call a function, Python adds the call to the *call stack*. Each function call adds another layer to the call stack. When an exception is raised, Python stores the call stack as a *traceback* that tells you exactly where the error occurred and the sequence of calls that got you there. (It doesn't, however, list the function parameters — you need to do your own logging for that.)

The following example program contains an error. When you run it, Python raises an exception, which generates a traceback:

```
### Three functions that call each other
def a():
    b()
def b():
    c()
```

```
def c():
    1/0      # Attempt at division by
             zero, will raise exception
### Run function a()
a()
```

When you run the program, the traceback lists the calls in the order they were received:

```
File "a.py", line 9, in <module>
    a()
  File "a.py", line 3, in a
    b()
  File "a.py", line 5, in b
    c()
  File "a.py", line 7, in c
    1/0      # Attempt at division by
             zero, will raise exception
ZeroDivisionError: integer division or
             modulo by zero
```

It works as follows:

1. Python runs the code in the `try` clause.
2. If no exception is found, Python finishes the `try` block and doesn't run the code in the `except` block.
3. If an exception occurs in the `try` clause, Python skips the rest of the `try` code and checks the exception against the exceptions named in the `except` statement. If there is a match, Python runs the `except` clause.
4. If an exception occurs in the `try` clause that doesn't match the `except` statement, Python looks for a matching exception handler in any code that the `try` block is nested in. If Python doesn't find a matching exception handler, then Python uses its built-in exception handler (that is, it prints those geekspeak error messages you saw earlier).

Handling multiple exceptions

You can process several different kinds of exceptions by using `try/except` code. If you want to catch more than one kind of exception in a `try/except` block, there are two ways to do it:

✔ **To handle all the exceptions the same way, list multiple exception classes within a single `except` clause.**

Pass the exceptions as a tuple (in parentheses, separated by commas), like this:

```
except (RuntimeError, TypeError, NameError):
```

✔ **To handle each exception a different way, use multiple `except` clauses.**

These clauses are tested in order; if there's a match in a clause, the rest of the clauses are skipped. Here's what two `except` clauses might look like:

```
except RuntimeError:
    some code
except TypeError:
    some different code
```

Following is a small program that checks for correct user input. It uses a `try/except` block with a single `except` clause that catches two kinds of exceptions.

```
try:
    x = raw_input("Enter an integer: ")
    y = int(x)
    print "Your number was", y
except (TypeError, ValueError):
    print "That didn't look like an integer to me."
```

Processing exception arguments

Some exceptions use arguments (associated data, like what functions and methods use):

✔ Exceptions usually have a string argument describing what sort of problem occurred. Here's an example:

```
try:
    x = int(x)
except TypeError:
    raise TypeError("%r is not a valid integer" % x)
```

✔ A few exceptions also have a tuple argument that stores several bits of information about the problem. This is an advanced feature we don't cover in this book.

To print or log the details of an exception, specify a name in the `except` statement to hold the exception instance. In the following example, the name `detail` is used to store the exception instance:

```
>>> try:
...     x = 1/0
... except ZeroDivisionError, detail:
...     print "Oops,", detail
...
Oops, integer division or modulo by zero
```

If you use more than one exception class in your except statement, put them in parentheses to differentiate from the exception instance name. Otherwise you'll get an unexpected result.

Dealing with exceptional exceptions

When using multiple `except` clauses, set up the last clause to catch any unexpected exceptions. A "catch-all" `except` clause (commonly called a *bare except*) should go at the highest level of your program. It should include code that logs the errors it catches. (It could also print the error and send it to a logging function and then re-raise the exception.) Logging is covered in Chapter 17.

Include code in your `except` clause that logs or prints the errors the `except` clause catches. Otherwise, Python swallows all the unexpected exceptions and you won't know what kinds of errors your program is really generating, which makes debugging harder.

When it comes to "or else"

A `try`/`except` block can have an `else` clause. The `else` clause runs only if the `try` block runs successfully and completely:

✔ No exception is raised.

✔ No `return` or other block-exiting statement is executed.

Use an `else` clause for code that needs to run if the `try` clause doesn't raise an exception. Put it after all the `except` clauses, like this:

```
try:
    some code
except SomeException:
    exception-handling code
else:
    necessary code
```

Using try/finally statements

If you need some code that *always* runs as part of a `try` block, and you want to handle exceptions elsewhere in your program, use the `try/finally` block.

The `finally` block is good for cleaning up — closing open files and releasing memory, for example. (Python usually does these things for you automatically, but in programs handling lots of data, it's useful to clean up as you go along.)

The `try/finally` block follows these steps:

1. Python runs the code in the `try` block.

2. If Python finds no errors, it leaves the `try` block and runs the code in the `finally` block.

3. If a `return`, `break`, or `continue` statement is executed in the `try` block, the `finally` clause runs on the way out.

4. If an exception occurs in the `try` block, Python skips the rest of the block but *saves the exception*. It runs the `finally` clause and then sends the exception up to higher levels of your program (that is, it *re-raises the exception*), where you should have exception-handling code.

A `try/finally` block looks like this:

```
try:
    some code
finally:
    cleanup code
```

When you use a finally clause, don't put initializing statements (for example, assignment statements) in the try block. In the following code, if open() raises an exception, the name f doesn't actually get created. Then when the finally clause runs, Python will produce a NameError complaining that f doesn't exist.

```
try:
    f = open('cheese_list')
    process(f)              # This line is pseudo-code
finally:
    f.close()
```

To avoid the problem, put the open() line before the try/finally block, like this:

```
f = open('cheese_list')
try:
    process(f)              # This line is pseudo-code
finally:
    f.close()
```

Because it's usually a good idea to do error-checking whenever you try to open a file, you might want to wrap the open() line in a separate try/except statement.

try/except/else/finally: Together at last

Starting in Python 2.5, you can write a single block that includes all the components discussed in the previous sections. This code works the same way as the old code did, and the guidelines for how to use the statements are the same — the only difference is that you don't have to nest two blocks if you want to use both except statements and a finally statement together.

The following example uses try, except, and finally together to create a function that tries to read a file and return its contents. But if there's an error reading the file, the function returns None instead. Whether or not the file read is successful, the function closes the file and returns a value:

```
def safe_read(filename):
    f = open(filename)
    try:
        data = f.read()
    except IOError:
        data = None
    finally:
        f.close()
    return data
```

It's easier to ask forgiveness than permission

Early in the history of programming, errors were often handled by trying to guess every error that might occur and then writing a lot of `if` statements to process them. This philosophy of error handling is called "Look Before You Leap" (LBYL for short). This is expensive in computer processing power because the error checking occurs every time the user does something (enters data, clicks something on the screen, chooses from a menu, and so on).

The `try` statement lets you assume that users will use your program correctly. It handles errors only when they actually occur. This philosophy of error handling is called "Easier to Ask Forgiveness than Permission" (EAFP for short). Props to Alex Martelli for the phrasing and tireless promotion of the philosophy, and

to Admiral Grace Murray-Hopper, architect of Cobol, who brought the concept into computers (albeit in a different context — she was commenting on a techie's relations with bureaucrats).

EAFP is more efficient than LBYL in several ways:

✔ You can handle all the errors in one place (the `except` statements).

✔ You can handle unexpected errors by using an `except` statement with a "catch-all" error handler.

✔ You handle errors only when they occur and not check for errors every time the program gets some input.

Raising Your Code to New Levels

When your program determines an error condition (such as depositing a negative amount to a bank account), the `raise` statement lets you force an exception even if Python doesn't detect an error. Raising an exception "pushes the error higher" in your program's code hierarchy.

To write a basic `raise` statement, type the word `raise` and the type of exception to raise. This example raises the `ValueError` exception:

```
raise ValueError
```

To include a value with an exception, specify the value in parentheses after the exception. The value is usually a string that gives a message about the error, as in this example:

```
raise NameError('What's your name again?')
```

You might also see this code written in the old style, with a comma rather than parentheses (for example, `raise NameError, 'What's your name again?'`), but parentheses are preferred, and the comma form won't be valid in Python 3.0 and later.

A `raise` statement can also include a traceback object, but we don't cover that in this book.

Sometimes, when Python has already raised an exception, you might want to do something with it now and also force higher levels of the program to deal with it (in geekspeak, this is known as "allowing the exception to propagate up the calling stack"). To save, or re-raise, an exception, type `raise` on a line by itself. For example, if you want to send an exception to a logging function and re-raise it, your code might look something like this:

```
try:
    some code
except ValueError:
    log_problem()    # replace this with your logging code
    raise
```

Use a bare `raise` only when there is an existing exception — otherwise you get an exception!

Making Your Program Exceptional

Python's exceptions are pretty general. Creating your own exceptions simplifies your error handling. It's much easier for users and other programmers to understand your code when you use an exception that describes what the error is, both at the point where the error occurs and when you handle it in an `except` clause.

To create your own exceptions, write a new exception class or class hierarchy that's derived from Python's `Exception` class or one of its subclasses.

Writing a base class for your exceptions

Here are some tips for writing an exception class:

- ✔ Use as a base class the Python exception that most closely resembles the exception you're writing.

- ✔ Most exceptions have names that end in `Error` to maintain consistency with Python's built-in error handling. Yours should, too.

- ✔ Keep exception classes simple. They should mostly only include attributes that can store information about the error. Separate handlers can extract this information and act on it.

For example, to define a class based on Python's Exception class, write something like this:

```
class MyModuleError(Exception):
    pass
```

Developing an exception hierarchy

If you're creating more than one kind of exception — perhaps as part of a module that handles several related functions — good practice is to start by creating a base class for the exceptions. Usually, the base class doesn't do anything. The code looks something like this:

```
class MyModuleError(Exception):
    """Base class for my exceptions."""
    pass
```

To make a subclass based on the base class, follow these steps:

1. **Name the subclass after its corresponding module or class, plus "Error", like this:**

   ```
   class InputError
   ```

   This helps you keep track of which modules your errors are coming from.

2. **Put the base class in parentheses in the class definition, and type a colon.**

   ```
   class InputError(MyModuleError):
   ```

3. **On the next line, indent four spaces, and write code for what you want the exception to do.**

   ```
   class InputError(MyModuleError):
       pass
   ```

Chapter 16

Tackling Some Advanced Features

In This Chapter
▶ Recognizing advanced Python code
▶ New features of Python 2.5

*T*his chapter describes some of the advanced features of Python, as well as some of the new features of Python 2.5.

If you don't understand parts of this chapter, don't worry. We're describing these things mainly so you will recognize them if you see them in someone else's code. As you work with Python, your understanding will improve until you're ready to use these features yourself!

What's That Idiom?

Table 16-1 shows you how some of the advanced and new features look in Python code. All these features are described later in this chapter.

Table 16-1	Recognizing Advanced Python Coding Idioms	
Keyword or Example	**Feature**	**Description**
`[X for X in mylist]`	List comprehension (listcomp)	Creates a new list; allows manipulation of list items)
`((x*2) for x in (2, 4, 6))`	Generator expression (genexp)	Creates a new iterator object; more efficient than a listcomp
`yield` in a function or method	Generator	Makes a function that remembers where it left off

(continued)

Table 16-1 *(continued)*

Keyword or Example	Feature	Description
`with exp as name:`	`with` statement	Adds context manage-ment to `try`/`finally` blocks)
`X if C else Y`	Conditional expression	Easier truth testing
`@`	Decorator	Creates function wrapper
`lambda a, b: a**b`	Lambda expression or anonymous function	An expression that returns a function

What to Do Next: Iterators and Generators

Lists are a useful Python feature that can take up a lot of memory and processing time. *Iterators* are tools that help make lists more efficient, and *generators* make creating iterators easy.

The itertools library

The `itertools` library, which was introduced in Python 2.3, includes functions for making lists more efficient both to write and to use. Each of the `itertools` functions creates a different type of iterator object. The objects are designed to work together. They also work with the tools in the `operator` module to produce high-speed results.

Here are some simple examples of `itertools` code.

This `itertools.imap()` code takes two lists and passes their elements (one element from each list at a time) to a `lambda` function (see the "Mary had a little lambda" section, later in this chapter), which multiplies the elements:

```
>>> n = [1, 3, 6, 4, 3, 6, 3, 234]
>>> m = [1, 2, 3, 5, 6, 7, 8, 9]
>>> for i in itertools.imap((lambda x, y: x*y), m, n):
...     print i,
...
1 6 18 20 18 42 24 2106
```

The inner lives of iterators

Iterators are used throughout Python, and if you understand them, you will have a good grasp on what Python is all about.

An *iterator* is a Python object that produces elements one at a time. An *iterable* is an object that can create an iterator. For example, the iterator created from a list returns the list elements one at a time, in order. The iterator for a dict returns the keys one at a time, unordered. Lists and dicts are examples of iterables.

As if things weren't confusing enough, some iterables (such as files) are also iterators. For example, a file simply returns itself when asked for an iterator (technically, it returns `self`). This means that all iterators are also iterables.

Finally, you can create functions and classes that either create iterators or are themselves iterators.

Iterators are useful because they simplify code and reduce memory usage. They can also make applications more responsive because they do only the calculations needed to produce one element at a time instead of doing the work of producing all the elements upfront.

The official Python tutorial available on the Python Web site at `http://www.python.org` contains further explanation of the inner workings of iterators:

Behind the scenes, the for statement calls iter() on the container object. The function returns an iterator object that defines the method next() which accesses elements in the container one at a time. When there are no more elements, next() raises a StopIteration exception which tells the for loop to terminate. This example shows how it all works:

```
>>> s = 'abc'
>>> it = iter(s)
>>> it
<iterator object at 0x00A1DB50>
>>> it.next()
'a'
>>> it.next()
'b'
>>> it.next()
'c'
>>> it.next()
Traceback (most recent call last):
  File "<stdin>", line 1, in <module>
StopIteration
```

This `itertools.count()` code creates an iterator that returns consecutive integers beginning with the argument you specify (0 by default). You can use `itertools.count()` with `itertools.imap()` in the preceding example to generate one of the lists, like this:

```
>>> n = [1, 3, 6, 4, 3, 6, 3, 234]
>>> for i in itertools.imap((lambda x, y: x*y), n, itertools.count()):
...     print i,
...
0 3 12 12 12 30 18 1638
```

The `itertools.islice()` function works on a slice of a list of numbers. This code creates a list of consecutive numbers between 0 and 61 (`xrange(62)`). It then takes a slice of that list (the argument 6 specifies the beginning of the slice and the argument 62 specifies the end) and prints every third number from the slice (the argument 3 specifies every third number):

```
>>> for i in itertools.islice(xrange(62), 6, 62, 3):
...     print i,
...
6 9 12 15 18 21 24 27 30 33 36 39 42 45 48 51 54 57 60
```

Generators: yield for faster processing

Generators look like functions — in fact, they are a special kind of function. They use the yield statement to return data (whereas regular functions use the return statement).

Generators are a convenient way to create iterators because they simplify the record-keeping needed for returning each element. (That is, you don't have to keep checking and reassigning values because the generator remembers the values it was assigned last.)

Generators are different from functions in two other ways:

- Calling a generator always returns the same thing: an iterator (usually called a *generator iterator* or *geniter*).

  Calling a function can return any data type, depending on what the function does.

- When Python encounters a yield statement, it doesn't exit the generator iterator. Instead, it remembers what was happening inside the function (including any values that were assigned).

  When Python encounters a return statement, it exits the function, and values assigned in the function are forgotten.

Because they make iterators, generators are usually used in loops. Here's how a generator works:

1. When you call a generator, you get a new iterator.

2. When you call the next() method of the generator iterator, the body of the generator function executes until it hits a yield statement.

   The for statement calls an iterator's next() method automatically.

3. The yield statement passes a new value to the next() method. The generator iterator doesn't exit. Instead, it preserves or remembers the *state* of the function body.

4. The next() method gets called again. Because the iterator remembers the state of the function, the values that were in effect before, remain in effect.

5. The cycle repeats until Python runs off the end of the generator, a `return` statement is executed, or an exception is raised.

6. If the generator ends normally, Python raises `StopIteration`.

Generators are sometimes called *resumable functions* or *generator functions*. People who call them *generator functions* usually call the thing that they return a *generator* rather than a *generator iterator*. (Python can add to your stock of tongue twisters as well as help you become a better programmer!)

The following code creates a generator function that filters out repeated items in a sequence — for example, repeated lines in a file. You prepare the file by reading it using the `readlines()` method and then sorting the resulting list of strings:

```
def uniq(input):
    prev = object()
    for line in input:
        if line != prev:
            yield line
        prev = line
```

In Python 2.4 and earlier, you can't use `yield` in the `try` clause of a `try/finally` statement.

Python 2.5 adds some esoteric features to generators. (We list them here so you won't be surprised if you see them in other people's programs.) All three features are new methods on geniters:

✔ `send()` allows you to pass values back into the generator.

A consequence of this change is that `yield` becomes an expression in Python 2.5, so code like this is allowed (in earlier versions, it raises an error):

```
foo = (yield foo)
```

Starting in Python 2.5, generators are also called *coroutines*.

✔ `throw()` raises an exception inside the generator.

✔ `close()` forces the generator to exit.

Expression and Comprehension: Listcomps and Genexps

List comprehensions (listcomps) and generator expressions (genexps) let you focus on data rather than control structures. (See also the "Focusing on Functions" section, later in this chapter.) They replace a `for` loop with an expression.

List comprehension and generator expression code can look intimidating if you don't know what's going on. But after you get used to them, you'll probably find them a lot easier and quicker to use than the multi-line statements they replace. Remember that you never *have* to use a listcomp or a genexp, but a lot of programmers use them, and it's best to have a basic understanding of how they work.

List comprehensions

A listcomp is a nifty shorthand way of creating a new list. You can create a new list in other ways, such as by using the map() function, but the listcomp syntax is more flexible, simpler to create, and often easier to read.

A list comprehension is enclosed in square brackets and always includes the keywords for and in.

As an example, if you have a list of strings and you want to make sure they are all lowercase, you could do something like this:

```
mylist = ['ABC', 'fOO', 'bar']
tmp = []
for x in mylist:
    tmp.append(x.lower())
mylist = tmp
```

That's a lot of code for a simple task! (Well, Java programmers might not think it's a lot of code, but Pythonistas are spoiled.) Plus, anyone reading the code would have to read the whole for loop carefully to understand that it was creating a new list.

Fortunately, you can use a listcomp instead. It does the exact same thing as the for loop, but it uses only one line of code.

Creating a simple listcomp

To create a simple listcomp, follow these steps:

1. **Type a name, =, and [**

   ```
   mylist = [
   ```

2. **Type the action you want done to create each list item.**

   For example, if you have a list of strings and you want to make sure they are all lowercase, you might use the lower() method of lists. Your line of code would now look like this:

   ```
   mylist = [x.lower()
   ```

3. **Type for and the same name you used in the action.**

   ```
   mylist = [x.lower() for x
   ```

4. **Type** `in`, **the name you typed at the beginning of the line, and** `]`

```
mylist = [x.lower() for x in mylist]
```

You should use a listcomp rather than a `for` loop when you want to focus on creating a list. That way, someone reading the code doesn't have to examine the `for` loop to find the purpose of the code.

Creating a listcomp that applies a filter

You've seen that you can use a listcomp to do something to each item in a list. Another thing you can do is apply *filters* to the items in a list to build a new list. The following listcomp produces a list of numbers divisible by 5 by using the filter `if x % 5 == 0`. Note that it uses the expression `range(50)` rather than a list name.

```
>>> filtered_list = [x for x in range(50) if x % 5 == 0]
>>> filtered_list
[0, 5, 10, 15, 20, 25, 30, 35, 40, 45]
```

Listcomps can get complex rather quickly. If your code is getting hard to read, use a `for` loop instead:

```
filtered_list = []
for x in range(50):
    if x % 5 == 0:
        filtered_list.append(x)
```

Generator expressions

In the earlier section, "Generators: yield for faster processing," we discuss generators, which are a special kind of function that makes processing in loops more efficient. Python 2.4 introduces *generator expressions*. Generator expressions (*genexps* for short) are a shorthand way of creating generator iterators.

Genexps look like listcomps, but they use parentheses rather than brackets. (However, if the generator expression is the only argument of a function, you can skip the parentheses.)

The difference between a genexp and a listcomp is:

✔ A genexp creates a generator iterator (also called a *geniter*).

✔ A listcomp creates a list.

One way to use a listcomp or a genexp is to give it as the argument to a function that takes an iterable. For example, a genexp is a handy way of building a dictionary by using the `dict()` constructor.

To write a simple genexp that creates a dict in which each number is associated with its square, follow these steps:

1. **Type the name of a function and** (.

   In this example we use the `dict()` function, which creates a dictionary out of two-item tuples.

   ```
   dict(
   ```

2. **Type** (, **a name for one item in the tuple, and a comma.**

   ```
   dict((x,
   ```

3. **Type an expression for the other item in the tuple, and then type**)

   ```
   dict ((x, x ** 2)
   ```

4. **Type** for **and the name of the first item in the tuple.**

   ```
   dict ((x, x ** 2) for x
   ```

5. **Type** in **and a tuple representing the values you want to assign to the first item in the tuple. Then type**)

   ```
   dict((x, x ** 2) for x in (2, 4, 6))
   ```

If you typed the above code into interactive mode, you'd get this result:

```
>>> dict((x, x ** 2) for x in (2, 4, 6))
{2: 4, 4: 16, 6: 36}
```

If the expression would evaluate to a tuple, it must be in parentheses. (This also applies to listcomps.)

With What, Your Bare Hands? (The Power of 'with' Statements)

In Python 2.5, the new `with` statement makes `try`/`finally` statements more powerful and easier to use. (Maybe even powerful enough to slay a fierce green dragon!) The syntax is as follows:

```
with EXPRESSION as NAME:
    BLOCK
```

The `with` statement works like this:

✔ EXPRESSION returns a value that the `with` statement uses to create a *context* (a special kind of wrapper object). This is similar to the way a `for` loop automatically creates an iterator. The context is used to execute the BLOCK. The block might end normally, get terminated by a break or return, or raise an exception. No matter which of those things happens, the context contains code to clean up after the block.

✔ The as NAME part is optional. If you include it, you can use NAME in your BLOCK. NAME is similar to the target of a for loop (that is, the i in for i in mylist).

To use the with statement in Python 2.5, put this code in your module:

```
from __future__ import with_statement
```

In Python 2.6 and later, the with keyword will automatically be recognized.

The protocol used by the with statement is called the *context management protocol,* and objects implementing it are *context managers.*

You can create a context manager with a decorated generator (see the later section, "Decorating Your Code"), like this:

```
from contextlib import contextmanager
@contextmanager
def opened(filename, mode="r"):
    f = open(filename, mode)
    try:
        yield f
    finally:
        f.close()
```

You might use the preceding code as follows:

```
with opened("/etc/passwd") as f:
    for line in f:
        print line.rstrip()
```

This canonical (standard) example is from the Python docs at www.python. org. The code creates a template for opening a file that ensures the file is closed when Python leaves the with block.

Making Exceptions for Yourself

The way you use standard exceptions and write custom exceptions changes slightly in Python 2.5. Here's the scoop:

✔ Python 2.5 turns all standard exceptions into new-style classes (see Chapter 14 for more about new-style classes) and introduces a new superclass called BaseException. All the standard exceptions you'll use in your programs still inherit from the Exception class, but the Exception class in turn is a subclass of BaseException.

✔ In Python 1.5 through 2.4, all standard exceptions are subclasses of the Exception class, but any (classic) class can be raised as an exception.

Two exceptions inherit from BaseException: KeyboardInterrupt and SystemExit. But you have no business catching those exceptions. You should let them behave the way they're supposed to so that the user can interrupt your program.

Any custom exceptions you write should be subclasses of Exception. (See Chapter 15 to find out how to write custom exceptions.) Although this rule isn't enforced now, it will be enforced in Python 3.0.

Early versions of Python (prior to 1.5) used string exceptions. Although Python still lets you create string exceptions, they won't be supported in the future. In Python 2.5 and later, string exceptions raise a PendingDeprecationWarning. Use them only in the (extremely unusual) case of code that needs to be compatible with versions earlier than 1.5.

Under One Condition

Conditional expressions were added to Python 2.5 to simplify choosing one of two options in an expression. (See Chapter 10.)

A conditional expression takes the following form:

```
X if C else Y
```

It works like this:

1. C is evaluated.

2. Action depends on whether C is true:

   • If C is true, then X is evaluated to give the result.

   • If C isn't true, Y is evaluated to give the result.

You can use parentheses in conditional expressions. Because parentheses identify the conditional expression as a single unit, they make it easier to read in context of other code, as in this example:

```
x = ("tiger" if fruit=="redcurrant" else "crocodile")
```

Although you can write nested conditional expressions, you shouldn't because they are hard to read. The following example is too hard to read as a single statement. It should be written as an if block instead:

```
# too-complex conditional expression
cleese = ("Hungarian tourist" if sketch == "Phrasebook Sketch" else
    ("Customer in search of parrot" if sketch == "Pet Shop Sketch" else
    "Fresh fruit sergeant")
    )

# easier-to-read if block
if sketch == "Phrasebook Sketch":
    cleese = "Hungarian tourist"
elif sketch == "Pet Shop Sketch":
    cleese = "Customer in search of parrot"
else:
    cleese = "Fresh fruit sergeant"
```

Decorating Your Code

Decorator syntax provides a way of modifying functions and methods. A *decorator* (also called a *function decorator* or *function wrapper*) is a function that takes a function as an argument and returns another function.

Before decorator syntax made its way into Python, programmers modified functions and methods by calling the decorator function and assigning the result back to the original name of the function.

A standard use for decorators is to implement a cache that stores the results of function calls. This is called *memoizing*. It works like this:

1. The first time you call the memoized function, the wrapper calls the original function to get the result. It returns the result but also stores it in the cache.

2. When the program calls the memoized function again with the same arguments, the stored value is returned.

This speeds up the program because the original function doesn't run again.

If you wrote a decorator function called memoize(), you would set it up to work with a function by using the following syntax. The @ character indicates a decorator. The decorator comes on the line before the function or method definition:

```
@memoize
def myfunc(myarg):
    some code
```

Without decorator syntax, you write the code this way:

```
def myfunc(myarg):
    some code
myfunc = memoize(myfunc)
```

When you pass `myfunc` as an argument to `memoize()` in the preceding code, `myfunc` doesn't have parentheses after it. That is because you aren't calling `myfunc()` as a function; you are passing *the function itself* as an argument.

Some memoizing decorator functions can be found in the Python Cookbook:

```
http://aspn.activestate.com/ASPN/Cookbook
```

Focusing on Functions

Several Python tools are designed specifically to work with functional programming, which is a kind of programming that works via functions.

Genexps, listcomps, and the `itertools` module are functional programming tools covered earlier in this chapter. This section introduces some more esoteric tools, mostly so you can recognize them in other people's programs.

If you made an easy A in calculus, you might enjoy functional programming. If you never made it to the calculus level, don't worry. The more complex types of functional programming aren't necessary for most types of programming tasks.

Python's functional programming tools include these features:

- `lambda` **expressions** create functions you can define in other function calls (this is useful if you don't want to create a whole separate function).

- **Higher-order functions** take functions as input and output a function.

  Decorators are an example of higher-order functions.

- **First-class functions** include functions that can be either

  - Stored in a data structure (for example, using the `pickle` module)

  - Passed as an argument to another function

- **List comprehensions,** which we discuss earlier in this chapter

- **The** `map()`, `reduce()`, `zip()`, **and** `filter()` **functions**

Mary had a little lambda

The `lambda` keyword creates *anonymous functions* — functions that don't have names. (The name *lambda* comes from LISP programming.) It creates a function object the same way the `def` keyword does, but the `lambda` function object has `<lambda>` in place of the name of a function, as shown.

```
>>> lambda x: x%5 is 0
<function <lambda> at 0x8211844>
```

This code uses the above lambda expression to make a list of the numbers from 0 to 75 that are divisible by 5:

```
>>> filter(lambda x: x%5 is 0, xrange(76))
[0, 5, 10, 15, 20, 25, 30, 35, 40, 45, 50, 55, 60, 65, 70, 75]
```

A couple of other differences between lambda functions and functions created with the `def` keyword are as follows:

✔ A `lambda` is an expression, not a statement, and it can appear anywhere that an expression is allowed.

✔ A `lambda` expression can't have statements in it (such as x = 2, or if or `try` statements).

Mapping it out

Another functional programming tool is the `map()` function. In its simplest form, using `None` as the first argument, it turns a sequence into a list, or multiple lists into a single list of tuples.

In the following example, the `map()` function turns a string into a list of single-character strings:

```
>>> mystring = "hello kitty"
>>> map(None, mystring)
['h', 'e', 'l', 'l', 'o', ' ', 'k', 'i', 't', 't', 'y']
```

✔ If you pass a function as the first argument, `map()` performs the function's action on each element of the list or sequence and stores the result in another list.

✔ If you pass more than one sequence, the function needs a parameter for each sequence.

✔ If the sequences have different lengths, `map()` substitutes `None` when there is no corresponding value in the shorter sequence.

If you don't need this sequence-extending behavior, you should use `zip()`, listcomps, or genexps rather than `map()`. They're simpler.

Applying filters

The `filter()` function takes a function (which can be a lambda) and a sequence. It processes each element using the function and returns a sequence of the items for which the result of the function is True. For example:

```
>>> data = [10, 2, 7, 5]
>>> filter(lambda x: x>5, data)
[10, 7]
```

You can also filter elements with listcomps. See "Creating a listcomp that applies a filter," earlier in this chapter.

Reductionism

The `reduce()` function takes a function (which can be a lambda) and a sequence. It returns a single value constructed as follows:

1. It calls the function by using the first two items of the sequence as arguments and returns the result.

2. It calls the function by using the result just returned and the next item of the sequence.

3. And so on until it runs out of items.

This example performs `x * y` on a list of 4 items:

```
>>> mylist = [2, 4, 6, 8]
>>> reduce(lambda x, y: x*y, mylist)
384
```

For most purposes, `reduce()` has been replaced by the built-in function `sum()`. The `sum()` function takes a sequence of numbers and adds them, as shown:

```
>>> sum(range(20))
190
```

Part IV
Libraries

The 5th Wave   By Rich Tennant

My job consists of working with the kernel all day.

In this part . . .

Y ou could almost write a Python program without ever writing any code of your own because Python comes with so many modules and packages that cover an enormous variety of situations. This part describes only a few of them.

Chapter 17 unfolds the most basic services that are included with Python. You find out how to talk to your computer's operating system and how to handle times and dates. Because computers make it easy to keep track of everything in case you want it later, we give you the lowdown on testing and logging services.

In Chapter 18, you find out a million (give or take) ways to search text, how to pretend strings are files, and how to get Python to wrap text like a word-processing program.

Computer programming languages wouldn't be much good if they couldn't get data out of computer files. Chapter 19 shows you how Python can copy and move files, deal with compressed files, and work with databases.

Python has some great tools for working with e-mail messages and Web sites. Chapter 20 introduces you to a few of them.

Chapter 17

Using Python's Primary Services

*I*n this chapter, you find out about many of the tools built into every installation of Python.

We call this the "primary services" chapter because almost every non-trivial
program uses some (but not all) of the features listed in this chapter.

Python: Batteries Included

The tools that come with Python are collectively called the *standard library*.
The standard library contains commands, modules, and packages.

Sometimes you'll see modules or packages that come with Python referred to
as *libraries*, which is short for *standard library module*. This book uses *module*
and *package*, though. Chapter 12 explains the difference between modules
and packages.

The standard library is like a basic education for Python, allowing it to work
with different operating systems (UNIX, Windows, and Mac OS, for example),
to handle many kinds of data, to navigate the Internet, to work with different
human language systems, and so on.

There are so many features that people often say that Python comes with
"batteries included."

Remember to import modules

Python's abilities come packaged in modules so you don't have to think about tools you aren't using right now. To use a tool, you usually have to import the module it's stored in.

The recommended way to import modules is to import the whole module by typing

```
import modulename
```

We describe other ways to import tools in Chapter 12.

This key point will save you many many many hours of coding:

Before you start writing a Python program to perform a function, check whether the function already exists in Python's libraries. Hundreds of programmers have developed these tools so you don't have to.

Each new version includes lots of feature upgrades and additions. So when you upgrade to a new version of Python, be sure to read the "What's New" Web page for the version at www.python.org/. The new features of Python 2.5 are available here:

```
http://docs.python.org/
```

You Get All This! — The __builtin__ Module

The tools in the __builtin__ module are available whenever you use Python. You don't have to import them. To see what's in the module, type dir(__builtins__). (Don't forget the 's' — although the module is called __builtin__, the alias for the module is __builtins__. If that bothers you, you can type import __builtin__ to use the actual module name.)

If you don't recognize most of the names, that's okay. A lot of what's in __builtin__ works behind the scenes, at least when you're just starting out. Curious? Get a description of a particular item in the library by typing help(name of item).

Most of the __builtin__ tools that you need to know about are described elsewhere in this book. This section describes a few additional tools you might find useful.

Seeing what's inside Python objects

The `dir()` function returns an alphabetized list of an object's attributes, such as functions or methods, constants, and the name of the object.

Here's how to use the `dir()` function:

✔ To see the names in the current namespace, type `dir()`.

If you type `dir()` immediately after starting Python's interactive mode, you will see something like this:

```
>>> dir()
['__builtins__', '__doc__', '__name__']
```

✔ To see all the attributes (named items) belonging to an object, type `dir(`*name of object*`)`. For example:

```
>>> dir(ArithmeticError)
['__class__', '__delattr__', '__dict__', '__doc__', '__getattribute__',
          '__getitem__', '__hash__', '__init__', '__new__', '__reduce__',
          '__reduce_ex__', '__repr__', '__setattr__', '__setstate__',
          '__str__', '__unicode__', 'args', 'message']
```

✔ To see the attributes of a specific attribute, separate the object name and the attribute name with a dot, like this:

```
dir(ArithmeticError.__doc__)
```

You can also see some attributes by typing `help` with the name in parentheses, for example:

```
>>> help(ArithmeticError)
```

The `dir()` function shows you these types of attributes:

✔ For a module, it returns the module's attributes.

✔ For a type or class object, it returns the object's attributes and those of its base classes.

✔ For any other object, it returns the object's attributes and the attributes of its class and base classes.

Reading and writing files

The `open()` function sets up a file object in Python. It returns a `file` data type.

The built-in documentation for `open()` for Python 2.2 through 2.4 has an error. It states (or implies) that because `open()` is an alias for `file()`, you should use `file()`. This is incorrect. Use `open()` rather than `file()` so that your code will work with all versions of Python.

The following sections describe most of the argument options and the methods of the open() function.

Options for the open() function

Here are the rules and options for open():

- ✔ You should give a name to the file you're opening, or else it will be difficult to do anything with it.

- ✔ The first item in the parentheses is a string containing the filename. If the file belongs in a particular directory, type the path to the directory. For example: 'my_dir/my_file'

- ✔ The second item in parentheses is a string representing the mode. If you leave this out, the mode defaults to 'r' for "read-only." The modes are described in Table 17-1.

So to open a file for reading, type code like this:

```
myfile = open(filename, 'r')
```

Table 17-1	Modes of the open() Function
Mode	**Meaning**
'r'	Open the file as read-only (allowing no changes). This is the default.
'w'	Open the file for writing. Create the file if it doesn't already exist.
	Warning: Using 'w' erases anything currently in the file.
'a'	Open the file for appending. Create the file if it doesn't already exist.
'b'	Treat the file's contents as binary.
	This code is used mostly with Windows. Most other OSes these days don't differentiate between text and binary files.
'+'	Allow both reading and writing. Add it to the 'r' or 'w' mode like this: 'r+'
'U'	Use universal newline support; for reading text files created on Mac, UNIX, or Windows. Works only with 'r'; doesn't work with '+'. Type it on its own or add it to 'r' mode like this: 'rU'

Saving changes to disk

To save file changes to disk, you need to use one or both of these methods:

✔ The `flush()` method forces Python to take data in the internal buffer and save it to the file. Use it when you want to write changes to disk without closing the file.

✔ The `close()` method closes the file object that is created with the `open()` method. You can't read from or write to the file after you close it. Use it when you're finished with the file.

Reading file contents

You can read the contents of a file in several ways. Which one you use depends on the format you want for the file's contents:

✔ For a string, use the `read()` method. It returns the whole file or up to a specified number of bytes as a string. This example returns 27 bytes:

```
>>> myquote = open('quotes.txt')
>>> myquote.read(27)
'If you like laws and sausag'
```

✔ For a list of strings (each string is one line of the file), use the `read-lines()` method. The following example reads the whole file.

```
>>> myquote.readlines()
['If you like laws and sausages, you should \n', 'never watch
either one being made. \n', '-- Prince Otto von Bismarck (attrib.)\n',
'\n', 'Not to mention web sites. \n', '-- SJM\n']
```

✔ For a string representing each line, use a `for` loop — which is also best if you want to read a file piecemeal rather than in a big gulp.

```
>>> for line in myquote:
...     print line.rstrip()
...
If you like laws and sausages, you should
never watch either one being made.
-- Prince Otto von Bismarck (attrib.)

Not to mention web sites.
-- SJM
```

In the preceding example, the string method `rstrip()` removes white space and the end-of-line character (`\n`) from the strings. Because `print` also appends `\n`, if you don't use `rstrip()`, the output will be double-spaced.

Writing information to a file

The `write()` method writes a specified string to the file. (The file must have been opened for writing or appending.)

Information written to a file may not appear in the disk copy of the file until you have flushed the buffer and closed the file.

This example creates a file object (`pithy_sayings`) and writes a string to it:

```
>>> pithy_sayings = open('myquote', 'w')
>>> mystring = "Entropy isn't what it used to be."
>>> pithy_sayings.write(mystring)
>>> pithy_sayings.close()
```

File objects don't support Unicode strings (see Chapter 6). To write a Unicode string to a file, you need to encode it as UTF-8 first, like this:

```
myfile.write(mystring.encode('utf-8'))
```

If you have a file (or file-like object) open for writing, you can use the `>>` operator with the `print` statement to redirect output to the file. The `print >>` statement is useful for logging or to make sure that a command-line program prints output to the screen when `stdout` is redirected elsewhere, like this:

```
print >> sys.stderr, "Danger! Danger!"
```

Working with attributes

To examine, specify, and change an object's attributes indirectly, you use the `hasattr()`, `getattr()`, and `setattr()` functions. One use for these functions is converting user input into an attribute of a class.

- To find out whether an object has a particular attribute, type `hasattr` and then, in parentheses, specify the name of the object and the attribute name as a string (separated by commas).

  ```
  >>> hasattr(math, 'cosh')
  True
  ```

  The result is `True` if the string matches the name of one of the object's attributes and `False` if not.

- To find out the value of an object's attribute, use `getattr()` with the object name and attribute name (again, as a string). If the attribute exists, Python returns its value.

  ```
  >>> getattr(math, 'pi')
  3.1415926535897931
  ```

  If the attribute doesn't exist, Python raises an `AttributeError` by default. But you can specify a third argument to the function: a value you want returned if the attribute isn't found. This value is often `None`.

```
>>> x = getattr(math, 'mary poppins', None)
>>> print x
None
```

An easier way to get the value of an attribute is by typing the object name, a dot, and the attribute name: `math.pi`. This returns an `AttributeError` if the attribute doesn't exist, so if you want to return a value instead, use `getattr()`.

✔ To assign a value to an object's attribute or to create a new attribute and assign a value at the same time, use the `setattr()` function.

In the parentheses, type the object name, the attribute name as a string, and the attribute's value, like this:

```
setattr(myobject, 'my attribute', 'my value')
```

If the attribute exists, the new value is assigned to it. If the attribute doesn't exist, Python creates it and assigns the new value.

Finding largest and smallest items

To find the largest item, use the `max()` function. In the parentheses, specify a sequence, like this:

```
>>> a = [1, 5, 3, 7]
>>> max(a)
7
```

To find the largest of several items, specify them all as arguments to the `max()` function. Separate arguments with commas. Here's an example:

```
>>> a = [1, 5, 3, 7]
>>> b = [100, 200, 500]
>>> max(a, b)
[100, 200, 500]
```

The `min()` function works the same way but returns the smallest item or argument.

Getting input from users

The `raw_input()` and `input()` functions read information from Python's standard input file (`sys.stdin`). You usually use them to collect input that a user types in response to a prompt or question.

raw_input ( )

The `raw_input()` function prints a prompt string to Python's standard output file, `sys.stdout`. (By default it writes output to the screen.) The function returns the user's input as a string. (The prompt string is optional, but you'll usually want to include one.)

You specify the prompt string as the argument, like this:

```
raw_input("How old are you? ")
```

input ( )

The `input()` function expects the user to enter a valid Python expression and then it evaluates that expression.

Unlike `raw_input()`, the `input()` function can return any valid Python object, not just a string.

It's safer to use `raw_input()` and have your program convert the string into a Python expression. Because the `input()` function calls `eval()`, it could be used to run malicious code. (See "Evaluating a string," later in this chapter.)

If `input()` doesn't receive a valid Python expression, it raises an exception, as in this example, in which the user input is `pi`:

```
>>> input("What is 3.1415? ")
What is 3.1415? pi
Traceback (most recent call last):
  File "<stdin>", line 1, in <module>
  File "<string>", line 1, in <module>
NameError: name 'pi' is not defined
```

Finding an object's type

To find an object's data type, use the `type()` function. In parentheses, give it the name of the object. It returns the object's data type — for example, string or function. This example returns the type of the function `round()`.

```
>>> type(round)
<type 'builtin_function_or_method'>
```

Reloading a module

The `reload()` function allows you to re-import a module without quitting and restarting Python. Reloading is useful when debugging a program that takes a long time to start up, when programming a GUI, or when Python is embedded in another application.

The reload() function should never be used in a live application because it does not modify existing references to the contents of a module.

Evaluating a string

The eval() function takes a Python expression in the form of a string, converts it into a code object, runs the code, and returns the result. You use it when you want to give your users direct access to Python.

The eval() function is a security risk, so if your code needs to be secure, it's better to use some other approach (for example, setattr() or a dictionary).

The eval() function also works with a code object, but that's an advanced feature we won't be documenting in this book.

This example uses eval() to solve an expression. (You wouldn't use this code in a real program, though — you'd simply type print x+1!)

```
>>> x = 1
>>> print eval('x+1')
2
```

You can use either of these optional arguments with the eval() function. They go after the string. You must pass them in this order:

✔ **A dictionary of global names,** used as the global namespace for evaluating the expression. This defaults to the current global namespace's dictionary.

✔ **A dictionary of local names,** used as the local namespace for evaluating the expression.

But Wait, There's More — The sys Module

The sys module is for interacting with and controlling the Python interpreter. It includes information about the operating system and the version of Python you're using. Most of the time, you don't interact directly with what's in the sys module, but you should know about a few tools it offers.

You must import the sys module before you use it.

```
import sys
```

To work with a feature in the sys module, type sys, a dot, and the name:

```
sys.exit()
```

These are the items in the sys module you'll probably use most often:

- sys.exit() **function:** Tells the Python interpreter to quit. It's the most direct way to end a Python script while it's running.

- sys.argv **list:** Stores any command-line arguments passed when you started Python. Also includes the name of the program you're running.

  Use sys.argv when writing utility scripts that accept parameters on the command line. This example shows the contents of sys.argv after you run a program called add.py and pass it the parameter 3.

  ```
  % python -i add.py 3
  >>> import sys
  >>> sys.argv
  ['add.py', '3']
  ```

The sys module also contains the following types of objects:

- **Input, output, and error files**

  - stdin: Used by the input() and raw_input() functions; accepts input from user

  - stdout: Used by the print statement; in interactive mode, prints to the screen

  - stderr: Stores error messages

- **Objects that store information specific to your version of Python.** Examples include pathnames, the list of available modules, and character encodings. Functions beginning with get and set let you access and change this information.

- **Debugging and exception-handling tools.**

Solving OS Incompatibility — The os and subprocess Modules

The os and subprocess modules include code that lets Python work with your operating system — they even run operating system commands.

These modules give Python ways of accessing the operating system that don't require you to write code specific to a particular operating system. Therefore, you should import and use them if you're writing a program that needs to work on more than one operating system.

The `os` module is best for the following tasks:

✔ Working with paths and permissions (test for access to a path, changing directories, changing access permissions and user/group IDs)

✔ Working with files (open, close, write, truncate, create links)

Another module that's useful for copying and moving files is `shutil` (which stands for "shell utility"). See Chapter 19.

The `subprocess` module, new in Python 2.4, lets you safely interact with the operating system to run commands and get information out of them.

Think of the `os` and `subprocess` modules as the way that Python does the same things you do with your operating system directly (such as starting programs and manipulating files). If you work on more than one operating system, you must remember different commands and syntax for filenames, for example. Python's `os` module helps Python remember these things. For example, the `os.path` module handles pathnames, so you don't have to write special code to handle both UNIX pathnames (which have forward slashes) and Windows pathnames (which have backslashes).

Working with the os module

This section lists some useful `os` functions and data. To find out more about the abilities of the `os` module, type `help(os)`.

Except where indicated in the following sections, all the tools of the `os` module work with UNIX, Mac, and Windows operating systems.

Manipulating directories and their files

Use these functions to work with directories and files on a computer system.

✔ `os.chdir()` changes the current working directory to the specified path. Specify the path as a string, like this:

```
os.chdir('/users/stef/Quote')
```

✔ `os.getcwd()` returns the current working directory as a string, like so:

```
>>> os.getcwd()
'/users/stef/Quote'
```

✔ `os.mkdir()` creates a directory with the path you specify. Specify the path as a string, as follows:

```
os.mkdir('MyNewDictory')
```

To set a directory's permissions, specify a four-digit octal permissions mode as the second argument. The default mode is usually `0777`, which gives everyone full access to the directory, but your operating system might override this default. Here's how to specify the default:

```
os.mkdir('MyNewDictory', mode=0777)
```

✔ `os.makedirs()` works like `os.mkdir()`, but it creates directories recursively. For example, if you're in directory A and you want to create directory B that holds directory C that holds directory D, type this:

```
os.makedirs('B/C/D')
```

`os.makedirs()` doesn't work with Windows Universal Naming Convention (UNC) paths, which use the `\\host\path` format.

✔ `os.remove()` deletes the item on the path specified. Specify the path as a string. It doesn't remove directories. In Windows it raises an error if the file is in use. The code looks like this:

```
os.remove('R/test')
```

✔ `os.rmdir()` removes a single directory on the path specified, and `os.removedirs()` removes multiple directories. We recommend using `shutil.rmtree()` rather than these functions. See Chapter 19.

✔ `os.walk()` creates a generator object that lists the files in a directory tree. It generates a three-item tuple (directory path, directory names, filenames) and examines the directory in top-down (default) or bottom-up order. To make and use the generator object, write code like this:

```
>>> for root, dirs, files in os.walk('quotes'):
...     print root, dirs, files
```

You use three names in the loop because the generator makes a three-item tuple.

✔ `os.tmpfile()` creates a new temporary file. The file is opened for writing and is binary (`"w+b"`). It's automatically deleted when you close it.

The `tempfile` module provides more tools for creating temporary files; use that instead of `os.tmpfile()` if you want more than the basics.

Wandering down the os.path

The `os.path` module is a submodule of `os`. It contains tools that handle filenames so that your program can work on multiple platforms.

We recommend that you import the whole `os` module when you need to use `os.path`. If you don't, Murphy's Law dictates that you'll need something else in the `os` module and forget you didn't import it and get an annoying error.

Many of the `os.path` functions don't work with Windows Universal Naming Convention (UNC) paths, which use the `\\host\path` format.

Descriptions of some important `os.path` tools follow. All these tools take pathnames as arguments. Use strings to specify pathnames.

✔ `os.path.join()` is one of the most important `os.path` tools. It takes one or more paths and joins them by using the current operating system's path separator. If any component is an absolute path, all previous components are thrown away. Here's an example:

```
>>> os.path.join('users', 'stef', 'Quote')
```

On UNIX this produces:

```
'users/stef/Quote'
```

On Windows it produces:

```
'users\\stef\\Quote'
```

On Windows, `os.path.join("c:", "foo")` creates a path relative to the current directory on drive `C:` instead of creating `c:\\foo`. To get an absolute path on Windows, use this syntax:

```
os.path.join('c:\\', 'foo')
```

✔ `os.path.abspath()` takes a relative pathname and returns the corresponding absolute pathname, like so:

```
>>> os.path.abspath('Quote')
'/users/stef/Quote/'
```

✔ `os.path.normpath()` converts path names in nonstandard formats to standard format. For example:

```
>>> os.path.normpath('stef//./Quote')
'stef/Quote'
```

✔ `os.path.split()` takes a pathname and returns it in two parts: the directory part and the filename.

```
>>> os.path.split('/users/stef/Quote/quote2.new')
('/users/stef/Quote', 'quote2.new')
```

If you specify a directory, it returns the path and an empty string, like this:

```
>>> os.path.split('/users/stef/Quote/')
('/users/stef/Quote', '')
```

On Windows systems using UNC, use `os.path.splitunc()` instead.

`os.path.split()` has two related functions:

• `os.path.dirname()` returns the directory name of the path (the first half of the pair that `os.split()` returns).

- os.path.basename() returns the filename (the second half of the os.split() pair). If no file was specified, the os.path.basename() function returns an empty string.

✔ os.path.splitext() (which stands for "split extension") splits the pathname into a pair of pathnames:

- The first part is the pathname, including the part of the filename before the extension.

- The second part includes a period and the file's extension.

```
>>> os.path.splitext('/users/stef/Quote/quote2.txt')
('/users/stef/Quote/quote2', '.txt')
```

If there is no extension or no file, the second part is an empty string.

This example puts os.path.split() and os.path.splitext() together:

```
>>> dirname, filename = os.path.split('users/stef/Quote/quote2.txt')
>>> basename, extension = os.path.splitext(filename)
>>> dirname, filename
('users/stef/Quote', 'quote2.txt')
>>> basename, extension
('quote2', '.txt')
```

✔ os.path.exists() returns True if the specified path exists; otherwise, it returns False. It also returns False for broken symbolic links.

✔ os.path.isdir() returns True if the specified path is an existing directory. It follows symbolic links.

Seeing environment variables

The os module includes a dictionary, os.environ, that stores your operating system's environment variables (which contain user and system preferences). The variables and their values are stored as strings. The dictionary is set up when you start Python. If you change your environment variables outside Python, the dictionary doesn't reflect the changes until you restart Python.

To see the value of an environment variable, type os.environ and then, in square brackets, type the name of the variable in quotation marks, like this:

```
>>> os.environ['HOME']
'/users/stef'
```

Although it's possible to change environment variables by changing the os.environ dictionary, it's not safe to do so. Use the Popen() function of the subprocess module to change environment variables instead. (The changes affect only the subprocesses.)

Subprocessing

The subprocess module, new in Python 2.4, lets you interact with the operating system to create new processes, pass information into and out of them, and get their return codes. It replaces a number of functions and modules available elsewhere in Python, including the following:

```
os.system
os.spawn
os.popen
popen2
commands
```

The subprocess module is safer than the preceding methods of starting new processes because its default is to create a new process directly rather than creating them through the shell. That means that, with subprocess, you can safely pass shell special characters.

There are two ways to use the subprocess module: by creating a Popen instance and by using the call() function. The Popen method is more complicated, so we only document the call() function here.

Introducing the call() function

The function subprocess.call() is a shortcut for one of the more common uses of the subprocess module. It runs a command, waits for the command to finish, and then returns its return code. This simple example lists the contents of a directory. The 0 after the directory listing is a *return code* — a status message that the subprocess sends. On UNIX, 0 indicates that the subprocess completed successfully.

```
>>> subprocess.call(['ls', 'MyDir'])
copyy.py        helloworld.pyc  mystuff.zip     stuff.zip
copyy.pyc       myspider.py     pagecount.py    stuff2.zip
helloworld.py   myspider.pyc    pagecount.pyc   x
0
```

Useful calling parameters

Here are some of the more useful parameters of the call() function:

✔ args, a string or sequence of program arguments. The program is the first item in the sequence, and the other items are any command-line arguments the program takes.

In the above example, args is a list. The program is 'ls' and the command-line argument is 'MyDir'.

On Windows, `args` is converted to a string; the converted value may not work with all Windows applications. (It works with applications that support the rules of MS C runtime.)

✔ `shell=True` specifies to run the command through the shell. The default shell is `sh` (UNIX) or whatever is specified by COMSPEC (Windows). To specify a different shell, use the `executable` parameter.

✔ `env` defines environment variables for the subprocess. These only apply to the subprocess; they don't change any environment variables defined in your main shell.

✔ `stdin`, `stdout`, and `stderr` define how data and error messages are transmitted to and from the child process. Values for these parameters include `PIPE`, an existing file descriptor (a positive integer), an existing file object, or `None`. `PIPE` creates a new pipe to the child. `None` specifies not to redirect messages (the child's file handles are inherited from the parent). To send error messages to the same place as other output, set `stderr=STDOUT`.

✔ `cwd` specifies a directory to change to before the child process runs.

Trying an OS command with call( )

This example code tries to run a command using `call()` and prints information about the success or failure of the attempt. The name `retcode` stands for the return code that the command sends. To use this `try` block in your own code, just fill in your command and argument in place of `"mycmd"` + `" myarg"`:

```
try:
    retcode = subprocess.call("mycmd" + " myarg", shell=True)
    if retcode < 0:
        print >>sys.stderr, "Child was terminated by signal", -retcode
    else:
        print >>sys.stderr, "Child returned", retcode
except OSError, e:
    print >>sys.stderr, "Execution failed:", e
```

Staying on Time with the datetime and time Modules

Computers usually store time as the number of seconds that have passed since some specific date (called the *epoch*). The exact date varies depending on the operating system. The UNIX operating system usually uses January 1, 1970.

Humans don't think of dates in terms of large numbers of seconds, so one of the functions of the datetime and time libraries is to convert this machine time into date and time information you can use.

Python has two primary modules with date and time tools:

✔ The datetime module includes tools for working with dates, times, and combinations thereof. It supports several different calendar systems and ways of presenting time zone information (but we don't cover time zones in this book).

✔ The time module includes tools for working with times and dates in the recent past to near future. It focuses mostly on manipulating time based on the computer's internal representations of time. For example, the time module includes a sleep() method, which lets you pause execution of your program while the computer counts down for you.

Using the datetime module

When you import the datetime module, you have available a datetime() object that stores both date and time information. You can also work with dates and times separately by using date() objects and time() objects. They work much the same way as the datetime() object, so we don't cover them here.

Components of a datetime() object

An object that stores date and time information looks like this:

```
datetime.datetime(1969, 7, 20, 22, 56)
```

Here's more information about the components:

✔ datetime.datetime is the type of object.

✔ The arguments are integers, separated by commas, in this order:

- Required arguments: year, month, and day of month

- Optional arguments (which default to 0): hours, minutes, seconds, microseconds. Another optional argument is time zone information, which defaults to None. (Using time zones in Python is an advanced feature beyond the scope of this book.)

The preceding object leaves out *seconds, microseconds,* and *time zone* information.

When you specify optional arguments, you must specify all arguments down to the level of precision you need by typing a number for any arguments to the left of the ones you want to specify. It's okay to leave out arguments to the right. For example, to specify no hours and 59 minutes, you type 0 for the hours and 59 for the minutes. You can leave out the seconds. The code looks like this:

```
datetime.datetime(1961, 12, 31, 0, 59)
```

Formatting date and time information

Python stores a datetime() object in exactly the same way you entered it:

```
>>> moonwalk = datetime.datetime(1969, 7, 20, 22, 56, 0)
>>> moonwalk
datetime.datetime(1969, 7, 20, 22, 56)
```

If you want the date and time in another format, you have a few built-in options, including the str() function, the ctime() method, and the isoformat() method (we don't document the latter two).

The most flexible way to display a datetime() object, however, is to use the strftime() method ("strftime" stands for "string-format time"). This method takes a string as an argument and uses % codes inside the string to specify how to format each element of the datetime() object. (The strftime codes work like the string interpolation codes described in Chapter 6, but the meanings of the codes themselves are different.) The datetime() formatting codes vary slightly by operating system.

Here's one way to format the moonwalk object:

1. **Type** moonwalk.strftime.

2. **On the same line, in parentheses, type the following string:**

   ```
   ("%A, %B %d, %Y  %I:%M:%S")
   ```

   This string tells Python to display the time using a long day of the week (%A), long month (%B), date of month (%d), four-digit year(%Y), and time. It uses commas and colons as punctuation.

   Here's the line of code and the result:

   ```
   >>> moonwalk.strftime("%A, %B %d, %Y  %I:%M:%S")
   'Sunday, July 20, 1969  10:56:00'
   ```

Adding time

When you perform arithmetic on datetime() objects, you get the result in a timedelta() object. Its attributes are *days*, *seconds*, and *microseconds*.

Here is the `timedelta()` object you get when you subtract the date of the moon walk from today's date (in this example, "today" is May 21, 2006, approximately 5:25 p.m.). The example shows that 13,453 days elapsed between the first moon walk on July 20, 1969, and May 21, 2006:

```
>>> now = datetime.datetime.today()
>>> moonwalk = datetime.datetime(1969, 7, 20, 22, 56)
>>> now - moonwalk
datetime.timedelta(13453, 66596, 407968)
>>> print now - moonwalk
13453 days, 18:29:56.407968
```

The `timedelta()` object works with the following operations: *addition, subtraction, multiplication, floor division,* and *absolute value.* The `timedelta()` object is immutable, so it works as a dictionary key.

When you create a `timedelta()` object, you don't have to use days, seconds, and microseconds. (That would be tedious for large time differences!)

Follow these steps to specify a `timedelta`:

1. **Type** `datetime.timedelta`.

2. **On the same line, in parentheses, specify any of the following keyword arguments, separated by commas:**

```
weeks, days, hours, minutes, seconds, microseconds, milliseconds
```

All the arguments are optional and if left out default to 0. For example, to specify one day, five minutes, and three seconds, type this:

```
datetime.timedelta(days=1, minutes=5, seconds=3)
```

This is the `timedelta` object created and Python's result. The result doesn't look exactly like what you entered because Python internally converts your data to days, seconds, and microseconds.

```
>>> datetime.timedelta(1,3,0,0,5)
datetime.timedelta(1, 303)
```

When printed as a string, the preceding `timedelta()` object looks like this:

```
>>> str(datetime.timedelta(1, 303))
1 day, 0:05:03
```

Taking your time

The `time()` module includes tools for working with the computer's internal representation of time. Tools depend on your operating system.

The time() module doesn't handle times or dates in either

✔ The far past (before 1900 A.D.)

✔ The far future

The future time and date of the cutoff depends on your operating system; for UNIX systems, it's 2038 A.D.

To work with far past or far future dates, use the datetime() module instead.

Using the time() object

A time() object is stored as a sequence of nine integers: *year, month, day of month, hour, minute, second, weekday, day of year,* and *whether daylight savings time is on (1) or off (0).*

The time() object is a tuple in Python 2.1 and earlier. In later versions, it is another data type called struct_time(). (We're telling you this because you might see an error message referencing struct_time() objects.) Time is also expressed as a floating point number, for example, by the time.time() method.

To create a time() object that stores the current time and date, type this (you'll get a different result, of course):

```
>>> time.localtime()
(2006, 2, 1, 18, 9, 4, 2, 32, 0)
```

To see the local time as a string, type this:

```
>>> time.asctime()
'Wed Feb  1 17:35:29 2006'
```

To format a time object as a string, use the strftime() method. See "Formatting date and time information," earlier in this chapter.

Let's pause for a moment

The time module's sleep() method is useful for programs that need built-in pauses. (Quiz shows, anyone?) The sleep() method pauses the execution of a program for a specified number of seconds.

The following example uses the sleep() method:

```
import time
for x in range(3):
    print "The time is now", time.asctime()
    print "Now sleeping for 2 seconds..."
    time.sleep(2)
```

This is the result of running the example code:

```
The time is now Sat Feb  4 17:28:08 2006
Now sleeping for 2 seconds...
The time is now Sat Feb  4 17:28:10 2006
Now sleeping for 2 seconds...
The time is now Sat Feb  4 17:28:12 2006
Now sleeping for 2 seconds...
```

Checking with the doctest Module

One approach for developing high-quality software is to write tests for each function as it is developed and to run those tests frequently during the development process.

Python has a unittest module as well as the doctest module we write about here. Skip unittest until you're more experienced with Python. The unittest module lets you write more formal tests under programmatic control. It's good for when you have complicated testing requirements.

Introducing the doctest module

The doctest module tests your code by using the following steps:

1. Search in a module for text that looks like an interactive Python session.

2. Run the text.

3. Print messages describing the results.

Use doctest when you want to

✔ **Check whether a module's docstrings are up to date.**

✔ **Verify that examples from a test file or object work as expected.**

   This verification is known as *regression testing*.

✔ **Write tutorial documentation with input and output examples.**

   Python's built-in module includes such examples in their docstrings. For example, type help(decimal) to access the decimal module's docstrings.

Adding interactive code to a module's docstrings

The simplest way to use `doctest` is to include interactive Python examples in your module's docstrings.

Here's example code in a module called `factorial.py`:

```
def factorial(x):
    """

    Calculate x!

    >>> factorial(2)
    2
    """
    if x < 0:
        raise ValueError("x must be positive")
    if x in (0, 1):
        return 1
    return x * factorial(x-1)
```

Adding doctest code to a module

After you've written your code and your examples, set up the module to work with `doctest`. The way you do this depends on your version of Python.

Python 2.3 and later

Type this code exactly as shown at the end of the module:

```
def _test():
    import doctest
    doctest.testmod()

if __name__ == "__main__":
    _test()
```

Python 2.2 and earlier

Type this code at the end of the module. Replace `factorial` on lines 2 and 3 with the name of your module:

```
def _test():
    import doctest, factorial
    doctest.testmod(factorial)

if __name__ == "__main__":
    _test()
```

In both versions, the line if __name__ == "__main__": tells Python to run the _test() function only if the module is started from the command line.

Testing a module

To test your module, start the module from the command line, like this:

```
% python factorial.py
```

Results of a successful test

When doctest finds no errors in your interactive code, nothing happens — you just get the command prompt again.

To make sure that doctest is working correctly, run it in verbose mode by adding -v after the module name, like this:

```
% python factorial.py -v
```

The verbose results for the preceding test are as follows:

```
Trying:
    factorial(2)
Expecting:
    2
ok
2 items had no tests:
    __main__
    __main__._test
1 items passed all tests:
    1 tests in __main__.factorial
1 tests in 3 items.
1 passed and 0 failed.
Test passed.
```

Results of an unsuccessful test

If the interactive code specified in the module's docstring doesn't match the results you would get if you ran the code in Python's interactive mode, doctest prints a detailed report about the errors.

If we change the interactive code in our module to the following . . .

```
def factorial(x):
    """
    Calculate x!

    >>> try: factorial(-1)
    ... except ValueError: print 'good'
```

```
... else: print 'bzzt!'
bzzt!
>>> factorial(2)
3
"""
```

... now the `doctest` function returns this result. (This is the result you get without specifying verbose mode. The verbose mode result includes a few more lines of information):

```
**********************************************************************
File "factorial.py", line 5, in __main__.factorial
Failed example:
    try: factorial(-1)
    except ValueError: print 'good'
    else: print 'bzzt!'
Expected:
    bzzt!
Got:
    good
**********************************************************************
File "factorial.py", line 9, in __main__.factorial
Failed example:
    factorial(2)
Expected:
    3
Got:
    2
**********************************************************************
1 items had failures:
   2 of   2 in __main__.factorial
***Test Failed*** 2 failures.
```

Keeping Track with the logging Module

The `logging` module is new in Python 2.3. Use it to set up log files or displays for the errors and debugging information for your programs. Python has very flexible logging features; we get you started with a few basic ways to use logging.

Getting started with basic logging

The tool that processes messages is called a *logger*. The default logger is called "root."

Log messages are tagged with priority codes, and each priority code has a method that produces a log message of that priority. The code methods are

```
debug(), info(), warning(), error(), critical()
```

To log a message, follow these steps:

1. **Type** `logging`, **a dot, and the method corresponding to the message priority, for example:**

   ```
   logging.warning
   ```

By default, the root logger doesn't do anything with debug or info messages. If you want to see your message without reconfiguring the logger, use one of these methods that indicate a higher priority message: `warning()`, `error()`, or `critical()`.

2. **On the same line, in parentheses, type a message as a string.**

   ```
   logging.warning("Watch out!")
   ```

   The following example tells the root logger to log a warning message and shows the result you get if you type this in interactive mode:

   ```
   >>> logging.warning("Watch out!")
   WARNING:root:Watch out!
   ```

The default behavior of the root logger is as follows:

✔ Process warning messages and higher, ignore debug and info messages

   If you try to use the `info()` method with the default root logger, you get no response:

   ```
   >>> logging.info("Try and see me")
   >>>
   ```

✔ Print messages as strings

✔ Log messages to `sys.stderr`

   In interactive mode, `sys.stderr` prints to the screen.

Changing the configuration of a logger

To change the default configuration of the root logger, or to set up the configuration of a logger you write yourself, use the `basicConfig()` function. Figure 17-1 illustrates some example `basicConfig()` code.

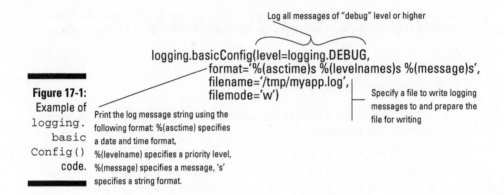

Log all messages of "debug" level or higher

logging.basicConfig(level=logging.DEBUG,
format='%(asctime)s %(levelnames)s %(message)s',
filename='/tmp/myapp.log',
filemode='w')

Specify a file to write logging messages to and prepare the file for writing

Figure 17-1:
Example of
`logging.`
`basic`
`Config()`
code.

Print the log message string using the following format: %(asctime) specifies a date and time format, %(levelname) specifies a priority level, %(message) specifies a message, 's' specifies a string format.

The keyword arguments for `basicConfig()` require Python 2.4 and later.

Designing your own logging system

If different parts of your program have different logging requirements, here's some guidance to get you started creating your own loggers.

Name your loggers according to the part of the program you're logging errors from and then configure your logger in these basic ways:

✔ **Levels of messages to process**

The levels are associated with integers, as follows:

- CRITICAL: 50
- ERROR: 40
- WARNING: 30
- INFO: 20
- DEBUG: 10

✔ **Format of the messages**

✔ **Handlers that determine where the messages should be logged.**

Most handlers are of the type `StreamHandler` or `FileHandler`. There's also `SMTPHandler` (sends error messages via e-mail), `HTTPHandler` (sends messages to an HTTP server), and more.

Seeing a few logging functions

These are the most useful basic functions available in the logging module:

✔ log()

Logs a message. Specify options in this order, separated by commas: priority level (as an integer), message (a formatting string with % codes), and the arguments to include in the string. Add exc_info at the end to include exception information in the message. This example logs a warning message by using % formatting:

```
>>> logging.log(30, "hello, is that %s?", "you")
WARNING:root:hello, is that you?
```

✔ disable()

Disables messages at the specified priority level and below. Overrides the levels specified in loggers. Specify the priority level as an integer.

✔ shutdown()

Shuts down the logging system. Flushes and closes all handlers.

Chapter 18

Processing Text

. . . .

In This Chapter

▶ Powerful searches with regular expressions

▶ Pretending your string is a file

▶ Wrapping text paragraphs

. . . .

There are whole books on Python's text-processing capabilities, so this chapter covers only the basics — three of the most important text-processing modules that come with Python. In this chapter, you find out about

✔ The `re` module, which brings the power of regular expression text searches to Python

✔ The `StringIO` library, which lets you work with strings as if they were files

✔ The `textwrap` library, which includes various tools for tidying up paragraphs

More text-processing information can be found in Chapter 6.

A Million Ways to re, You Know That There Are

The `re` module supports searching text files by using *regular expressions* (*regexes* for short) — strings that specify a set of match rules.

The following sections describe

✔ The character codes that you use to build regexes

✔ The search abilities of Python's `re` library

TIP

When not to use a regex

Python's data types include a number of easy-to-use text-search methods. We recommend that you get familiar with these methods and use them rather than the re module if they will fit your needs.

Regular expressions are complex and hard to use, and it's easy to make mistakes when using them.

For example, if you have a file of quotations, each separated by '%%\n', you could use a regex to split the file into separate quotes. But it would be better to use the split() method of strings.

Writing a basic regex

To create a regex, just write it as a string — that is, enclose some text in quotation marks. You can use single or double quotation marks, or even triple quotes. Your string can be just a set of characters to look for, or it can include special instructions.

The following string, if used with one of the re methods or functions, uses the [] characters to give special instructions to search for either monty or minty (but not mointy, a city in Kazakhstan):

```
'm[oi]nty'
```

TIP

Both regexes and Python strings often use the backslash (\) to indicate special treatment for a character. The re module recognizes Python's \ codes, like \n for newline. (We discuss these codes in Chapter 6.) But to avoid conflicts, you should usually write regexes as raw strings by prepending r to the string. The r tells Python's string data type to ignore any backslashes inside the string and save them for the re method or function to process.

Setting up a basic regex search

The following code gives the name zipcode to a regex (specified as a raw string) that looks for the text Zip: followed by any number of white space characters (\s*) and five digits (\d):

```
>>> zipcode = r'Zip:\s*\d\d\d\d\d'
```

To use the `zipcode` regex to search for a zip code in a string, type code like this:

```
>>> addr = "Street address:    342 Anywhere Rd \n Zip:    32433"
>>> re.search(zipcode, addr)
```

✔ If the search is successful, it returns an object of the type `_sre.SRE_Match`, like this:

```
<_sre.SRE_Match object at 0x8202640>
```

✔ If there is no match, it returns `None`.

```
>>> mystring = "foo"
>>> print re.search(zipcode, mystring)
None
```

Regular expression characters and codes

The search rules in a regular expression can be simple (the simplest useful regex is a single character) or complex. Complex rules are implemented by using characters that have special meanings in regular expressions. We describe these characters and codes in the following sections.

Special characters

Table 18-1 shows the most commonly used of the characters that have special meanings in regexes.

Table 18-1	Regular Expression Special Characters	
Character	*Action*	*Example and Notes*
. (dot)	Matches any single character except a newline.	`'p.thon'` matches `python`, `p!thon`, `p2thon`, but not `pyython`.
[ ]	Encloses a set of characters to match (a *character class*). A match occurs if *any one* of the characters is found. You canenclose specific characters or a range of characters, such as all the uppercase letters: `[A-Z]`	`'T[iy]ger'` matches `Tiger` or `Tyger` (but not `Tiyger`).
		If you want to match a hyphen inside a character class, it must be the first or last character.
		`[\s.-]` matches space, period, or hyphen.

(continued)

Table 18-1 *(continued)*

Character	Action	Example and Notes
^ (caret)	At the beginning of a character class, ^ stands for "not." Outside of a character class, ^ matches the beginning of a line.	`'[^a]'` matches any character that isn't 'a'. `'^A'` matches `'America'` but not `'Canada'`.
$	Matches the end of a line or string, depending on the MULTIMODE flag. (See Table 18-3.)	`'t$'` matches `'bright'` but not `'tender'`.
regex1 | *regex2*	Matches either of two regexes, starting with the leftmost and stopping when it finds a match. You can use multiple | characters to join several regexes.	`'python'` | `'asp'` first looks in a string for `'python'`. If `'python'` is not found, it then looks for `'asp'`.
{number}	Matches the preceding regex only if the regex occurs a certain number of times consecutively.	`'y{3}'` matches `'pyyython'` but not `'python'`.
( )	Encloses a regex group. You can refer to groups by number. The first group is referred to by \1, the second by \2, and so on.	`r'Phone: (\d{3})-(\d{3}-\d{4})'` looks for a phone number, with the area code in group 1 and the number in group 2. \1 refers to the area code group in the above regex.
\	Escape code — treats the character that follows as special, or treats a special character as text. See the following section.	`'\$'` searches for the $ character in text instead of treating $ as an "end of line or string" code.

Escape codes with special meanings

When you use \ in front of some characters in a regex, it creates a code with a special meaning. Table 18-2 lists these special regex codes. The re module also recognizes the Python escape codes — for example, \n for newline.

Table 18-2	Regex Codes with Special Meanings
Code	*Action*
\number	Matches the contents of the group with that number
\A	Matches only at the start of a string
\b	Matches an empty string at the beginning or end of a word
\B	Matches an empty string in the middle of a word
\d	Matches any digit (0-9)
\D	Matches any character that is *not* a digit
\s	Matches any white space character
\S	Matches any character that is *not* white space
\w	Matches any alphanumeric character
\W	Matches any character that is *not* alphanumeric
\Z	Matches only at the end of a string

Finding repeats

One common regex task is to find repeats of a character or other match. You write a regex to find repeats by using the characters +, *, ?, or {}.

Python lets you search for repeated characters in a number of ways:

- ✔ * matches the previous character any number of times, *including none*.

  py*thon **matches** pthon, python, pyython, **and so on.**

- ✔ + matches the previous character one or more times.

  py+thon **matches** python **and** pyython, **but not** pthon.

- ✔ ? matches the previous character zero or one times.

  py?thon **matches** pthon **and** python, **but not** pyython.

Numbers enclosed in curly braces ({}) create a range of repeated characters, like this:

- ✔ py{5}thon **matches an exact number of repeats:** pyyyyython

- ✔ py{1,3}thon **matches a range of repeats:** python, pyython, **and** pyyython. **It doesn't match** pthon **or** pyyyython.

> If you leave out the first number of the range (for example, `py{,3}thon`), the first range defaults to 0. This example would match `pthon`, `python`, `pyython`, or `pyyython`. If you leave out the last number of the range (for example, `py{1,}thon`), any number of repeats equal to or larger than the first number will match.

Regexes support two kinds of repeating searches: *Greedy* and *non-greedy*.

Greedy searches

A greedy search tries to match as many of the search characters as possible.

The following regex greedily searches for one or more `y` characters in a row. It finds all three `y` characters in the string `'pyyython'`:

```
>>> p = 'pyyython'
>>> greedy_re = 'y+'
>>> mymatch = re.search(greedy_re, p)
>>> mymatch.group()
'yyy'
```

Non-greedy searches

A non-greedy search stops after it finds one match.

To specify a non-greedy search, add `?` after either

✔ The repeat character

✔ The end brace of a range

The following regex searches for one or more `y` characters in a row, but the `?` character specifies a non-greedy search. As soon as this search finds one `y`, it's finished:

```
>>> p = 'pyyython'
>>> non_greedy_re = 'y+?'
>>> mymatch = re.search(non_greedy_re, p)
>>> mymatch.group()
'y'
```

Regex groups

Regexes can be complicated to read and to type. One way of making regexes easier to read is to enclose a portion of a regex inside parentheses to make a *regex group*. This also makes the regex easier to use later because you can refer to the group by typing a number or name instead of retyping the whole regex.

Python deals with two types of regex groups:

✔ **Numbered groups:** Whenever you group part of a regex inside parentheses, it automatically gets a number — 1 for the first group, 2 for the second, and so on.

✔ **Named groups:** To name a group, begin the statement inside parentheses with this code (substituting your name):

```
?P<groupname>
```

Follow it with the regex and then type a closing parenthesis.

The following example creates a group named `zip` that searches for the text `Zip:` followed by any number of spaces and exactly five digits.

```
(?P<zip>Zip:\s*\d\d\d\d\d)
```

You can refer to a numbered or named regex group in several ways:

✔ You can refer to a group in any `MatchObject` method that takes a regex as an argument. In the examples below, the `groupdict()` method returns a dictionary containing the group name `'zip'` and its matches. The `group()` method returns the matches of the second group:

```
>>> my_regex = r'(?P<zip>Zip:\s*\d\d\d\d\d)\s*(State:\s*\w\w)'
>>> addrs = "Zip: 10010 State: NY"
>>> y = re.search(my_regex, addrs)
>>> y.groupdict('zip')
{'zip': 'Zip: 10010'}
>>> y.group(2)
'State: NY'
```

✔ When writing a regex, you can refer to the `'zip'` group by using the following syntax: `(?P='zip')`

✔ You can use a group when specifying replacement text: `\g<zip>`.

For an example of a regex with multiple groups, see "Making regexes more readable," later in this chapter.

Using the regular expression module

There are two ways to use the `re` module:

✔ Use *functions* to perform regex operations on a string.

✔ With the `compile()` function, turn the regex into an object (called a *regular expression object*; in some Python messages, it's called an *SRE_Pattern object*) and use the object's *methods* to work with the regex.

Functional versus methodical

If you want to use a simple regex only once, it's okay to use the functions. But for code that uses regexes heavily, we recommend using the compiled form of regexes for two reasons:

✔ The compiled object works faster.

✔ Remembering the order of arguments is easier if you always use the compiled form.

Using a regex function

To use a regex function, type these elements:

✔ The function name

✔ Parentheses

Pass any arguments inside the parentheses, separated by commas. *The regex is always the first argument.*

This example uses the `findall()` function to return a list of all the vowels in a string.

```
>>> mystring = 'Your father smelt of elderberries!'
>>> print re.findall('[aeiou]', mystring)
['o', 'u', 'a', 'e', 'e', 'o', 'e', 'e', 'e', 'i', 'e']
```

Some regex functions return a match object. See "Querying the match object," later in this chapter.

Using a regex method

To use a regex method, type these elements:

✔ The name of the regex object that you created by using the `compile()` function

See the next section, "Compiling regular expressions."

✔ A dot

✔ The method name

✔ Parentheses

Pass any arguments inside the parentheses, separated by commas.

This example creates a regex object that finds vowels and uses the `findall()` method to return a list of all the vowels in a string.

```
>>> mystring = 'Your father smelt of elderberries!'
>>> vowels = re.compile('[aeiou]')
>>> vowels.findall(mystring)
['o', 'u', 'a', 'e', 'e', 'o', 'e', 'e', 'e', 'i', 'e']
```

Compiling regular expressions

To turn a regex string into a *regular expression object*, you use the `compile()` function. `compile()` takes a regex string and optional flags (see Table 18-3) as arguments. Here's an example:

```
>>> my_regex = re.compile('py+thon', re.IGNORECASE)
>>> my_regex
<_sre.SRE_Pattern object at 0x82200e0>
```

The object contains the following data attributes:

- ✔ `flags`: A number corresponding to the flag used when the `re` object was compiled. See Table 18-3. This is `0` if no flags were used.

  ```
  >>> my_regex.flags
  2
  ```

- ✔ `groupindex`: A dictionary mapping any group names to group numbers. The dictionary is empty if no group names were specified.

- ✔ `pattern`: The regex from which the object was compiled.

  ```
  >>> my_regex.pattern
  'py+thon'
  ```

Tools of the re module

The following regex functions and methods are the most useful.

findall()

`findall()` returns a list of all the occurrences of a regex in a string. It also takes an optional flag argument (Table 18-3 lists the flags).

`finditer()` does the same thing as `findall()` but returns an iterator object rather than a list.

Table 18-3		Optional Flags for Regexes
Long Name	*Short Name*	*Meaning*
IGNORECASE	I	Matches are case-insensitive.
LOCALE	L	Matches depend on the current locale.
MULTILINE	M	Allows ^ and $ to match linefeeds (\n) inside a string. Without it, they match only the beginning (^) and end ($) of a string.
DOTALL	S	Dot (.) matches any character including newline.
UNICODE	U	Matches depend on the Unicode locale.
VERBOSE	X	Allow spaces and comments in regexes. This makes them easier for humans to read.

match ( )

To find a single occurrence of a regex at the *start* of a string, use match():

✔ match() takes a string and an optional flag as arguments (Table 18-3 lists the flags).

✔ match() returns either

- A MatchObject instance (if there is a match)

  See "Querying the match object," later in this chapter.

- None (if there is no match)

It's easy to confuse match(), which matches only at the beginning of a string, and search(), which matches anywhere in a string. (See the following section.) One way around this problem is to always use search(), specifying ^ in your regex to match only at the beginning of a string.

search ( )

To find a single occurrence of a regex *anywhere* in a string, use search().

✔ search() takes a string and an optional flag as arguments (Table 18-3 lists the flags).

✔ search() returns either

- A MatchObject instance (if there is a match)

  See "Querying the match object," later in this chapter.

- None (if there is no match)

split ( )

To split a string wherever a regex is found, use split().

✔ split() takes these arguments:

- A string

- An optional integer specifying the maximum number of times to split the string

✔ split() returns a list of the substrings.

This example shows the workings of the split() function:

```
>>> cow1 = "I never saw a purple cow, @@ I never hope to see one;"
>>> re.split('', cow1)      # function
['I never saw a purple cow, ', ' I never hope to see one;']
```

This example uses the split() method with the same regex:

```
>>> cow2 = "But I can tell you anyhow, @@ I'd rather see than be one."
>>> sep = re.compile('@@')
>>> sep.split(cow2)
['But I can tell you anyhow, ', " I'd rather see than be one."]
```

sub()

To find all occurrences of some text in a string and substitute other text, use sub():

✔ When sub() finds a match, it substitutes the replacement string.

✔ sub() returns either

  • The changed string (if any changes were made)

  • The original string (if no changes were made)

sub() takes these arguments:

✔ A replacement string

✔ The original string

✔ An optional integer

  The integer specifies the maximum number of replacements. If you leave the integer out, all matches are replaced.

The following code shows the result of replacing part of a string:

```
>>> mystring = "European swallow"
>>> myregex = re.compile("European")
>>> myregex.sub("African", mystring)          # method
'African swallow'
>>> re.sub('European', 'African', mystring)  # function
'African swallow'
```

Querying the match object

A successful regex search returns a Python object called a MatchObject, as illustrated in the following example:

```
>>> my_regex = re.compile('py+thon')
>>> mystring = "pyyython is a suuuper programming language"
>>> mymatch = my_regex.match(mystring)
>>> mymatch
<_sre.SRE_Match object at 0x82c6c28>
```

The MatchObject stores information about where in the string the match starts and ends, the substring(s) that were matched, and so on. To get access to this information, you use the following methods:

- group(): Takes the group index number as an argument; this defaults to 0, or the first group, which returns the matched string.

  ```
  >>> mymatch.group(0)
  'pyyython'
  ```

- groups(): Returns a tuple containing the match found for each regex group. Takes an optional argument to return for the regex groups that didn't match anything; this defaults to None.

  The regex for the following MatchObject has two groups, one named group for zip code and one numbered group for the string 'USA'.

  ```
  >>> y.groups()
  ('Zip: 94101', 'USA')
  ```

- groupdict(): Returns a dictionary containing all the named subgroups of the match. The keys are the subgroup names. Takes an optional argument to return for nonparticipating groups; this defaults to None.

  ```
  >>> y.groupdict()
  {'zip': 'Zip: 94101'}
  ```

- span(): Returns a tuple containing the starting and ending index numbers that were matched. Takes the group index number as an argument; this defaults to 0, or the first group.

  ```
  >>> mymatch.span(0)
  (0, 8)
  ```

You can get just the starting position with start() and just the ending position with end(). Both of these also take the group index number argument.

Additional regex resources

The "Regular Expression HOWTO" Web page at www.amk.ca/python/howto/regex/ includes a basic tutorial on regular expressions.

Regex *debuggers* can help clarify regex problems. Kodos, the Python Regular Expression Debugger (available at http://kodos.sourceforge.net/), is one such tool.

A tool for practicing and testing regexes comes with Python 2.4. It's part of the GUI tool kit Tkinter, and it's usually installed at Tools/scripts/redemo.py.

Kiki, which comes with the WxPython installer, has nice coloring for grouping in regexes. More info about WxPython can be found at www.wxpython.org/.

When you're writing a program that uses a regex to search a string, you usually want to check whether there was a match. To do this, you check whether the match object is `None`. For example, you might use this code (remember that `if mymatch` is short for `if mymatch is not None`):

```
if mymatch:
    print 'Match found'
else:
    print 'No match'
```

Making regexes more readable

You can use the `VERBOSE` flag when you write a regex to make it more readable. With this flag, you can use comments and white space in your regex. Here's how it works:

✔ The regex interpreter ignores any white space that is *outside* square brackets.

✔ Anything following the # character on a line — as long as # isn't inside square brackets — is considered a comment rather than part of the regex.

✔ Using a raw string with triple-quotes is the simplest way to write a multi-line regex with comments.

This example searches text for a phone number. It finds numbers with or without parentheses around the area code, and with or without a space, period, or hyphen as a separator.

```
>>> phone_re = re.compile(r'''
...     \(?                     # optionally match begin parenthesis
...     (?P<area>\d{3})         # match/name group for area code
...     \)?                     # optionally match end parenthesis
...     [\s.-]?                 # optionally match space, period, or hyphen
...     (?P<prefix>\d{3})       # match/name group for prefix
...     [\s.-]?                 # optionally match space, period, or hyphen
...     (?P<suffix>\d{4})       # match/name group for suffix
...     ''', re.VERBOSE)
>>> phone_re.sub(r'\g<area>-\g<prefix>-\g<suffix>', '(213)555-1212')
213-555-1212
>>> phone_re.sub(r'\g<area>-\g<prefix>-\g<suffix>', '213.555.1212')
213-555-1212
```

Strings Disguised as Files

The `cStringIO` and `StringIO` modules support "string buffers" (also called *memory files*) that let you pretend that a string is a file. This is useful because some Python library modules, such as the `tarfile` module, work with files but not with strings. Python holds the "file" in memory instead of writing the file to disk.

StringIO versus cStringIO

The cStringIO module implements the same functionality as StringIO. cStringIO is faster, but it has a couple of limitations:

✔ cStringIO doesn't support subclassing.

Use StringIO if you need to write a subclass of StringIO.

✔ If you give Unicode strings to cStringIO, you must encode them as UTF-8 (see Chapter 6).

Creating a StringIO object

There are two ways to create a StringIO object:

✔ **Pass it a string as an argument.** This is called *initializing the buffer.*

Do this if you want to read or otherwise process an existing string.

✔ **Leave out the argument,** which creates the object with an empty buffer.

Do this if you want to write to the object.

To create a StringIO object, follow these steps:

1. **Type** from cStringIO import StringIO.

2. **On the next line, type code like one of the following lines.**

Substitute the name of your file and your string (or its name).

To create an empty buffer, type this:

```
pretend_file = StringIO()
```

To initialize the buffer with an existing string, type this:

```
pretend_file = StringIO("mystring")
```

StringIO special methods

The methods for working with StringIO files are the same as the methods for working with regular files (described in Chapter 17).

Here are two differences:

✔ The `StringIO` object includes the `getvalue()` method, which returns the entire contents of the memory file as a string:

```
>>> pretend_file.getvalue()
'mystring'
```

✔ The `StringIO` `close()` method frees up the memory buffer.

A regular file object's `close()` method writes the contents to disk.

Paragraph Dumplings: Filling and Wrapping Text

The `textwrap` module, new in Python 2.3, is for formatting paragraphs of text. You can perform three basic formatting tasks with it: unindenting ("dedenting"), wrapping, and filling. You can also create a customized `TextWrapper` object.

Removing indentation from strings

To remove white space that appears in front of every line of the string, use the `dedent()` function. It takes a string as an argument.

Dedent is meant to be the opposite of *indent*.

One use for this function is to make triple-quoted strings in a Python program — docstrings for example — line up with the left margin, even though they are indented in the source code. Here's an example:

```
>>> mystring = '''   Tyger, Tyger, burning bright
...    In the forests of the night'''
>>> print mystring
   Tyger, Tyger, burning bright
   In the forests of the night
>>> print textwrap.dedent(mystring)
Tyger, Tyger, burning bright
In the forests of the night
```

Wrapping text by splitting it up

To turn a long string into a list of strings, one for each line of text, use the `wrap()` function. It takes a string as an argument, and it also takes an optional `width` argument, specifying the maximum length of any line (it defaults to 70 characters). The strings returned don't have newline characters.

The following example shows the use of the `wrap()` function on a long string:

```
>>> metaphor = """\
... Worse, many abandon the pearl which exists in the present in favor
... of a caravan of dreams which always recedes across the desert. -- Mixed
... Metaphor Hall of Fame"""
>>> m = textwrap.wrap(metaphor, width=40)
>>> m
['Worse, many abandon the pearl which', 'exists in the present in favor of
a','caravan of dreams which always recedes', 'across the desert. -- Mixed
Metaphor', 'Hall of Fame']
```

You could use a `for` loop to print the result of the `wrap()` function:

```
>>> for i in m:
...     print i
...
Worse, many abandon the pearl which
exists in the present in favor of a
caravan of dreams which always recedes
across the desert. -- Mixed Metaphor
Hall of Fame
```

Here's a shorter idiom for accomplishing the same thing:

```
print '\n'.join(m)
```

Wrapping text by adding newline characters

To add newline characters to a long string, use the `fill()` function. It takes a string as an argument and returns a string. It also takes an optional `width` argument, specifying the maximum length of any line (it defaults to 70 characters).

Here's an example of wrapping text with the `fill()` function:

```
>>> longstring = '''
... But once you build some islands of peace into your daily routine, they
... help serve as beachheads against the full-court press of life.
... --Mixed Metaphor Hall of Fame'''

>>> wrappedstring = textwrap.fill(longstring, width=40)
>>> wrappedstring
```

```
' But once you build some islands of\npeace into your daily routine,

they help\nserve as beachheads against the full-\ncourt press of

life. --Mixed Metaphor\nHall of Fame'
>>> print wrappedstring
But once you build some islands of
peace into your daily routine, they help
serve as beachheads against the full-
court press of life. --Mixed Metaphor
Hall of Fame
```

Creating a TextWrapper object

The `wrap()` and `fill()` functions work by creating a `TextWrapper` instance and calling a single method on it.

This instance goes away after you use it, so for applications that format many text strings, it's more efficient to create your own `TextWrapper` object.

TextWrapper attributes

When you create a `TextWrapper` object, you can specify any of the following arguments. You can also use them as keyword arguments for the `wrap()` and `fill()` functions.

- ✔ `width`: The maximum length of a wrapped line. The default is 70 characters.

- ✔ `expand_tabs`: Changes tabs to an equivalent number of spaces (between 1 and 8). Default `True`. If set to `False`, tabs are treated as single characters.

- ✔ `replace_whitespace`: Changes all white space characters to spaces. Default `True`.

  What counts as a white space character is defined by the `whitespace` data attribute of the `string` module. This depends on your locale and operating system. Here's our result:

  ```
  >>> import string
  >>> string.whitespace
  '\t\n\x0b\x0c\r '
  ```

  The meanings of the codes are: `\t` (tab), `\n` (newline), `\x0b` (vertical tab), `\x0c` (form feed), `\r` (carriage return), `' '` (space).

If you set `expand_tabs` to `False` and `replace_whitespace` to `True`, tabs are converted to single space characters.

✔ `initial_indent`: Set this to a string of five spaces or so to get an indented line at the beginning of a paragraph. The default is an empty string.

✔ `subsequent_indent`: This string is added at the beginning of all wrapped lines after the first. Default is an empty string.

✔ `fix_sentence_endings`: Puts two spaces between sentences.

What `textwrap` thinks a sentence is might not match what you think a sentence is. For example, `fix_sentence_endings` puts two spaces after "Dr." Default is `False`.

✔ `break_long_words`: Breaks words longer than the `width` attribute. If set to `False`, lines with long words may exceed the specified width. Default is `True`.

Example of a custom TextWrapper object

Here's an example of a custom `TextWrapper` object. This object specifies a 40-character line and indents each line after the first one 4 spaces.

```
>>> mywrapper = textwrap.TextWrapper(width=40, subsequent_indent="    ")
>>> indented_string = mywrapper.fill(longstring)
>>> print indented_string
 But once you build some islands of
    peace into your daily routine, they
    help serve as beachheads against the
    full-court press of life. --Mixed
    Metaphor Hall of Fame
```

Chapter 19

Digging into Disk Data

Python includes a variety of modules and packages for working with data files on disk. In this chapter, you find out how to

✔ Use Python to work with files on your hard drive, including compressed Zip files.

✔ Use Python to communicate with databases.

✔ Turn Python objects (such as dictionaries) into formats that can be stored or sent over the Internet.

Shell Game: Copying and Moving Files

The shutil module lets you use Python to manipulate, copy, and remove files on your hard drive ("shutil" stands for "shell utility").

You can use the os module to work with hard drive files, but shutil is usually simpler because it does a lot of the path manipulation behind the scenes.

If you're working on a Mac or your program will run on a Mac, use the macostools module, not shutil, to copy files and directories. On Mac OS, the shutil module does not recognize resource forks and other metadata. If you use shutil to copy files on a Mac, the files' resources, file types, and creator codes may not be correct.

Some of the useful `shutil` functions are described in the following list. All the functions take pathname arguments (as strings) — source pathname first, followed by destination pathname (if any):

✔ `copy()`: Copies the source file and its permissions to the destination.

The `copy()` function has these rules:

- The destination can be a file or a directory.

- If the destination is a directory, the copy has the same name as the source file.

This example copies the file `'myspider.py'` to `'copyy.py'` within the same directory:

```
>>> import shutil
>>> shutil.copy('myspider.py', 'copyy.py')
```

✔ `copy2()`: Like `copy()`, but also copies the last access time and last modification time.

✔ `copymode()`: Copies the permissions of the source file to the destination file. Does not change the file contents, owner, or group.

✔ `copytree()`: Copies the entire contents of the source directory to the destination. The destination cannot already exist. Uses `copy2()` to copy files. This example copies the contents of `'MyDir'` to `'MyNewDir'`:

```
>>> shutil.copytree('MyDir', 'MyNewDir')
```

This function also takes an optional third argument, `symlinks`, specifying what to do with symbolic links:

- `True` creates symbolic links in the new directory tree.

- `False` (the default) copies the contents of symlinked files.

Starting in version 2.3, Python raises an `OSError` if any problems occur while implementing `copytree()`. (In earlier versions, Python printed a message.) The `OSError` looks something like this:

```
>>> shutil.copytree('MyDir', 'MyNewDir')
Traceback (most recent call last):
  File "<stdin>", line 1, in ?
  File "/System/Library/Frameworks/Python.framework/Versions/2.3/lib/
python2.3/shutil.py", line 102, in copytree
OSError: [Errno 17] File exists: 'MyNewDir'
```

✔ `move()`: New in Python 2.3. Moves the source to the destination.

The `move()` function has these rules:

- The destination cannot already exist.

- If the source and the destination are on different file systems, `move()` first does a copy to the destination and then deletes the source.

- The paths can be files or directories.

This example moves a directory:

```
shutil.move('MyNewDir', '../MyNewDir')
```

✔ `rmtree()`: Deletes the specified directory and its contents.

Error messages depend on the optional argument `ignore_errors`:

- When set to `True`, `ignore_errors` suppresses any error messages.
- The default is `False`, which causes Python to raise an exception if it discovers an error while executing `rmtree()`.

An advanced feature also lets you customize the exception handling.

This example removes the directory that we moved in the previous example:

```
shutil.rmtree('../MyNewDir')
```

Zipping and Unzipping

The `zipfile` and `gzip` modules support data compression and expansion.

zipfile

The `zipfile` module provides access to Zip files, which are created with WinZip (the most common Windows file compression utility), the Mac OS "Create Archive" command, or the UNIX `zip` utility.

In Windows XP, Mac OS, and UNIX, Zip files are similar to folders (because they can hold files and folders). If you select a folder in Windows XP and make it a compressed folder, it's compressed as a Zip file.

The `zipfile` module lets you use Python to create, read, write, append, and list a compressed Zip file.

The `zipfile` module doesn't work with either

- ✔ Zip files with appended comments
- ✔ Zip files that span multiple disks

Finding out whether a file is a Zip file

To identify a file as a Zip file, import `zipfile` and use the `is_zipfile()` function:

- ✔ Its argument is a pathname string.
- ✔ It returns `True` if the file is a valid Zip file.

This example checks a file called `'stuff.zip'`:

```
>>> import zipfile
>>> zipfile.is_zipfile('MyDir/stuff.zip')
True
```

Don't make incorrect assumptions if `is_zipfile()` returns `False`. It also returns `False` if the file doesn't exist.

Creating a ZipFile object for reading or writing

To read or write to a compressed Zip file, you create a `ZipFile()` instance.

To create a `ZipFile` object, follow these steps:

1. **Type a name for the object and** `= zipfile.ZipFile(`.

2. **Type the path to your Zip file (as a string).**

3. **If you want to *write* to the Zip file, type a comma and** `'w'`.

   Using `'w'` erases whatever is currently in the file, so make doubly sure that you don't need to keep what is already in the Zip file before you go appending `'w'`.

   There is another mode, `'a'` for append. This is an advanced feature we don't expound on in this book.

   If you don't want to compress the stored data, skip to Step 5.

4. **If you want to compress the data, specify a compression type by typing a comma and** `compression= ZIP_DEFLATED`.

   `ZIP_STORED` (the default) stores data without compression.

   The `zlib` module must be available if you want to compress the data.

5. **End by typing** `)`.

   If you fill in both optional parameters, your instance might look like this:

```
>>> myz = zipfile.ZipFile('MyDir/x.zip', 'w',
          compression=zipfile.ZIP_DEFLATED)
>>> myz
<zipfile.ZipFile instance at 0x780a8>
```

Working with a ZipFile object

`ZipFile` instances are similar to file objects. They have these methods:

✓ `close()` and `read()`: Work like the `file()` object methods of the same names (see Chapter 17).

✔ `getinfo()`: Takes a string specifying the name of an item in the archive and returns a `ZipInfo()` object containing information about the item.

```
>>> myz.getinfo('pagecount.py')
<zipfile.ZipInfo instance at 0x79fa8>
```

One way to see the attributes of the `ZipInfo()` object is to use the `dir()` function. The following example looks at the contents of a `ZipInfo()` object called `myinfo` and then looks at its file size:

```
>>> dir(myinfo)
['CRC', 'FileHeader', '__doc__', '__init__', '__module__', 'comment',
'compress_size', 'compress_type', 'create_system', 'create_version',
'date_time', 'external_attr', 'extra', 'extract_version', 'file_offset',
'file_size', 'filename', 'flag_bits', 'header_offset', 'internal_attr',
'orig_filename', 'reserved', 'volume']
>>> myinfo.file_size
4220L
```

✔ `infolist()`: Returns a list of `ZipInfo()` objects for all items in the order they're stored in the archive.

✔ `namelist()`: Returns a list of strings — the names of the items in the archive — like so:

```
>>> myz.namelist()
['copyy.py', 'helloworld.py', 'myspider.py', 'pagecount.py', 'x']
```

✔ `printdir()`: Lists the items in the archive to `sys.stdout`.

```
>>> myz.printdir()
File Name                          Modified             Size
copyy.py                    2006-03-07 16:56:54         4220
helloworld.py               2005-07-05 15:01:28           22
myspider.py                 2005-11-06 21:29:02         4220
pagecount.py                2005-10-10 15:01:10          367
x                           2006-02-24 13:49:46            0
```

✔ `testzip()`: Examines the checksums (CRCs) of all the items in the archive. Returns as a string the name of the first bad file detected; if all files are good, returns `None`.

✔ `write()`: Takes as an argument a string specifying a pathname and writes the specified file to the archive.

The archive must be open for writing or appending. `write()` takes two optional arguments:

- `arcname`, a string specifying the name for the file in the archive (it defaults to the filename)

- A compression type, either `ZIP_STORED` or `ZIP_DEFLATED`

This example writes the file `'helloworld.py'` to the archive and stores it with the name `'foo'`:

```
myz.write('MyDir/helloworld.py', arcname='foo')
```

✔ `writestr()`: Writes a data string to the archive. The archive must be opened with mode `'w'` or `'a'`. Takes two arguments:

- A string specifying the name that the written data string will have in the archive (or a `ZipInfo()` instance with at least a filename, a date, and a time)

- A string containing the data to store

```
myzipf.writestr(info, "my_data")
```

The `ZipFile()` instance has a data attribute, `debug`, which specifies the level of debug output to print to `sys.stdout`. The options range from `0` (no output) to `3` (the most output). The default is `0`.

Zipping up a Python library

`PyZipFile()` instances create zip archives containing Python libraries. Python can import modules from Zip files. Putting the modules your program uses into Zip files is one way of delivering a smaller program.

To create a zip archive with Python files, follow these steps:

1. **Create a `PyZipFile()` instance.**

   Use the instructions in "Creating a ZipFile object for reading or writing," earlier in this chapter. Open the archive for writing or appending.

   Your code will look something like this:

   ```
   mypz = zipfile.PyZipFile('foo.zip', 'w')
   ```

2. **On the next line, type the name of your instance, a dot, and** `writepy(.`

3. **On the same line, type a file or directory pathname and** `)`.

   If you type a filename, the suffix must be `.py`. This example uses a directory pathname:

   ```
   mypz.writepy('MyDir')
   ```

How `writepy()` works depends on the pathname you type:

✔ If you type a filename, the file is added to the archive.

✔ If you type a directory name, all the Python files in the directory with the suffixes `.py`, `.pyo`, or `.pyc` are added to the archive. The file locations depend on the path's location:

- If the path is a regular directory, the files are added to an archive at the top level of the directory.

- If the path is a package directory, the files are added under the package name and subdirectory names (if any).

PyZipFile() objects use the same methods as ZipFile() objects.

gzip

The gzip module reads and writes compressed files that are compatible with the GNU program gzip. To your program's users, the contents of these files look like ordinary files (that is, not zipped).

The gzip module doesn't support all the formats that the GNU gzip utility supports. For example, compress and pack aren't supported.

To use Python's gzip module, use its open() function to create a GzipFile() instance. The instance works like a file object, but with these differences:

✔ The GzipFile() instance doesn't support the readinto() or truncate() methods.

✔ The close() method does not close the file object the instance is using. It closes the instance only.

This feature allows you to do something to the file object after working with it as a GzipFile() instance. For example, if the file object is a StringIO object, you can use the StringIO.getvalue() function to retrieve the contents after closing the GzipFile() instance.

To create a GzipFile() instance from a file on disk, follow these steps:

1. **Type** gzip.open(

2. **On the same line, type the path to your gzipped file as a string. For example,**

```
gzip.open('filename.gz'
```

If you don't want to write to the file, skip to Step 4.

3. **If you want to write to the file, type a comma and** 'w'.

Using the 'w' mode erases whatever is currently in the file, so make sure that you don't need to keep what is already in the file before you go appending 'w'.

There is another mode, 'a' for append. This is an advanced feature we don't document in this book.

If you want the file to open and close faster, you can tell gzip to create a *faster, larger* file:

   a. *Type a comma.*

   b. *Type* `compresslevel=.`

   c. *Type an integer from* 1 *(fastest, largest file) to* 9 *(slowest, smallest file).*

   By default, the `compresslevel` value is 9 (slowest, smallest file).

4. End the line of code by typing `)`.

If you fill in both optional parameters, your code and the result might look like this:

```
>>> import gzip
>>> myfile = gzip.open('quote2.new.gz', mode='w', compresslevel=8)
>>> myfile
<gzip open file 'quote2.new.gz', mode 'wb' at 0x4b5c0 0x5d490>
```

It's also possible to create a `GzipFile()` instance from a file or file-like object (such as a `StringIO` object) already opened in Python. This works much like using the `open()` function, but the order of the arguments is different:

1. Mode (optional, defaults to the mode of the Python file object)

2. Compression level (optional, defaults to 9 or slowest/smallest)

3. The name of the Python file object (required)

   The creation of a `GzipFile()` instance might look something like this:

```
>>> gfile = gzip.GzipFile(mode='w', compresslevel=8, fileobj=myfile)
```

Sussing Out SQL Databases

The `sqlite3` module gives you an easy way to store your data by using the SQLite library, an implementation of the universal database language SQL. (SQL is pronounced "sequel" and stands for Structured Query Language. SQLite is pronounced "sequel-ite"). `sqlite3` is a new standard module in Python 2.5. If you have Python version 2.2 through 2.4, you can download the essentially similar `pysqlite` module from `http://pysqlite.org/`.

We don't have the space for detailed information on using SQL — SQL is a whole programming language all by itself. But in the sections that follow, we show you the basics of using `sqlite3` as well as some quick tricks for using SQL. (*SQL For Dummies*, 5th Edition, by Allen Taylor has more information.) The Web site `www.sqlite.org/` also has lots of documentation.

Installing SQLite and sqlite3

The `sqlite3` module is automatically installed when you install Python 2.5. On Windows, the Python 2.5 installation also includes SQLite itself. On other platforms, make sure that SQLite is installed before you build Python 2.5. See the `README` file in your Python download for details.

Setting up a SQLite database

To create or use a SQLite database, you open a *connection* to the database (it's like opening a file) and create a *cursor* to access the database.

You can open a connection in two ways:

✔ **Disk-based connection:** Allows you to write changes to the database file on disk.

✔ **In-memory database:** The connection works faster, but you can't write changes to disk. It's most useful for loading some data into memory and then running a bunch of queries.

To open a connection to a database on disk, follow these steps:

1. **Type** `import sqlite3`.

2. **On the next line, type the code to open the connection:**

   • For a disk-based connection, type the name of the database in the parentheses:

   ```
   conn = sqlite3.connect('my_database')
   ```

   • For an in-memory database, type the special string `':memory:'` in the parentheses.

   You can type a pathname to an existing database or type a new filename to create a new database.

   ```
   conn = sqlite3.connect(':memory:')
   ```

3. **On the next line, create a cursor by typing code like this:**

   ```
   cursor = conn.cursor()
   ```

   The cursor is like a bookmark telling you where you are in the database.

Working with a SQLite database

This section describes some basic tasks you can do with the database: creating a table, adding data to a table, and getting data out of a table.

Creating a table

A *table* is an area in a database where you store related information. A table consists of records (sets of information), which in turn contain fields (each field is one bit of information of a particular *type*). To create a table, you write a *query* (instructions to the database), and then use the cursor's `execute()` method to run the query. To create a table to store addresses, you might use code like this:

```
query = """                     -- sqlite queries are strings; comments use "--"
    create table address        -- create a table named "address"
    (                           -- begin creating a record
        name varchar,           -- create a field called "name", with type "varchar"
        street varchar,
        city varchar
    )                           -- end of this record
    """                         # end of query
```

The above code is formatted so that it's easier for humans to read. SQL doesn't care about indentation in query strings. The text after -- on each line represents comments. Python ignores these.

The code `varchar` in the preceding example is a *type* (a declaration of the kind of information to be stored in that field). `varchar` specifies that the field contains text of varying length. SQLite requires you to define a type for each field. (SQLite doesn't care much about types, but most other SQL databases do.)

Think of SQL tables as being like Python classes except that they only contain data, not methods. A SQL database can have multiple tables. A *record* or *row* (the section within parentheses in the above example) is like a class instance. The *fields* or *columns* of a record (each line inside the parentheses is one field) are like instance data attributes, except that all records have exactly the same attributes (the data associated with the fields can be different). In contrast, class instances can have different attributes, although most of the time they don't.

Actually, most modern SQL databases do allow for creating methods, but they're an advanced and complicated feature. So pretend we didn't mention them.

Populating a table with data

After you have a table, you can *populate* the table (add data to it), like this:

1. **Create a list of tuples.**

   Each element in a tuple should correspond to a field in one of the database's records. For example:

   ```
   addresses = [
       ('Pet Shops Ltd', '123 Main St', 'Notlob'),
       ('Similar Pet Shops Ltd', '321 First St', 'Bolton'),
       ]
   ```

For help arranging data into the proper format, see Chapter 8.

2. **Use the** `execute()` **method in a** `for` **loop to write the addresses into the database.**

```
for addr in addresses:
    cursor.execute("insert into address values (?, ?, ?)", addr)
```

The `execute()` method's first argument is a string with the SQL command `insert into`, the name of the table, and `values` followed by a set of query parameters in parentheses. Question marks (?) stand for query parameters; `sqlite3` passes in an argument for each parameter. The number of question marks must match the number of elements in the second argument. Lucky us — in the example above, there are three question marks and three elements in each `addr` tuple. The second argument is the target of the `for` loop.

Use double quotation marks or triple quotes for all Python strings that contain SQL queries. SQL requires string values to be surrounded by single quotation marks (see the example in the "Getting a subset of the values" section), so you'll make life easier for yourself if you avoid using single quotation marks for Python strings when working with SQL.

Getting field values from a table

To get field values from a table, you execute a query specifying the data you want and then use the `fetchall()` method to retrieve the data. (You may have noticed by now that most SQLite tasks involve executing a query.)

Getting all the values

This example retrieves a list of all the values stored in our table's `name` field:

```
>>> cursor.execute("select name from address")
<sqlite3.Cursor object at 0x66830>
>>> print cursor.fetchall()
[(u'Pet Shops Ltd',), (u'Similar Pet Shops Ltd',)]
```

The `fetchall()` method returns a list of tuples. Because each tuple in the result has only one element, the tuples end with a comma. See Chapter 8 for a review of tuples.

SQLite stores text data as Unicode strings. See Chapter 6 for more info about Unicode.

Getting a subset of the values

The real power of a database lies in its ability to give you the subset of information that matches your needs. In this example, we get the records that have "Bolton" in the `city` field. If you know that the `*` character stands for "all fields," it's pretty easy to understand what this query does:

```
>>> cursor.execute("select * from address where city='Bolton'")
<sqlite3.Cursor object at 0x66830>
>>> print cursor.fetchall()
[(u'Similar Pet Shops Ltd', u'123 Main St', u'Bolton')]
```

When you're starting out with `sqlite3`, you should probably stick with storing and retrieving simple strings, numbers, and dates. But when you get more comfortable, you can store Python objects in the database by using the `pickle` module's `dumps()` function. See the next section, "Pickling Your Data (And Relishing the Outcome)." Note that you won't be able to share your database with non-Python programs if you store pickled data.

`sqlite3` follows the Python Database API Specification v2.0 (for more details, see Python Enhancement Proposal PEP249 at `www.python.org/dev/peps/pep-0249/`). Because Python database modules are all designed to work consistently, when you need a more powerful database (such as PostgreSQL or Firebird), it should be easy to upgrade your code: You need only change the `connect()` function call.

Pickling Your Data (And Relishing the Outcome)

The `pickle` and `cPickle` modules let you store data between runs of a program, the way a word processor allows you to save formatted documents and edit them later even if you quit the program. This is called *pickling* because it's a way of *preserving* your data.

Storing a Python object in a file makes it a *persistent object*. You could write your own code to store and read Python objects, but if your data includes complex objects, it's easier to use pickling because it automatically converts data back and forth between strings and Python objects.

Python includes the following support for persistent objects:

✔ The `cPickle` and `pickle` modules convert Python objects to and from string representations.

Pickling is commonly used when working with persistent databases, which store Python objects so that they can be accessed by keys.

✔ The `shelve` module (see the next section) supports persistent dictionaries whose values can be arbitrary Python objects. It works with the `pickle` and `anydbm` modules.

Pickled data is a security risk because it might include malicious code. Make sure you unpickle data only from a trusted source.

The module of choice for the majority of pickling tasks is `cPickle`, which is simpler and faster than the `pickle` module. The only reason to use `pickle` is if you need access to its advanced features (which we don't cover in this book).

Pickling an object

To pickle a Python object, follow these steps:

1. **Type** `import cPickle`.

2. **Open a file for writing. For example,**

   ```
   mypicklefile = open(myfile, 'w')
   ```

3. **Type** `cPickle.dump` **and in parentheses specify the name of the object you want to pickle and the name of the file you opened (which is where the pickled object will be stored).**

   ```
   cPickle.dump(myobj, mypicklefile)
   ```

4. **Close the file.**

   ```
   mypicklefile.close()
   ```

Pickling restrictions

Most Python data types can be pickled, with the following exceptions:

✔ Functions, built-in functions, and classes defined at a level other than the top level of a module can't be pickled.

✔ A class with a __dict__ attribute or a __setstate__() method that isn't compatible with pickling can't be pickled.

✔ Tuples, lists, sets, and dictionaries that contain non-picklable objects can't be pickled.

✔ Pickling stores only the names of functions and classes, not any code or attributes from them. So when you unpickle a module, its functions must be available for importing on the system you're unpickling from.

✔ When instances are pickled, class attributes aren't pickled along with them.

The following functions pickle a Python object. The function you use depends on what type of data you want returned.

dumps ( )

The dumps() function pickles a Python object and returns a string. It's useful for storing Python objects in databases, such as SQLite (see the previous section, "Sussing Out SQL Databases.")

This function takes a Python object as an argument.

dump ( )

The dump() function pickles the object and writes the pickled object to an open file (or a file-like object like StringIO).

This function takes two arguments:

- ✔ A Python object
- ✔ A file object opened for writing

The dump() and dumps() functions take one optional parameter that specifies the pickling version to use. The following subsections show the right parameter for your version of Python.

Python 2.3 or later

If you're using Python 2.3 or later, the pickling version parameter for the dump() and dumps() functions is called protocol.

You can specify the pickling protocol version by entering one of the values from the sidebar, "All about pickling protocols."

All about pickling protocols

There are three pickling protocols:

- ✔ 0 is an *ASCII* protocol. It's compatible with earlier versions of Python.

  0 is the default value.

- ✔ 1 is a binary protocol (also compatible with earlier versions of Python).

- ✔ 2 works more efficiently with Python's new-style classes (discussed in Chapter 14).

You can also specify this version by entering HIGHEST_PROTOCOL or any *negative* integer.

Protocol version 2 is new in Python 2.3.

Older Python versions

If you're using a version of Python older than 2.3, the optional pickling version parameter is called `bin`. It specifies to pickle the data in a binary format. (The default version is text, which is less efficient.)

Don't use `bin` in your code unless your program must be compatible with earlier versions of Python.

Unpickling an object

The loading function for a pickled Python object depends on whether it's a file or a string.

Unpickling files

The `load()` function takes a file object (or a file-like object such as `StringIO`) as an argument. The file should be opened in read mode. `load()` reads the contents of the file object and unpickles it. The result is the original object that you pickled.

To unpickle a Python object from a file, follow these steps:

1. **Import** `cPickle`.
2. **Open for reading the file containing the pickled object.**

   ```
   mypicklefile = open(myfile, 'rb')
   ```

3. **Type a name for the object,** `= cPickle.load`, **and in parentheses the name of the file you opened.**

   ```
   myobj = cPickle.load(mypicklefile)
   ```

Unpickling strings

The `loads()` function takes the name of a string as an argument. It reads the contents of the string and unpickles it. The result is the original object that you pickled.

Using shelve with DBM-style databases

This section is for people who need to store Python data on disk using Python 2.4 or earlier, or who need to use the Berkeley DB database library. (Berkeley DB and its relatives are called *DBM-style databases*.) If you have Python 2.5, read "Sussing Out SQL Databases," earlier in this chapter, instead. It's easier to use. (You can also download `pysqlite` for Python 2.2 through 2.4.)

Storing pickles on a shelf

The `shelve` module is a "wrapper" around several DBM-style database modules available in Python. The shelve module works like this:

1. You create a `shelve` object and tell it to open a database file.

2. The `shelve` object looks at your database file on disk and decides which Python database module to use.

3. The Python database module accesses your database file.

The `shelve` module and its tools have the following features:

✔ The `open()` function automatically chooses an available database module when you open a file.

✔ Shelve objects behave like dictionaries (see Chapter 9), with a few minor differences (see "Properties of a shelve object" later in this chapter).

✔ Shelve objects allow you to store pickled Python objects as values. (See "Pickling Your Data (And Relishing the Outcome)" earlier in this chapter.)

A shelve object is called a _persistent dictionary_ because it can store and reconstitute Python objects from a disk file.

Creating a shelve object

To create a `shelve()` object, follow these steps:

1. **Type** `import shelve`.

2. **On the next line, type a name for the shelf,** =, **and** `shelve.` `open('mydatabase'`.

   Substitute the name of your DBM-style database file.

3. **To open the file as read-only, to open an existing file as read-write, or to create a new, empty database, type a comma and a flag:**

   The flags are:

   `'r'`   read only

   `'w'`   read and write

   `'c'`   create database if it doesn't exist (default)

   `'n'`   create new empty database

If the file exists, typing `'n'` erases its contents.

```
myshelf = shelve.open('mydatabase', 'w'
```

4. **If you have Python 2.3 or later and you want to use one of the advanced pickling protocols, type a comma,** `protocol=` **and one of the following:**

   For more about the protocols, see "Pickling Your Data (And Relishing the Outcome)" earlier in this chapter.

   - 1   binary protocol
   - 2 or HIGHEST_PROTOCOL   advanced protocol; works more efficiently with Python's new-style classes

   ```
   myshelf = shelve.open('mydatabase', 'w', protocol=2
   ```

5. **To allow changes to mutable objects in the database, type a comma and** `writeback=True`.

   ```
   myshelf = shelve.open('mydatabase', 'w', protocol=2, writeback=True
   ```

   This feature makes the database slow to close.

   If you don't turn on the `writeback` feature, you can still make changes to mutable objects by using a three-step process described in the sidebar, "Changing mutable objects in a shelve database."

6. **Type the end parenthesis.**

   ```
   myshelf = shelve.open('mydatabase', 'w', protocol=2, writeback=True)
   ```

Changing mutable objects in a shelve database

When you create a `shelve` object, by default changes to mutable objects are not stored in the database file, because allowing this makes the database slow. To allow such changes, you can set `writeback=True` when opening a `shelve` object (see "Creating a shelve object"). But if you leave it turned off, you can use this three-step process for making changes to mutable objects. These steps assume you've already opened a `shelve` database object.

1. Access the mutable value by using its key, and give it a temporary name. In this example, the mutable value is a list and its key is `'mylist'`:

   ```
   temp = myshelf['mylist']
   ```

2. Make changes to the copy. In this example, we append a string to the list.

   ```
   temp.append('foo')
   ```

3. Assign the changed copy back to the same database key.

   ```
   myshelf['mylist'] = temp
   ```

Properties of a shelve object

The objects created by the shelve module are like a cross between a dictionary and a file object. As with a dictionary, you can retrieve, store, search for, and delete keys and values. As with a file object, you can open and close a shelve object and direct it to write changes to a file on disk. shelve objects have these unique features:

- ✔ Keys must be strings.

- ✔ Values can be strings or picklable Python objects.

- ✔ Changes to mutable objects are not written to disk unless you set writeback=True when you create the shelve object.

  See the sidebar, "Changing mutable objects in a shelve database," for some workaround ways of changing mutable objects.

- ✔ The sync() method writes changes to disk. (Writing happens automatically when you use the close() method.)

- ✔ When you write changes to disk by using the sync() or close() method, an extension might be added to the filename and more than one file might be created.

  Whether these happen depends on the underlying database shelve is using.

Chapter 20

Accessing the Internet

· ·

· ·

Python has an array of tools for working with information over the Internet. This chapter introduces tools for handling Web page addresses, downloading and parsing data from Web pages, building XML data structures, creating and sending e-mail messages, and writing and installing CGI scripts (for processing Web forms).

This chapter introduces concepts for working with Internet modules, but we assume that you have basic knowledge of Web, XML, and e-mail protocols.

Downloading Web Data

The following sections cover opening URLs, reading their contents, and submitting form data to a Web server.

Python has two modules for performing these tasks: `urllib` and `urllib2`. Each has specific strengths. We focus on the simpler `urllib` module in this section, but we recommend the `urllib2` module for opening and fetching data from Web pages because it has better error handling.

Opening a URL

The function `urlopen()` creates objects that behave a lot like files, but it has two important differences from the `open()` function, which creates files:

✔ urlopen() takes a Web page address (Uniform Resource Locator, or URL) as an argument (rather than as a filename).

✔ urlopen() opens the URL only for reading, not for writing.

Both the urllib and the urllib2 modules support the urlopen() function. The function works the same way in both, but the urlopen() function in urllib2 has better error reporting on problems that occur when opening Web pages.

Using urllib2.urlopen() to open a URL

To open a URL, follow these steps:

1. **Type** import urllib2.

2. **On the next line, type a name for the object and** = urllib.urlopen(.

3. **Type the URL (as a string) and close the parentheses by typing**).

   Your code should look something like this:

   ```
   page = urllib2.urlopen('http://www.python.org/doc/current/modindex.html')
   ```

If all goes well, the Web page opens. If you examine the object you just created, you'll see something like this:

```
>>> page
<addinfourl at 137848780 whose fp = <socket._fileobject object at 0x837c1b4>>
```

Reading text from a URL

To read text from an opened URL, use a for loop. This example prints the text to <sys.stdout> one line at a time:

```
for line in page:
    sys.stdout.write(line)
```

Understanding Web page errors

If there's a problem opening the page, Python raises an exception specifying the kind of error. Sometimes the message is long, so we won't reproduce the whole thing here. The critical part of the message is the last line. Here's part of the message you get if the site exists but the page doesn't exist:

```
>>> page=urllib2.urlopen('http://www.python.org/idontexist.html')
[...]
urllib2.HTTPError: HTTP Error 404: Not Found
```

Detailed error reporting is useful when you want to write code that handles different Web errors in different ways. For example, you might write code that checks a Web page's links and logs whether the link is still valid, whether it redirects to another page, or whether the linked page no longer exists. (The spider.py program in Chapter 4 uses this functionality.)

Finding information about a URL

Python has two useful tools for getting the scoop on a URL.

info ( )

To get meta-information (server type, last-modified date, content type, and so on) about a URL you've opened, use the info() method, like this:

```
>>> print page.info()
Date: Sun, 21 May 2006 07:52:15 GMT
Server: Apache/2.0.54 (Debian GNU/Linux) DAV/2 SVN/1.1.4 mod_python/3.1.3
           Python/2.3.5 mod_ssl/2.0.54 OpenSSL/0.9.7e
Last-Modified: Mon, 17 Apr 2006 12:04:05 GMT
ETag: "240110-8ac5-3811b740"
Accept-Ranges: bytes
Content-Length: 35525
Connection: close
Content-Type: text/html
```

geturl ( )

To get the actual URL that was opened when you made your request, use the geturl() method, like this:

```
>>> redirect = urllib2.urlopen('http://www.livejournal.com/users/firecat')
>>> redirect.geturl()
'http://firecat.livejournal.com/'
```

Use geturl() to find out whether the URL you opened redirected you somewhere else.

Processing special characters in a URL

To process special characters (such as a space or tilde) in a URL, use the urllib module's quote_plus() function.

Although the functions quote() and unquote() are similar to quote_plus(), we recommend using quote_plus() to avoid problems with URLs that contain + and space characters.

The quote_plus() function has a required argument and an optional argument.

Required argument

The quote_plus() function requires a URL string (or part of a URL) as an argument and does the following:

- ✔ Replaces special characters (anything but letters, digits, underscores, dots, and hyphens) by using the "%xx" escape format
- ✔ Replaces spaces with + (required for quoting HTML form contents)
- ✔ Escapes + characters in the original string

This example processes a URL with slash characters and a tilde (~):

```
>>> import urllib
>>> urllib.quote_plus('http://cat-and-dragon.com/~stef')
'http%3A%2F%2Fcat-and-dragon.com%2F%7Estef'
```

To reverse this process, use unquote_plus(). (This function doesn't use any optional parameters.)

Optional argument

The quote_plus() function takes an optional safe argument, which specifies characters to leave alone.

The following example processes the same URL as the preceding example, but the slash character has been designated as *safe:*

```
>>> urllib.quote_plus('http://cat-and-dragon.com/~stef', safe='/')
'http%3A//cat-and-dragon.com/%7Estef'
```

Submitting form data

When communicating via HTTP, the urlopen() function usually makes a GET request to the HTTP server. A GET request limits your URL (address and data) to 1,024 bytes. To send more data — for example, to submit the results of a form — you need to make a POST request.

Sending data via a POST request requires the following steps. Note that these steps require you to import both urllib (for the urlencode() function) and urllib2 (for the urlopen() function):

1. Type the following:

```
import urllib, urllib2
```

2. **Use the** `urllib.urlencode()` **function to encode the data.**

   The function takes one of the following arguments:

   - A mapping object (such as a dictionary of form fields)

   - A sequence of two-element tuples

   The function converts its argument to the format `application/x-www-form-urlencoded`. Here's an example:

   ```
   >>> mylist = [('1', 'one'), ('2', 'two'), ('3', 'three')]
   >>> mydata = urllib.urlencode(mylist)
   >>> mydata
   '1=one&2=two&3=three'
   ```

3. **Call** `urllib2.urlopen()` **and pass the data from** `urlencode()` **as the second argument, like this:**

   ```
   x = urllib2.urlopen('http://www.company.com', mydata)
   ```

Taming the Wild URL

The `urlparse` module splits URLs into components, combines components into a URL, and converts a relative URL to an absolute URL.

To split a URL string into components, pass it to the `urlparse()` function. There are two optional parameters for `urlparse()`:

✔ `default_scheme`: Used if the URL doesn't include an addressing scheme, for instance, `'http'`. The default is an empty string (which means it's off).

✔ `allow_fragments`: Allows URLs with elements following a # character (designating a location somewhere inside a page). Defaults to 1, which means to allow them.

The `urlparse()` function returns a six-item tuple of strings containing

1. Addressing scheme (`http` or `ftp`)

2. Network location (`www.python.org`)

3. Path (`/doc/2.4.2/lib/module-urlparse.html`)

4. Parameters (`;type="a"`)

5. Query (`?filter=16400`)

6. Fragment identifier (`#top`)

The tuple items don't include delimiters (colons and slashes), except for a leading slash in the path component. If any of the items isn't part of the URL being parsed, the tuple contains an empty string for that item.

The following example contains an addressing scheme, network location, and path, but doesn't contain parameters, a query, or a fragment identifier:

```
>>> urlparse.urlparse("http://python.org/doc/2.4.2/lib/module-urlparse.html")
('http', 'python.org', '/doc/2.4.2/lib/module-urlparse.html', '', '', '')
```

The `urlparse` module has a couple of other capabilities:

- ✔ To turn a tuple created by `urlparse()` back into an URL string, pass the tuple to `urlunparse()`.
- ✔ To stick together a base URL and a relative URL to create a complete URL, use `urljoin()`. It takes the base URL and relative URL as strings. It also takes the optional `allow_fragments` argument. This example joins a single Web page to its location:

  ```
  >>> urlparse.urljoin('http://python.org/doc/2.4.2/mac/', 'mac.html')
  'http://python.org/doc/2.4.2/mac/mac.html'
  ```

Getting Hip with Hypertext

To read and output HTML-formatted text files and to find links in HTML documents, use the `htmllib` module. It supports all of XHTML 1.0, all of HTML up to 2.0, and much of HTML 3.0 and 3.2.

Of parsers, formatters, and writers

Reading and outputting an HTML file is a three-step process. Here's what's going on inside Python while it's happening:

1. A parser receives information from an HTML-formatted file. This file might be an HTML document you have on disk, or it might be a Web page you've opened with `urllib2.urlopen()` (see "Downloading Web Data," earlier in this chapter).

   When the parser encounters an opening tag, it stores whatever is inside that tag in a buffer until it encounters the matching closing tag.

2. The parser passes the information to a formatter, which reformats it into a human-readable form by reading the HTML tags and applying instructions to them.

3. The formatter passes the reformatted information to a writer, which outputs the information.

Setting up a read-and-output process

The parser, formatter, and writer are all instance objects, so you need to create the instances before they can act. The parser works on the contents of the file or Web page, so you have to open and read a file or Web page before the parser, formatter, and writer can act.

To set up a read-and-output process, follow these steps:

1. **Import the** `htmllib`**,** `formatter`**, and** `StringIO` **modules, like so:**

   ```
   import htmllib, formatter
   from cStringIO import StringIO
   ```

2. **Open an HTML-formatted file:**

   ```
   myfile = open("memo.html", 'rb')
   ```

3. **Read the file:**

   ```
   html = myfile.read()
   ```

4. **Create a writer instance.**

   The simplest writer is `DumbWriter()`, which outputs plain text.

   ```
   dumdum = formatter.DumbWriter(StringIO())
   ```

5. **Create a formatter instance and pass it the writer instance.**

   `AbstractFormatter()` is the most commonly used formatter class.

   ```
   fermat = formatter.AbstractFormatter(dumdum)
   ```

6. **Create an** `HTMLParser` **instance and pass it the formatter instance.**

   ```
   parsley = htmllib.HTMLParser(fermat)
   ```

7. **Feed the file contents to the parser.**

   ```
   parsley.feed(html)
   ```

8. **Close the parser and the file.**

   ```
   parsley.close()
   myfile.close()
   ```

Outputting the links of a Web page

After the parser has read the document, the document's links are available in the data attribute `anchorlist`.

```
>>> parsley.anchorlist
['http://www.portmeirion-village.com/']
```

Getting help for messy HTML

If you have to deal with badly formatted HTML (and there's a lot of it out there), don't despair; a third-party tool can help. It's called Beautiful Soup (after the poem in *Alice's Adventures in Wonderland*), and full details are available at www.crummy.com/software/BeautifulSoup.

The Great XML

Python comes with modules that support Extensible Markup Language (XML), a mechanism for creating structured documents in plain text.

Although we wrote *plain text* above, XML is actually often encoded in UTF-8. See Chapter 6 for details about character encoding.

Both HTML and XML data include *tags* — text surrounded by brackets (<>). But they use tags *differently:*

- In HTML, tags are *specific formatting instructions*. For example, <p> starts a new paragraph and <b> marks boldface type.
- In XML, tags label *kinds of data.*

  An XML tag can also have subtags for kinds of data that are *part* of a larger group — <address> data can include <name> and <street>; <item> data can include <price>, and so on. These tags clarify the data structure, so it's easy for a computer to separate the data into parts.

If XML tags and subtags remind you of Python's classes and their data attributes, you might be on to something. . . .

The ElementTree XML implementation

The best way to use XML in Python is with ElementTree.

- ElementTree is included as xml.etree in Python 2.5.
- ElementTree is available for download from http://effbot.org.zone/element-index.htm if you're using an earlier version of Python.

ElementTree is based on an Element data type, which stores hierarchical data structures (such as XML) in memory.

TECHNICAL STUFF

Ordering up some XML

Here's an application for which XML is useful. Suppose you need to send an order. If you were writing it on a piece of paper, it would look something like this:

```
Order:
Eric Half-a-Bee
123 Main St
Anytown, CA, 95432
Items:
Foo     1     $12     $12
Bar     2     $15     $30
Subtotal: $42
Shipping: $5
Total: $47
```

In XML, it would look something like this:

```
<?xml version="1.0" encoding="ISO-8859-1"?>
<order>
    <recipient>
        <name>Eric Half-a-Bee</name>
        <street>123 Main St</street>
        <city>Anytown</city> <state>CA</state> <zipcode>95432</zipcode>
    </recipient>
    <items>
        <item>
            <prodcode>Foo</prodcode>
            <qty>1</qty> <price>12</price> <total>12</total>
        </item>
        <item>
            <prodcode>Bar</prodcode>
            <qty>2</qty> <price>15</price> <total>30</total>
        </item>
    </items>
    <subtotal>42</subtotal>
    <shipping>5</shipping>
    <total>47</total>
</order>
```

Importing ElementTree

How you import ElementTree depends on your version of Python.

   ✔ In Python 2.5, type this:

```
from xml.etree import ElementTree as ET
```

✔ In earlier versions, after you download ElementTree, type the following:

```
import elementtree.ElementTree as ET
```

(You don't have to use the as ET part, but it will help if you are follow-ing along with our examples.)

Creating an element

An ElementTree structure consists of Element instances.

✔ An Element instance must have a *tag* — a string identifying the element type.

✔ An Element instance can have these options: *attributes, a text string,* and *subelements* (child elements).

To create an element, type ET.Element and pass the tag string as an argu-ment, like this:

```
tree = ET.Element("tree")
```

Element attributes

Element attributes are dictionary key:value pairs. (The keys must be unique.)

Assigning attributes

To assign attributes to an existing element, use the attrib() method, like this:

```
branch = ET.Element("branch")
branch.attrib["one"] = "1"
branch.attrib["two"] = "2"
```

Manipulating attributes

To manipulate attributes, use the following methods, which work a lot like dictionary methods (see Chapter 9):

✔ To assign attributes when creating an element, use keyword arguments, like this:

```
branch = ET.Element("branch", one="1", two="2")
```

✔ To return attribute values, use the get() method with the key:

```
branch.get("one")
```

✔ To get a list of attribute keys, use the keys() method, like so:

```
branch.keys()
```

✔ To get a list of attributes (key:value tuples), use the items() method:

```
branch.items()
```

✔ To set attribute values, use the `set()` method, like this:

```
branch.set("third", "3")
```

✔ To set an element's `text` attribute, assign it a string, like so:

```
branch.text = "this element also contains text"
```

Subelements

Element instances can have subelements, also called child elements.

Creating subelements

There are a couple of different ways to build a tree:

✔ **The** `SubElement()` **function:** You can create subelements and attach them to the parent element by using the `SubElement()` function. The resulting code looks like this:

```
ET.SubElement(tree, "branch")
```

✔ **The** `append()` **method:** You can attach subelements to a parent element with the `append()` method, like this:

```
tree.append(ET.Element("branch"))
```

Subelements (child elements) are stored as a list, so you can access, add, and delete them by using list methods, like this:

```
>>> tree.insert(0, ET.Element("fruit flies"))
```

Searching for subelements

To search for or within subelements, use these methods:

✔ `find(pattern)` returns the first matching subelement.

✔ `findtext(pattern)` returns the value of the text attribute for the first matching subelement.

✔ `findall(pattern)` returns a list of all subelements.

The `pattern` argument in `find()` can be either

✔ **A tag:** If you use a tag, only subelements of that tag are checked.

✔ **A path:** You can use a path to search the entire subtree.

To search the whole tree, use the `getiterator()` method. `getiterator(tag)` returns a list of all subelements with the tag; `getiterator()` (without an argument) returns a list of all subelements in the subtree.

`getiterator()` searches the tree in depth-first order; that is, it searches down one branch to the end, and then down the next branch, and so on.

Using XML files

ElementTree is designed to automatically read XML files, represent their structures, and write them to disk or to a Python file object.

Loading documents

To load an XML document and turn it into an `ElementTree` instance, use the `file` keyword argument to create a tree from a file in a single operation, like this:

```
order = ET.ElementTree(file='order.xml')
```

Writing an Element tree to disk as an XML file

To save an `ElementTree` instance back to disk, use the `write()` method. It takes either a filename or a file object. The output might not be human-readable.

```
order.write(output_file)
```

To save an `Element` structure to disk, use the following code:

```
ET.ElementTree(tree).write(output_file)
```

Other useful XML modules

Python includes a few other XML modules:

- ✔ `xml.dom`: New in Python 2.0. Supports Document Object Model (DOM), a method for reading and modifying XML documents that works in a variety of programming languages.

    DOM creates XML documents in a tree structure and is useful for random-access reading.

- ✔ `xml.dom.minidom`: Supports Document Object Model (DOM) but is simpler and smaller than the full `xml.dom` module.

- ✔ `xml.sax`: This package implements Simple API for XML (SAX). It's good for huge XML documents because it doesn't read the whole thing in one chunk. However, SAX is more difficult to use than the other modules, so we recommend you use it only when you really need it.

MIME-ing Success: Managing E-Mail Messages

The email package is a library that includes tools for reading the text of e-mail messages, transforming messages from text to Python objects and back again, and generating e-mail objects, including MIME documents.

The email package doesn't send messages; the smtplib module sends them.

Representing an e-mail message in Python

In Python, e-mail objects are represented as instances of the Message class. A Message instance has two parts:

- **Message headers:** Addressing information, subject, date, and so on are stored in a dictionary-like format (a mapping), but there are a few differences from dictionaries:

  - Duplicate message headers are possible.

  - Message headers are stored in the order they appeared in the original message.

- **Payload:** The body of the message can be either a *string* (a text-only message) or a *list of* Message *objects* (a multipart message; for instance, a message that has text, HTML, a GIF file, and so on).

Creating e-mail and MIME objects

To build a message structure, you create a Message instance and add attachments and headers.

Creating a Message object

The simplest way to create a Message object is to use the message_from_string() or message_from_file() function.

To create a Message object from a string, use message_from_string(). Pass the function a string or StringIO instance, like this:

```
>>> import email
>>> msg = email.message_from_string(mystring)
```

To create a Message object from a file, use message_from_file(). Pass the function an open file object.

Creating MIME objects via subclasses

The `email` module's MIME submodules are for attaching particular kinds of data, such as formatted text documents, to an e-mail message. The subclasses automatically set up some of the MIME headers for you.

The name of the class is always the same as the name of its corresponding submodule. To import a class from a MIME submodule, type the following line of code (substitute the name of the class/submodule you want to import):

```
from email.MIMEBase import MIMEBase
```

To create an instance of the class after using the preceding import statement, type code like this:

```
mime_msg = MIMEBase(parameters)
```

The following MIME subclasses create messages that include MIME objects.

MIMEMultipart()

The `MIMEMultipart()` subclass is an outer layer for MIME messages that have multiple parts.

To use `Message` objects (or other MIME subclass instances), you can either

✔ Specify the objects as payload subparts when you create an instance of the `MIMEMultipart` subclass.

✔ Add the objects later by using the `Message.attach()` method.

The `MIMEMultiPart` subclass is new in Python 2.2.2.

MIMEBase()

The `MIMEBase()` subclass is for creating MIME messages with message parts that aren't of specific other MIME types (text, audio, or image).

`MIMEBase()` requires two `Content-Type` arguments:

✔ Major type (for example, `application`)
✔ Minor type (for example, `msword`)

If you aren't sure what types to use, import the `mimetypes` module and use the `guess_type()` function, like this:

```
>>> mimetypes.guess_type('foo.doc')
('application/msword', None)
>>> x = email.MIMEBase.MIMEBase('application', 'msword')
```

To attach a Word document to an e-mail message, use the `MimeBase()` subclass:

1. **Import the modules you need, like so:**

   ```
   >>> from email.MIMEBase import MIMEBase
   ```

2. **Open the Word file for reading:**

   ```
   >>> word_file = file('foo.doc', 'rb')
   ```

3. **Read the file, and then close it:**

   ```
   >>> file_contents = word_file.read()
   >>> word_file.close()
   ```

4. **Make a** `MIMEBase()` **object by typing this:**

   ```
   >>> mime_msg = mime_msg = MIMEBase('application', 'msword')
   ```

5. **Set the payload of the** `MIMEBase()` **object:**

   ```
   >>> mime_msg.set_payload(file_contents)
   ```

Specifying a character set

To specify the character set of a payload, use the `set_charset()` method.

The `set_charset()` method argument can be either

- A `Charset()` instance
- A string with the name of a character set
- `None` (which removes the `charset` parameter from the `Content-Type:` header)

The following line specifies the character set using a string:

```
>>> msg.set_charset('ISO-8859-1')
```

Adding and changing message headers

`Message` object headers are stored in a dictionary-like object:

- The header field is the key.
- The content of the header is the value.

To create or change a header, or to add a value, use the key, like this:

```
>>> msg['Subject'] = 'Pictures of My Cat'
```

The `add_header()` method creates a new header, a value, and optional parameters for the value:

```
>>> msg.add_header('MyCat', 'Angus', coat='Tuxedo')
```

The set_param() method sets or changes a parameter in the Content-Type: header, creating the header if it doesn't exist.

Adding content to an existing message

To add a payload to a multipart e-mail message that already has an existing payload, use attach() and pass it a list of Message objects.

If the message doesn't have any payload yet, use set_payload() to add a payload stored as a string.

If the message already has a payload, the set_payload() method replaces it.

Generating MIME documents from message structures

After you have set up an e-mail message as a structure of Python objects, you need to convert it to plain text if you want to send it or print it. This is called *flattening* the message. There are several ways to flatten a message object. We discuss two of them.

Printing a message object as a string

The easiest way to print the text of a message is to use the as_string() method of Message() objects, like so:

```
>>> print littlemsg.as_string()
Date: Wed, 5 Jul 2006 01:04:42 -0700
From: Professor Grue
To: Geography 101 students
Subject: Islands of the world

Farallons:
Seal Rock
Maintop Island
```

Encoding binary data into string data

The Encoders module includes functions for turning binary data into data that can be sent as e-mail. Two of its functions are

- ✔ encode_quopri(): Use for a message that has mostly text but some unprintable characters.

- ✔ encode_base64(): Use for a message that has mostly binary (unprintable) data. The format is more compact than quoted-printable, but humans can't read it.

The encoding functions add a `Content-Transfer-Encoding:` header. They change a message in place and return `None`. To encode the `Message()` object `littlemsg` as base 64, type this code:

```
>>> import email.Encoders
>>> email.Encoders.encode_base64(littlemsg)
>>> print littlemsg
From nobody Wed Jul  5 01:04:42 2006
From: Professor Grue
To: Geography 101 students
Subject: Islands of the world
Content-Transfer-Encoding: base64

RmFyYWxsb25zOgpTZWFsIFJvY2sKTWFpbnRvcCBJc2xhbmQKCgoK
```

Reading e-mail messages

This section shows how Python can read and manipulate existing e-mail messages.

Getting information and payloads

The simplest way to return an e-mail message as a text string is to use the `as_string()` method of a `Message()` instance. To include an envelope header in the string, specify `unixfrom=True` as the argument.

```
mymessage.as_string(unixfrom=True)
```

To find whether the e-mail message has multiple parts, use the `is_multipart()` method. It returns `True` or `False`. `False` means the message is a string.

To see a message's payload, use the `get_payload()` method. If the message is multipart, it returns a list of `Message()` objects. If not, it returns a string.

```
>>> msg.get_payload()
[<email.Message.Message instance at 0x82e26ec>,
<email.Message.Message instance at 0x82e260c>]
>>> littlemsg.get_payload()
'Farallons:\nSeal Rock\nMaintop Island\n
```

Parsing e-mail messages

The classes of the `Parser` module process more complex messages. When you already have the whole message as a string or file, use its "classic" `Parser` class. Follow these steps:

1. **Import the `Parser` module, like so:**

```
>>> import email.Parser
```

2. Create an instance of the `Parser()` **class:**

```
>>> p = email.Parser.Parser()
```

Use the `parse()` method for a file (pass it a file object) or the `parsestr()` method for a string (pass it a string).

The text must be a block of headers followed by the body of the message (which can have MIME-encoded subparts). To read only the headers, pass the optional parameter `headersonly=True`.

```
>>> x = p.parse(fp)
>>> print x
From nobody Wed Jul  5 01:04:42 2006
From: Professor Grue
To: Geography 101 students
Subject: Islands of the world

Farallons:
Seal Rock
Maintop Island
```

Using e-mail utilities

The `email.Utils` module includes the following message tools:

✔ **Functions for managing quotation marks and other delimiters**

- `quote()` takes a string and escapes backslashes and double quotes by preceding them with `\`.

- `unquote()` removes double quotes and angle brackets from the beginning and end of a string.

✔ **Functions for reading address headers**

- `parseaddr()` splits the header into two parts — real name and e-mail address. It returns a tuple.

- `formataddr()` takes the `parseaddr()` tuple and turns it back into a string suitable for an address header.

- `getaddresses()` takes a list of headers and returns a parsed list of addresses found in the headers.

  This code gets all the addresses in a message's `To:` header:

  ```
  from email.Utils import getaddresses
  to_addrs = msg.get_all('to', [])
  to_recips = getaddresses(to_addrs)
  ```

✔ **Tools for working with dates**

- parsedate() reads a date in a message header and returns a nine-item tuple that works with time.mktime() (see Chapter 17). If the date doesn't follow the standard format, parsedate() tries to guess how the date is formatted.

- formatdate() takes a floating point time value (or uses the current time) and returns a date string of the following format:

```
Fri, 09 Nov 2001 01:08:47 -0000
```

✔ **Functions for decoding and encoding character sets**

- decode_rfc2231() decodes a string according to RFC 2231.

- encode_rfc2231() encodes a string and accepts optional character set and language arguments.

- collapse_rfc2231_value() turns a get_param() three-item tuple (character set, language, and value) into a Unicode string.

- decode_params() decodes a list of two-item tuples in the format (content-type, string-value).

Simply SMTP

The email package only generates and processes e-mail messages. To send e-mail messages, you need the smtplib module. SMTP stands for *Simple Mail Transfer Protocol.*

The primary way to use the smtplib module is to create an instance of the SMTP class (its parameter is a hostname); then use the sendmail() and quit() methods in that order. The sendmail() method requires the following arguments:

✔ From-address string

✔ List of to-address strings, or a string containing a single to-address

✔ Message (a text string — usually a flattened email.Message object)

The optional arguments for sendmail() are advanced, and we don't cover them in this book.

The response from sendmail() depends on the following factors:

✔ If the server accepts the mail for at least one of the to-addresses, sendmail() reports success.

✔ If any of the to-addresses didn't receive the message, sendmail() returns a dictionary containing one entry for each recipient who didn't get the mail, along with error codes.

To end the SMTP session and close the connection with the server, use the `quit()` method.

The simplest code for sending a message is the following:

```
import smtplib
server = smtplib.SMTP('localhost')
server.sendmail(fromaddr, toaddrs, msg)
server.quit()
```

CGI: Gateway to the Web

Common Gateway Interface, or CGI, is a standard scripting language for Web sites. CGI scripts work like this:

1. A browser makes a request to a Web server.
2. The Web server executes a CGI script.
3. The CGI script output is returned to the browser as a Web page.

You can write CGI scripts in Python. The `cgi` module includes tools that let your scripts work with Web pages and receive data from form fields. Debugging tools are also provided.

Setting up CGI output in Python

A CGI script usually outputs two sections of text separated by a blank line.

To generate this text from your Python program, use the `print` command:

1. The first section contains headers describing the type of data in the second section. Code for this section might look like this:

```
print "Content-Type: text/html"
```

2. Use an empty `print` command to generate the blank line separator:

```
print
```

3. The second section usually includes HTML-formatted text that generates the Web page, like this:

```
print "<TITLE>Message in a browser</TITLE>"
print "<H1> Hello, world!</H1>"
print "<P> Help! I'm trapped in this Web browser"
print "and I can't get out! </P>"
```

Reading data from Web input

CGI scripts usually process input from a Web form created with the HTML tag `<form>`. Form fields can contain data of various types, but you usually want to treat the data as a string or a file.

Reading data from form fields

To get form data, you create an instance of the `FieldStorage()` class (without arguments):

✔ The instance reads form contents from standard input or from the appropriate environment.

✔ The instance stores data in a dictionary-like structure in which a field name is associated with its value.

Unlike Python dictionaries, instances of the `FieldStorage()` class allow for multiple keys with the same name. They support such methods as `has_key()`, `keys()`, and `len()`. After you've stored the data, the easiest way to get the values out of individual fields is to use the `getfirst()` and `getlist()` methods.

These methods protect against the possibility that a user entered too many values in a field.

getfirst ( )

If a field is supposed to have only one value, use the `getfirst()` method of the `FieldStorage` instance to return a single value. Pass the name of the form field as an argument, like this:

```
addr = form.getfirst("addr")
```

The `getfirst()` method takes an optional parameter specifying what to return if the form field doesn't exist or has no value. It defaults to `None`.

getlist ( )

To return a list of all the values associated with a form field, use the `getlist()` method and pass the name of the form field. If there is only one value in the field, the method returns *a one-item list*. If there are no values or the form field doesn't exist, it returns *an empty list*.

To process the list of values, use a `for` loop, like this:

```
for item in form.getlist("field_header"):
    do_something(item)
```

Maintaining security when using HTML forms

Forms on HTML pages are vulnerable to security problems — malicious code can be entered. If you are planning to use form data in a shell command on your computer (via the `os.system()` function, for example), include tests in your script to make sure the data contains only alphanumeric characters, dashes, underscores, and periods. *Specifically do not allow spaces.*

Whenever possible, use Python functions (for instance, `shutil.move()`) instead of calling `os.system()` with data entered by end users.

Similarly, when sending user-entered data back to the browser, make sure to strip HTML tags, especially if you have a Web site where users can see data entered by other users (such as a blog).

Reading files from form fields

To find whether a field stores a file, test the `file` data attribute of the `FieldStorage` instance with an if statement, like this:

```
fileitem = form["userfile"]
if fileitem.file:
    # do something
```

Setting up and installing a CGI script

Your script must follow certain guidelines to work in the Web environment. The following instructions show how to write and install your script.

Writing a script to work in the Web environment

Type the following code as the *first line* of the script (replace the pathname with the pathname of the Python installation on your Web server):

```
#!/usr/local/bin/python
```

Use absolute paths in your script to access programs or files.

To load modules from a location not on the default Python search path, use `sys.path.insert()` to add their pathnames to `sys.path`. Use 0 as the first argument to have this path searched first. For example, you might type

```
import sys
sys.path.insert(0, "/usr/home/stef/python_modules")
```

Checking for syntax errors

Run your script from the command line to see whether it contains syntax errors. This step makes sure your script contains valid Python code:

```
% python script.py
```

Installing a script and setting permissions

Your CGI script usually goes in the `cgi-bin` directory of your Web server. Check the documentation for your Web host provider to find out any requirements for the script — for example, some ISPs require that all CGI scripts end with `.cgi`.

After you've installed the script in the appropriate directory, you need to set permissions so that users of your Web site can access it. Here's how:

1. **Change the permissions for the script to let the "others" group read and execute the script.**

   On UNIX, the command for giving the "others" group read and execute access is `chmod 0755 scriptname`.

2. **If the script uses any files, change those file permissions so that the "others" group can read or write the files (depending on how the script uses the files).**

   • *Reading the files:* The UNIX command for making files readable by the "others" group is: `chmod 0644 filename`.

   • *Writing the files:* The UNIX command for allowing the "others" group to write to files is `chmod 0666 filename`.

Debugging CGI scripts

CGI scripts don't handle Python's error tracebacks the same way that Python itself does, so you need to follow special procedures for debugging your CGI scripts. The rest of this chapter shows you how.

Check for syntax errors

Before doing any other debugging steps, double-check your script for syntax errors (yes, even if you already did it once). Follow the instructions in "Checking for syntax errors," earlier in this chapter.

Make sure your script is installed correctly

Use these two steps to install and check the script:

1. **Install a copy of the** `cgi.py` **module in the location of your script.**

2. **Run the** `cgi.py` **module by typing code like this into your browser (replacing** `hostname/cgi-bin/` **with the path to your** `cgi-bin` **directory):**

   ```
   http://hostname/cgi-bin/cgi.py?name=My+Name&addr=Cyber
   ```

The results show whether the script is installed in the correct directory:

- ✔ If the directory is correct, some diagnostic text, including the text after the `?` in the above line of code, appears in the Web browser.

- ✔ If you see a 404 error or a message that the page can't be found, then the scripts are installed in the wrong directory.

  You might get a different error if the script is in the right directory but installed incorrectly.

Test your code

If your script doesn't work, and you've verified that it's installed in the correct directory, these steps test your code by using the `cgi.test()` function:

1. **In a text editor,** *comment out* **the main body of your code (put a # character at the beginning of every line) and add this line of code:**

   ```
   cgi.test()
   ```

2. **Run the altered script by typing code like this into your browser (replace** `hostname/cgi-bin/` **with the path to your** `cgi-bin` **directory and replace** `scriptname` **with the name of your script):**

   ```
   http://hostname/cgi-bin/scriptname.py?name=My+Name&addr=Cyber
   ```

   If the diagnostic text and the text after the `?` in the above line of code appears in the Web browser, then the script is installed correctly, and any problems you're having are probably with your script's code.

   If the `cgi.test()` code doesn't work, then the script probably isn't installed correctly. Go back to "Installing a script and setting permissions," earlier in this chapter. You might need to ask your Web hosting company for the path of your `cgi-bin` directory.

Include debugging code in your script

If your script is executing *some* code but works incorrectly, set up your script to display helpful debugging messages. Use one or both of the following methods.

Seeing CGI script errors

The `cgitb` module displays error information for CGI scripts. Import and enable the `cgitb` module by including one of the following code lines near the top of your script, after the `#!/usr/local/bin/python` line:

✔ This line displays errors in the Web browser:

```
import cgitb; cgitb.enable()
```

✔ This line saves errors to a temporary file:

```
import cgitb; cgitb.enable(display=0, logdir="/tmp")
```

Seeing traceback information

If your script isn't working correctly, it might be producing traceback information (the error messages that Python normally prints when you run a program from the command line or from interactive mode). Depending on the configuration of your Web host, the traceback messages sometimes appear in the HTTP server's log files. How you access these files depends on the server setup. Contact the support team for your Web host to find out more.

If you don't want to dig through the log files, you can set up your script so that traceback information is displayed in your Web browser. Include this code near the top of your script:

```
import sys
sys.stderr = sys.stdout
print "Content-Type: text/plain"
print
```

Part V
The Part of Tens

The 5th Wave   By Rich Tennant

"Well, here's your problem. You only have half the ram you need."

In this part . . .

*L*ists, lists, and more lists! *For Dummies* readers know that they can count on the Part of Tens to provide yummy tidbits of information, and this Part of Tens is no different.

In this part, you get ten chunks of code that solve annoying little programming problems in elegant ways; just drop them into your programs. We also show you ten free resources you can use to find out more about Python and hook up with the rest of the Python community.

Chapter 21

Ten Critical Python Idioms

In This Chapter

▶ Playing games with random numbers

▶ Tricks with dicts

▶ The Borg Pattern: Resistance is futile

▶ And other clever timesavers

*H*ere are ten little code snippets that illustrate how to handle some common problems in Python. They are arranged roughly in order of difficulty.

Some of these idioms are from the Python Cookbook, and you'll find more:

```
http://pythoncookbook.activestate.com
```

Collecting Globs and Globs of Files

The glob module provides a single function, also called glob, which lets you get a list of files from a directory (you can also find directory names). The glob function recognizes the same wildcard search characters that the UNIX shell recognizes, except for tilde (~).

On Mac and Unix systems, glob searches are case-sensitive.

Here's how to find all the Word documents (which end with the suffix .doc) in a directory called MyDocs:

```
>>> import glob
>>> docs = glob.glob('MyDocs/*.doc')
  ['MyDocs/helloworld.doc', 'MyDocs/myspider.doc', 'MyDocs/pagecount.doc']
```

The following example finds files beginning with . (a dot). These files aren't found in wildcard searches.

```
>>> glob.glob('.*')
['.hidden_file']
```

Rolling Dice and Shuffling Cards

Python's `random` module is good for generating simple random numbers (and for sophisticated random number problems, but we won't get into that — we're just as eager to avoid statistics as everybody else).

Making a saving throw

Here's a simple dice-roller function. To use it, just call it with an optional integer argument:

```
import random
def roll(d=6):
    return random.randint(1, d)
```

```
>>> roll()      # rolls a 6-sided die
4
>>> roll(20)    # rolls a 20-sided die
17
```

Playing the dealer

Now suppose you have a list representing a deck of cards. Here is some code that would create such a list:

```
def make_deck():
    suits = ['spades', 'hearts', 'diamonds', 'clubs']
    values = ['ace', '2', '3', '4', '5', '6', '7', '8', '9', '10', 'jack',
        'queen', 'king']
    deck = []
    for s in suits:
        for v in values:
            deck.append(v + ' of ' + s)
    return deck
```

To get a single card, run the function to make a deck and pick a card with `random.choice()` like this:

```
>>> deck = make_deck()
>>> random.choice(deck)
'3 of diamonds'
```

If you want to pick a few cards, use `random.shuffle()` and then use the `pop()` method of lists to retrieve cards one at a time.

```
>>> newdeck = make_deck()
>>> random.shuffle(newdeck)
>>> hand = []
>>> for c in range(5):
...     hand.append(newdeck.pop())
...
>>> hand
['5 of diamonds', '6 of diamonds', 'ace of spades', 'ace of
clubs', 'king of hearts']
```

Because `shuffle()` and `pop()` change the list in place, you should make a new deck each time you deal.

In Python 2.2 and earlier, `shuffle()` works well only with small lists. Python 2.3 uses a new random number algorithm so that `shuffle()` to work correctly with lists containing as many as 2,000 elements. But someone forgot to update the docs for Python 2.3 and 2.4; they don't reflect this change.

Uniquely Ordered Lists

Python's set data type makes it easy to find all the unique items in a list. (See Chapter 9 to find out about sets.) But sets don't work well if you want to keep the order of items. This function takes a list and returns a new list containing only its unique items, in the same order as the original list:

```
def unique(items):
    tmp = []
    cache = set()
    for item in items:
        if item not in cache:
            tmp.append(item)
            cache.add(item)
    return tmp
```

If you're concerned about memory usage, you can use a generator version of the preceding function (see Chapter 16):

```
def unique(items):
    cache = set()
    for item in items:
        if item not in cache:
            cache.add(item)
            yield item
```

Here's how they work:

```
>>> menu = ['egg', 'bacon', 'egg', 'sausage', 'bacon', 'egg',
'spam', 'egg', 'bacon', 'spam', 'egg', 'bacon', 'sausage',
'spam', 'spam', 'bacon', 'tomato', 'spam',
'lobster thermidor with truffle pate, brandy, and a fried egg on top',
'spam', 'baked beans']
>>> unique(menu)          # preserves item order
['egg', 'bacon', 'sausage', 'spam', 'tomato', 'lobster thermidor with truffle
pate, brandy, and a fried egg on top', 'baked beans']
```

Reversing Your Way to Success

The `unique` function in the previous section keeps the first item it finds and throws away subsequent duplicates. What if you want the last matching item? Most of the time, adding the double-reverse technique does what you want:

```
my_data.reverse()
my_data = unique(my_data)
my_data.reverse()
```

Note that the `sort()` method of lists and the `sorted()` built-in function, which puts list items in alphanumeric order, both have a `reverse` parameter (new in Python 2.4). See Chapter 8 for the lowdown on `sort()` and `sorted()`.

Exceptional Type-Testing

Sometimes it's a good idea to check the type of data that is being put into your function to make sure it's the type of data you want. You can use `isinstance()` or `issubclass()` to do this. But that's not the ideal test for code that's intended to work with user-defined classes based on built-in data types. Python's duck-typing (see Chapter 13) makes it possible to create an object that has an `append` method, for example, that isn't an instance or subclass of the list data type. This object might work in your function but would not pass the `isinstance()` or `issubclass()` test.

If you want your function to process such objects, it's better to use a `try`/`except` block to verify that the object *behaves* the way you need it to. For example, you might test whether an object supports the `append()` and `pop()` methods and whether it allows indexing. (If so, there's a good chance it will support other list operations.) Here's a code block that performs such a test:

```
def foo(l):
    try:
        l.append('foo')
        l[0]
        l.pop()
    except StandardError:
        raise TypeError("Not a valid list object: %r" % l)
```

This code catches `StandardError` in the `except` statement. `StandardError` is the class from which almost all exceptions derive (except for `SystemExit` and `KeyboardInterrupt`). Catching it also catches any exception that derives from it. We then translate the exception into a `TypeError` for the purpose of logging the result or printing a message.

Use this checking only with critical code. Usually, this level of checking is overkill, and you can assume that your users will follow the documentation you provided with your function (you did provide documentation, right?).

Classes Just for Data

Python class instances are a lot like dicts — both can store keys and associated values. In fact, in many ways, instances are simply a thin wrapper around dicts, and attribute syntax is easier to read than dict syntax.

```
foo.bar    # a class attribute
foo['bar'] # a dictionary key
```

Python programmers commonly create classes with no methods (a *data-only class*) for manipulating key/value data. Here's a class that makes it easy to initialize the class instance with some values (courtesy of Alex Martelli):

```
class Bunch:
    def __init__(self, **kwargs):
        self.__dict__.update(kwargs)
```

When creating the instance, you just pass it one or more keyword arguments. In this example, we create an instance of `Bunch` and store the current working directory by using the keyword `start_dir`:

```
>>> import os
>>> config = Bunch(start_dir=os.getcwd())
>>> config.start_dir
'/Users/firecat'
```

For more info about `Bunch`, see this Web page, part of the Python Cookbook:

```
http://aspn.ActiveState.com/ASPN/Cookbook/Python/Recipe/52308
```

Getting Close Enough with difflib

People often make mistakes when entering text. The `difflib` module gives you a way to find strings that are close but not exact matches to a given string:

```
>>> import difflib
>>> right = 'The quick brown fox'
>>> wrong = 'THe quack brown fix'
>>> matcher = difflib.SequenceMatcher(None, right, wrong)
>>> print matcher.ratio()
0.842105263158
```

The `ratio()` method returns a floating point number between 0 and 1 that indicates how close the match is. Higher numbers indicate a closer match. A match higher than 0.6 is usually considered "good" (maybe not by medieval manuscript-illuminating monks, but good enough for the modern world).

To compare a single word against a list of words, use the `difflib` module's `get_close_matches()` method. It finds the words with the highest match ratio:

```
>>> import difflib
>>> mylist = ['quick', 'quack', 'quark', 'quart']
>>> difflib.get_close_matches('quote', mylist)
['quart']
```

DSU! DSU! Rah rah DSU!

DSU stands for "decorate, sort, undecorate," and it's a clever trick for sorting sequence objects by one of their elements.

This use of the word *decorate* doesn't have anything to do with the *decorator* feature discussed in Chapter 16. Python has just gotten so big that it's having to recycle the words it uses to describe tools!

Suppose you have a list of address tuples, like this:

```
addresses = [
            ('123 Main St', 'Anytown', '12345'),
            ('123 Second St', 'Othertown', '54321'),
            ('456 Second St', 'Nowhereville', '11111'),
            ('777 Morris St', 'Filenes Basement', '99999')
            ]
```

Now suppose you want to sort them by zip code. The sort() method of lists lets you pass a comparison function, but we don't recommend that because it's clumsy and slow. A better way is to create a new list that is *decorated* with the zip field, so that each tuple becomes a 2-tuple where the first element is the zip code and the second element is the old tuple:

```
('12345', ('123 Main St', 'Anytown', '12345') )
```

After you have the list of 2-tuples, you can sort the list and then *undecorate* it (remove the extra zip field).

These two functions do DSU on such a list. The first one uses a list comprehension to create the tmp list and the return value. (See Chapter 16 for more on list comprehensions.)

```
def dsu_zip(addresses):
    tmp = [(x[2], x) for x in addresses]
    tmp.sort()
    return [x[1] for x in tmp]
```

Here's what happens when you run the function:

```
>>> dsu_zip(addresses)
[('456 Second St', 'Nowhereville', '11111'), ('123 Main St',
'Anytown', '12345'), ('123 Second St', 'Othertown', '54321'),
('777 Morris St', 'Filenes Basement', '99999')]
```

There's another way to perform a DSU sort. Python 2.4 adds a new key parameter to the sort() method and the sorted() built-in function. Use this with the itemgetter() class from the operator module for a simpler DSU-type solution:

```
>>> import operator
>>> third_item = operator.itemgetter(2)  # get 3rd item from tuple
>>> addresses.sort(key=third_item)
>>> addresses
[('456 Second St', 'Nowhereville', '11111'), ('123 Main St',
'Anytown', '12345'), ('123 Second St', 'Othertown', '54321'),
('777 Morris St', 'Filenes Basement', '99999')]
```

The key parameter requires a function, which itemgetter() supplies. A similar attrgetter() function works with class instances to retrieve attribute values based on their names.

Simplifying Choices Using Dicts

Typing lots of `if`/`elif`/`else` statements can get rather tedious, as the following example shows. In the example code, `account_type` is a string and `CheckingAccount`, `SavingsAccount`, and `GenericAccount` are classes or functions (for this purpose it doesn't matter which):

```
if account_type == 'checking':
    new_account = CheckingAccount()
elif account_type == 'savings':
    new_account = SavingsAccount()
else:
    new_account = GenericAccount()
```

If you're checking a single expression against a bunch of constants, as in the preceding code, using a dict to store the constants makes more sense:

```
accounts = {
            'checking': CheckingAccount,
            'savings': SavingsAccount,
           }
new_account = accounts.get(account_type, GenericAccount)()
```

The preceding line of code contains a few useful techniques:

✔ The `get()` method of dicts lets you specify a value to return if the key isn't found. Here, if the account type isn't in the `accounts` dict, the `get()` method returns `GenericAccount`.

✔ `CheckingAccount` and `SavingsAccount` don't have parentheses after them inside the dict because they're being stored rather than called.

✔ The set of parentheses at the end of the line after the `get()` call specify that the function or class that `get()` returns should be called.

Singles Going Steady

Sometimes you want to make sure that there is only one of an object (called a *singleton*) within your program. A common example might be an object that holds configuration info. There are two standard ways to do this in Python: creating a singleton object and creating a Borg Pattern.

Using a singleton object

One way to make sure you have a unique object is to create a type of object that's a always a singleton. Python has two: modules and classes. (*Classes* are singletons, but instances aren't.) The following example creates a class called `Config` and stores an attribute in it. You can't create another `Config` class in your module, so you can be sure that `Config.start_dir` is unique.

```
class Config:
    pass

config.start_dir = os.getcwd()
```

Calling in the Borg Pattern

You can make a special kind of class so that all of its instances share the same state (which makes them functionally identical). That means whatever you do to one instance is also done to all the other instances.

To create this class, use the following brilliant code from Alex Martelli called the *Borg Pattern:*

```
class Config:
    __shared_state = {}
    def __init__(self):
        self.__dict__ = self.__shared_state
```

Here's what happens when you test it. This code shows that the two `Borg` instances are different objects (they are stored in different locations):

```
>>> borg1 = Config()
>>> borg2 = Config()
>>> borg1
<__main__.config instance at 0x584e0>
>>> borg2
<__main__.config instance at 0x584b8>
```

This code shows that both instances share state — when an attribute is assigned to `borg2`, the same attribute now exists in `borg1`.

```
>>> borg2.start_dir = os.getcwd()
>>> print borg2.start_dir
/Users/firecat/StefPythonProgs
>>> print borg1.start_dir
/Users/firecat/StefPythonProgs
```

For more about the Borg Pattern, see

```
http://aspn.ActiveState.com/ASPN/Cookbook/Python/Recipe/66531
```

Chapter 22

Ten Great Resources

his chapter lists ten resources to check out to find out more about Python, to get more help with your programs, and to get involved with the Python community.

The Mothership: www.python.org

The Python mothership on the Web is docked at www.python.org. If you have questions about Python, you should go here first. It includes the latest versions of Python for download, along with documentation, FAQs, introductions, tutorials, a Wiki (an encyclopedia-type structure that anyone can edit), mailing list archives, announcements, links to third-party modules, and more.

A search box is available on most of the main pages of python.org. If you want to search specific parts of the site or specify lots of search criteria, use the search page, available here:

```
www.python.org/search/
```

The following sections highlight important parts of the python.org Web site.

We're glad you asked that: Python FAQs

Python FAQs (Frequently Asked Questions) and a Spanish translation can be found at http://python.org/doc/faq/. The FAQs cover such topics as

✔ What Python is, how to get a copy, who uses it and for what, and Python's design philosophy

- How-tos for common programming tasks
- Installing and using third-party libraries
- Writing extensions to Python in other languages
- Python's behavior in Windows
- Graphical User Interface (GUI) programming

Official documentation

You can always find the documentation for the latest version of Python at www.python.org/doc/current/. Documentation for earlier versions of Python is also available. You can view the docs on the Web site or download them in a variety of formats.

In addition to the docs for specific versions, you can find general guides covering a variety of subjects:

- Beginner's guides (for people who haven't programmed before)
- Introductions to Python (some for people who have used other languages and some for beginners; tutorials are also included)
- A PythonInfo Wiki — a collection of pages that anyone can edit
- Topic guides — articles about databases, parsers, scientific uses of Python, Web programming, XML, and more
- A list of books and reviews of books written about Python, organized by topic

Python Enhancement Proposals (PEPs) are documents of the process of adding new features to Python. An archive of PEPs for features added to previous versions of Python is available. PEPs aren't documentation per se, but they usually include an explanation of a feature's benefits, which can be very helpful for understanding its uses. Summaries of arguments for and against the feature shed light on the philosophy behind the Python language. An index of PEPs is here:

```
www.python.org/dev/peps/
```

If you're a history buff, you'll like PEPs because they include background information about how proposals developed.

tutor@python.org and help@python.org

The Tutor mailing list is for beginning and intermediate Python programmers to ask and answer each other's questions. Its Web page is here:

```
http://mail.python.org/mailman/listinfo/tutor/
```

You can post a message to it by sending e-mail to tutor@python.org. We recommend that if you post a message, you also subscribe to the list! You can do so via a form on the above Web page.

Tutor mailing list archives are at http://mail.python.org/pipermail/tutor/. When you use the search box on the Python home page, you get results from the Tutor Archives as well as from other pages on the site.

If you have a question that you want answered privately, and you can't find information about it by searching the Python Web site, you can send e-mail to help@python.org, which is staffed by volunteer Python experts.

The comp.lang.python Newsgroup

The comp.lang.python Usenet newsgroup is the main source for a variety of discussions about Python. Both beginners and advanced programmers post to the group, and contents include examination of programming problems, discussions of Python compared with other languages, discussions (often vociferous!) of proposed new Python features, and more.

You can read comp.lang.python either with netnews software or as a mailing list. Because it receives hundreds of posts a day, we recommend reading it via Usenet; news-reading software generally handles complex message threading better than e-mail software.

Cheese Shop: Online Collection of Python Modules

Cheese Shop, formerly called PyPI, maintains a collection of third-party Python modules. It lives on the python.org Web site. Its home page is here:

```
http://cheeseshop.python.org/
```

As of this writing, it contains 1,429 packages. Most of them are available for free (but check the licensing scheme before you distribute them or use them in commercial applications). You can search packages by name or by keyword, and you can browse a list of packages organized by topic and by type (for example, you can browse for packages that work on a particular operating system). You can also submit your own packages.

Cheese Shop is named after the Monty Python sketch of the same name, in which a customer discovers that the cheese shop doesn't, in fact, have any cheese for sale at all.

Random Access Reference at wiki.python.org

The Web page `http://wiki.python.org/` contains links to two Wikis: the Python Wiki (for Python) and the Jython Wiki. (Jython is Python for Java.)

A Wiki is a collection of Web pages that anyone can edit. Wikis usually make heavy use of hyperlinks, and you gather information by jumping from one page to another as you find linked topics that interest you.

The front page for the Python Wiki contains a list of starting points for jumping in. This includes a Code page that lists bits of useful code that are too small to count as modules. One of the items on the Code page extracts a useful bit of information about string formatting that's buried in the official documentation for sequence types:

```
http://wiki.python.org/moin/StringFormatting/
```

The Python Wiki is a work in progress and doesn't include all the information available on other pages of the `python.org` Web site. But it does contain some information that isn't available on other parts of the site. It can be a good place to explore if you like to learn by ingesting small chunks of information. As you become more comfortable with Python, you might want to contribute your own pages.

The Python Cookbook Web Site

The Python Cookbook, part of the ActiveState Programmer Network Web site, collects a variety of recipes, or short bits of code or programs that perform particular tasks and can be freely used in your own programs. The home page is here:

```
http://aspn.activestate.com/ASPN/Cookbook/Python/
```

Editors review submissions to the Cookbook, and you have the option of searching the editors' favorites, approved, and not-approved recipes. The recipes are periodically collected into a dead-trees book.

Each recipe is displayed on its own page with a description, source code, and discussion. Members of ASPN can add comments to the page.

The Latest News

The Python newsgroup `comp.lang.python` is an excellent resource for finding out about Python and joining in the community. But if you don't have time to read 200+ posts every day, you can find out what's going on in the Python community in the following ways.

Dr. Dobbs' Python-URL

Dr. Dobbs' Python-URL is a weekly summary of hot topics in `comp.lang.python` and other doings. It's posted weekly to `comp.lang.python` and `comp.lang.python.announce`.

You can get past issues from Google Groups, an archive of Usenet newsgroup postings. Go to `http://groups.google.com/groups/` and type `dr dobbs python-url!` in the Search box.

Daily Python URL

Daily Python URL is a blog (*Web log*) from `pythonware.com` that includes links to news about Python, additions to the Cheese Shop module library, and more. Read it here:

```
www.pythonware.com/daily/
```

comp.lang.python.announce

The `comp.lang.python.announce` newsgroup is a moderated forum for Python-related announcements. Availability of new modules and programs and requests for comments on Python Enhancement Proposals (PEPs) are posted here. This newsgroup receives only a few messages a day, so it's easier to keep up with than `comp.lang.python`.

Being a PUG-nosed PIGgie: Local User Groups

Python user groups gather in what computer nerds call "meatspace" in cities throughout the world. Such groups welcome beginners and provide demonstrations, lectures, and time for questions and socializing. (Sometimes you get free food, too!) The groups often have the acronym *PIG* ("Python Interest Group") or *PUG* ("Python User Group") in their names.

A list of local user groups can be found on the Python Wiki here:

```
http://wiki.python.org/moin/LocalUserGroups/
```

The Python Wiki might not be up-to-date, so if you don't see a group in your area, be sure to search the Web and/or post to `comp.lang.python` to see if others know of a group there.

Many local user groups maintain mailing lists in which you can read announcements about local meetings and participate in discussions about Python. Some of the groups have archives of past messages that are available to non-subscribers so you can check out whether the group meets your needs.

Part VI

Appendixes

The 5th Wave   By Rich Tennant

In this part . . .

If you weren't lucky enough to have Python already installed on your computer, Appendix A shows you how to download and set up Python for your operating system.

Appendix B describes the new features in each new version of Python starting with Python 2.0.

Appendix A

Getting and Installing Python

• •

In This Appendix

▶ Installing and using Python on Windows, Mac OS, and UNIX

▶ Using embedded Python

• •

*T*his Appendix contains instructions for installing Python and its modules, the Python development environment (IDLE), and Python documentation on the three major operating systems: Windows, Mac OS, and UNIX. This chapter also provides tips for using Python when it is embedded in your application.

All versions of Python are available for download here:

    www.python.org/download

Operating Systems

To install Python on your Windows, Mac OS, or UNIX computer, follow the instructions in the appropriate subsection below.

Windows

You can find out whether Python is already installed on your Windows system. If you haven't already installed Python, or if you have an older version of it, we show you how to install the latest version.

Checking for Python

There are three ways to find out whether Python is installed on your Windows system:

- ✔ Look for Python in the Start menu.
- ✔ Use the Search command to search for `python.exe`.
- ✔ Type `python` in the Command Prompt window.

Installing Python documentation

If you are using Python and you see a message that documentation was not found, you can download the docs from the `python.org` site and then set the PYTHONDOCS environmental variable to the directory you stored them in.

The Python 2.5 docs are available in either CHM (a help format for Windows) or HTML format from this Web page:

`www.python.org/download/releases/2.5/`

When you find where `python.exe` is stored, add the path to that directory to your computer's PATH variable. How you do this depends on your Windows version.

Adding a directory to the PATH variable for Windows XP, 2000, and NT

If your computer uses Windows XP, 2000, or NT, follow these steps to add the Python directory to the PATH variable:

1. **Right-click My Computer and select Properties from the pop-up menu.**

2. **On the Advanced tab, click the Environment Variables button.**

3. **Add the following string to the PATH environment variable (substitute the name of your Python directory — ours was** `C:\Program Files\Python25`**):**

```
;C:\python directory
```

Adding a directory to the PATH variable for Windows ME, 98, and 95

On older versions of Windows, edit the `C:\AUTOEXEC.BAT` file to include the following line (substituting your Python directory):

```
PATH C:\python directory;%PATH%
```

Installation

All versions of Python are available for download here:

```
www.python.org/download
```

Starting with Python 2.4, the Windows Python installer is a Windows Installer (`.msi`) package. Most systems already have MSI installed.

If your Windows system doesn't have the Windows Installer program, you can download it from www.microsoft.com/downloads/. For the best installation experience, follow these rules when installing Python from the MSI file:

✔ If you're an admin user, you have the option to either Install for All Users or Install Just for Me. Select the Install for All Users option.

✔ Follow these steps to make Python start faster:

   1. When you see the Customize Python screen, shown in Figure A-1, click the Advanced button.

   The Advanced Options screen opens.

   2. On the Advanced Options screen, select Compile .py Files to Byte Code after Installation.

✔ Install all the files that come with Python.

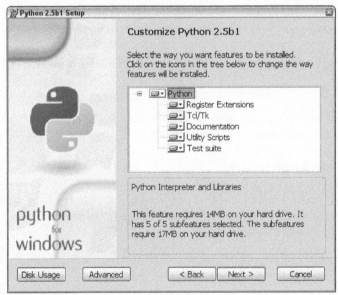

Figure A-1:
The Customize Python screen of the Windows Python installer.

Working with IDLE

Python's own development environment, called IDLE (Integrated DeveLopment Environment), is automatically installed along with Python. To start IDLE, select it from the Start menu, or right-click a Python file and select Edit with IDLE.

Chapter 2 shows how to use IDLE.

Mac OS X

The latest versions of Mac OS X (10.3 and later) already have Python installed. This section shows you how to check which version is installed and how to download the latest version without messing up the preinstalled version.

We also provide instructions for installing Python on pre–OS X Macs.

Finding out which Python is installed

Mac OS X 10.3 and 10.4 come with Python already installed.

To check whether Python is installed on your Mac, follow these steps:

1. **Open the Terminal application (in Applications/Utilities).**

2. **Type** `python` **at the command prompt and press Return.**

   ```
   % python
   ```

   If Python is installed, you'll see something like this. The Python version appears on the first line (version 2.3.5 in this example):

   ```
   Python 2.3.5 (#1, Mar 20 2005, 20:38:20)
   [GCC 3.3 20030304 (Apple Computer, Inc. build 1809)] on darwin
   Type "help", "copyright", "credits" or "license" for more information.
   >>>
   ```

If Python isn't installed, or if you want to install a later version of Python, the sidebar "Downloading the latest Mac version" shows you how.

Using the latest version

MacPython is automatically installed in a different location than Apple's pre-installed Python. The result is that after you install it, typing `python` into the Terminal window still starts up Apple's preinstalled version. There are several ways to use the new version:

✔ Open it from the Terminal window by typing the following:

   ```
   % /usr/local/bin/python
   ```

✔ Add `/usr/local/bin/` to your PATH environment variable.

   Make sure it comes before `/usr/bin/`. (The way you do this depends on the shell you're using.) If you do this, then

   • The new Python version starts automatically when you type `python`.

   • You can start the old version by typing `/usr/bin/python`.

✔ Start IDLE (see Figure A-2). IDLE is installed in the MacPython folder in Applications. For more about IDLE, see Chapter 2.

   Both programs support Python interactive mode.

Downloading the latest Mac version

We encourage you to install the MacPython package:

✔ It's a later version of Python than Apple's preinstalled Python.

✔ It contains tools that aren't part of Apple's preinstalled Python (including the IDLE development environment).

The universal installer for MacPython 2.5 works on Mac OS X 10.3 and later on PPC and Intel Macs.

The Mac OS X download is a .dmg (disk image) file. It's available from this page:

www.python.org/download/releases/2.5

To install MacPython, download the .dmg file, double-click it to mount it, and then double-click the MacPython.mpkg file to start the installer. Follow the instructions on-screen.

Figure A-2:
The MacPython IDLE application.

Don't delete the preinstalled version or install a new version in /usr/bin/ python. Some of the Mac OS system software relies on the preinstalled version of Python.

Installing Python on older Mac operating systems

To install Python on Mac operating system version 10.2 and earlier, follow the instructions at this URL:

www.python.org/download/mac/

You may need to install the Tkinter and Tcl/TkAqua packages (which in turn might need other packages) in order to use IDLE on versions of OS X earlier than 10.4. The documentation at http://tcltkaqua.sourceforge.net shows you how to install these packages.

UNIX and Linux

Many UNIX and Linux installations already include Python. If Python isn't installed on your system, you may be able to install it by using your system's package manager. To install from source instead, follow these steps:

1. **Download the source file for your system:**

   All versions of Python are available for download here:

   www.python.org/download/

   • If your operating system supports `bzip2` files, you can download the `tar.bz2` file.

   `tar.bz2` files are smaller than `tgz` (gzipped) files, so they download faster.

   • If your system doesn't support `bzip2`, download the `tgz` file.

2. **Unpack the file:**

   • If you have the `tgz` file, type `tar -zxv python-2.5.tgz`.

   Replace `2.5` with the version number of the Python package you're installing.

   • If you have the `tar.bz2` file, type `tar-xjvf python-2.5.tar.bz2`.

   Replace `2.5` with the version number of the Python package you're installing.

   If you get errors unpacking, try installing the GNU tar utility.

3. **Change to the directory that was created when you unpacked the file.**

4. **Run these commands to compile and install Python:**

```
./configure
make
make install
```

   If you already have Python installed on your system, use `make altinstall` rather than `make install`.

If Python is preinstalled on your UNIX or Linux system, don't *delete* it. Make sure to install a newer version in a different location. Many UNIX distributions rely on Python for their system scripts.

Using Embedded Python

If you have an application that uses Python as its scripting language, you're in luck! Python makes it easy to customize your application.

You'll be able to use the full power of the Python language as described in this book, but there are some issues to be aware of:

- ✔ **The embedded Python might not include all the standard Python modules.** You won't be able to use the modules that aren't included in scripts for your application.

- ✔ **You won't be able to upgrade the embedded version of Python.** You'll have to wait for an upgrade to the application itself.

   You can still install a newer version of Python elsewhere on your system. But be sure not to overwrite the version that the application uses.

- ✔ **You may want to test your scripts outside the application.** Depending on how the application is set up, a mistake in your script could cause the application to crash or hang.

Appendix B

Python Version Differences

. . . .

In This Appendix

▶ Differences between Python versions

▶ Importing new features from the __future__ module

. . . .

*T*his Appendix describes the new features in each version of Python going back to 2.0. If you don't have the latest version, check out this Appendix to find out what features you have access to. The list of goodies will also encourage you to upgrade!

Each new version of Python adds features. Some of the modules and packages added to a particular version of Python can be used with earlier versions by downloading the modules or packages from the Web. We've given the URL for the module or package when appropriate, but because Web sites change, you should look around if these URLs don't work.

Some features must be imported from the __future__ module in the version that first introduces them. Usually in the next version, you no longer have to import from __future__. Exceptions are noted in the following lists.

Python 2.5

New features in Python 2.5 include

- **Many performance improvements**
- **Conditional expressions:** X if C else Y (Chapter 16)
- **Absolute imports:** Use from __future__ import absolute_import. (Chapter 12)
- **Updated exception hierarchy** (Chapter 16)
- with **statement** (Chapter 16)
- **Unified** try-except **and** try-finally **to** try-except-finally (Chapter 15)

- ✔ **Boolean functions** `any()` **and** `all()` (Chapter 10)

- ✔ **Generators have** `send()`, `throw()`, **and** `close()` **methods**

- ✔ `__index__` **special method**

- ✔ `partition()` **and** `rpartition()` **string methods**

- ✔ `sqlite3` **package** (`http://pysqlite.org`) (Chapter 19)

- ✔ `ctypes` **package** (`http://starship.python.net/crew/theller/ctypes`)

- ✔ `ElementTree` **package** (`http://effbot.org/zone/element-index.htm`) (Chapter 20)

Python 2.4

New features in Python 2.4 include

- ✔ **Built-in** `set` **and** `frozenset` **objects** (rather than the `sets` module) (Chapter 9)

- ✔ **Generator expressions** (Chapter 16)

- ✔ **Function/method decorator syntax** (Chapter 16)

- ✔ `reversed()` **built-in function** (Chapter 8)

- ✔ `sorted()` **built-in function** (Chapter 8)

- ✔ `subprocess` **module** (`http://www.lysator.liu.se/~astrand/popen5/` or the Windows version at `http://effbot.org/downloads/#subprocess`) (Chapter 17)

- ✔ `cookielib` **library supports client-side handling for HTTP cookies** (`http://wwwsearch.sourceforge.net/ClientCookie/`)

- ✔ `Decimal` **package for true decimal (calculator) arithmetic** (`www.taniquetil.com.ar/facundo/bdvfiles/get_decimal.html`) (Chapter 7)

Python 2.3

New features in Python 2.3 include

- ✔ **Extended slices:** Sequences now support step argument (Chapter 10)

- ✔ **New built-in type,** `bool`, **with two constants,** `False` **and** `True` (Chapter 10)

✔ **Ability to import Python modules from zip archives** (Chapter 19)

✔ **Universal newline support** (Chapter 17)

✔ **Improved** in **operator for string searches (allows multicharacter substrings)**

✔ **Python files can be in arbitrary encodings**

✔ **Unicode filename support for Windows NT/XP**

✔ **IDLE runs code in subprocess**

✔ **Sockets support timeouts**

✔ enumerate() **built-in function** (Chapter 16)

✔ sum() **built-in function**

✔ datetime **module** (Chapter 17): Use mxDateTime in earlier versions or download datetime.py from this Web page: http://svn.python.org/view/sandbox/trunk/datetime/.

✔ itertools **module** (Chapter 16)

✔ sets **module** (Chapter 9)

✔ timeit **module** (Chapter 17)

✔ logging **package** (www.red-dove.com/python_logging.html) (Chapter 17)

Python 2.2

New features in Python 2.2 include

✔ **True division (float division) for** / **operator:** Use // for integer (floor) division. To activate these features, use from __future__ import division. True division requires a __future__ statement in Python 2.X; this will change in Python 3.0. (Chapter 7)

✔ **Iterators and generators:** For generators, use from __future__ import generators. (Chapter 16)

✔ **Very large** int **type numbers automatically converted to** long (Chapter 7)

✔ **New-style classes** (Chapter 17)

✔ help() **available in interactive mode** (Chapter 2)

Python 2.1

Features new in Python 2.1 include

- **Rich comparisons**
- **Nested scopes:** Use `from __future__ import nested_scopes`. (Chapter 11)
- `doctest` **module** (Chapter 17)

Python 2.0

Features new in Python 2.0 include

- **Native Unicode support** (Chapter 6)
- **List comprehensions** (Chapter 16)
- **Augmented assignment** (Chapter 7)
- **String methods** (Chapter 6)
- **Improved memory management through automatic "garbage collection"**
- `zip()` **function** (Chapter 8)
- `print` **command can print to any file-like object, not just** `sys.stdout`
- **Function calls accept** `*args/**kwargs` (Chapter 11)

Index

• J •

• K •

• L •

• *M* •

BUSINESS, CAREERS & PERSONAL FINANCE

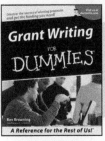

Grant Writing FOR DUMMIES
A Reference for the Rest of Us!
0-7645-5307-0

Home Buying FOR DUMMIES
A Reference for the Rest of Us!
0-7645-5331-3 *†

Also available:
- Accounting For Dummies †
  0-7645-5314-3
- Business Plans Kit For Dummies †
  0-7645-5365-8
- Cover Letters For Dummies
  0-7645-5224-4
- Frugal Living For Dummies
  0-7645-5403-4
- Leadership For Dummies
  0-7645-5176-0
- Managing For Dummies
  0-7645-1771-6

- Marketing For Dummies
  0-7645-5600-2
- Personal Finance For Dummies *
  0-7645-2590-5
- Project Management For Dummies
  0-7645-5283-X
- Resumes For Dummies †
  0-7645-5471-9
- Selling For Dummies
  0-7645-5363-1
- Small Business Kit For Dummies *†
  0-7645-5093-4

HOME & BUSINESS COMPUTER BASICS

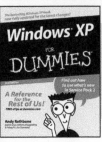

Windows XP FOR DUMMIES
A Reference for the Rest of Us!
0-7645-4074-2

Microsoft Office Excel 2003 ALL-IN-ONE DESK REFERENCE FOR DUMMIES
9 BOOKS IN 1
0-7645-3758-X

Also available:
- ACT! 6 For Dummies
  0-7645-2645-6
- iLife '04 All-in-One Desk Reference
  For Dummies
  0-7645-7347-0
- iPAQ For Dummies
  0-7645-6769-1
- Mac OS X Panther Timesaving
  Techniques For Dummies
  0-7645-5812-9
- Macs For Dummies
  0-7645-5656-8

- Microsoft Money 2004 For Dummies
  0-7645-4195-1
- Office 2003 All-in-One Desk Reference
  For Dummies
  0-7645-3883-7
- Outlook 2003 For Dummies
  0-7645-3759-8
- PCs For Dummies
  0-7645-4074-2
- TiVo For Dummies
  0-7645-6923-6
- Upgrading and Fixing PCs For Dummies
  0-7645-1665-5
- Windows XP Timesaving Techniques
  For Dummies
  0-7645-3748-2

FOOD, HOME, GARDEN, HOBBIES, MUSIC & PETS

Feng Shui FOR DUMMIES
A Reference for the Rest of Us!
0-7645-5295-3

Poker FOR DUMMIES
A Reference for the Rest of Us!
0-7645-5232-5

Also available:
- Bass Guitar For Dummies
  0-7645-2487-9
- Diabetes Cookbook For Dummies
  0-7645-5230-9
- Gardening For Dummies *
  0-7645-5130-2
- Guitar For Dummies
  0-7645-5106-X
- Holiday Decorating For Dummies
  0-7645-2570-0
- Home Improvement All-in-One
  For Dummies
  0-7645-5680-0

- Knitting For Dummies
  0-7645-5395-X
- Piano For Dummies
  0-7645-5105-1
- Puppies For Dummies
  0-7645-5255-4
- Scrapbooking For Dummies
  0-7645-7208-3
- Senior Dogs For Dummies
  0-7645-5818-8
- Singing For Dummies
  0-7645-2475-5
- 30-Minute Meals For Dummies
  0-7645-2589-1

INTERNET & DIGITAL MEDIA

Digital Photography FOR DUMMIES
A Reference for the Rest of Us!
0-7645-1664-7

Starting an eBay Business FOR DUMMIES
A Reference for the Rest of Us!
0-7645-6924-4

Also available:
- 2005 Online Shopping Directory
  For Dummies
  0-7645-7495-7
- CD & DVD Recording For Dummies
  0-7645-5956-7
- eBay For Dummies
  0-7645-5654-1
- Fighting Spam For Dummies
  0-7645-5965-6
- Genealogy Online For Dummies
  0-7645-5964-8
- Google For Dummies
  0-7645-4420-9

- Home Recording For Musicians
  For Dummies
  0-7645-1634-5
- The Internet For Dummies
  0-7645-4173-0
- iPod & iTunes For Dummies
  0-7645-7772-7
- Preventing Identity Theft For Dummies
  0-7645-7336-5
- Pro Tools All-in-One Desk Reference
  For Dummies
  0-7645-5714-9
- Roxio Easy Media Creator For Dummies
  0-7645-7131-1

* Separate Canadian edition also available
† Separate U.K. edition also available

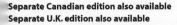

WILEY

SPORTS, FITNESS, PARENTING, RELIGION & SPIRITUALITY

0-7645-5146-9

0-7645-5418-2

Also available:

- Adoption For Dummies
  0-7645-5488-3
- Basketball For Dummies
  0-7645-5248-1
- The Bible For Dummies
  0-7645-5296-1
- Buddhism For Dummies
  0-7645-5359-3
- Catholicism For Dummies
  0-7645-5391-7
- Hockey For Dummies
  0-7645-5228-7

- Judaism For Dummies
  0-7645-5299-6
- Martial Arts For Dummies
  0-7645-5358-5
- Pilates For Dummies
  0-7645-5397-6
- Religion For Dummies
  0-7645-5264-3
- Teaching Kids to Read For Dummies
  0-7645-4043-2
- Weight Training For Dummies
  0-7645-5168-X
- Yoga For Dummies
  0-7645-5117-5

TRAVEL

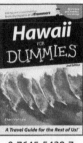

0-7645-5438-7

0-7645-5453-0

Also available:

- Alaska For Dummies
  0-7645-1761-9
- Arizona For Dummies
  0-7645-6938-4
- Cancún and the Yucatán For Dummies
  0-7645-2437-2
- Cruise Vacations For Dummies
  0-7645-6941-4
- Europe For Dummies
  0-7645-5456-5
- Ireland For Dummies
  0-7645-5455-7

- Las Vegas For Dummies
  0-7645-5448-4
- London For Dummies
  0-7645-4277-X
- New York City For Dummies
  0-7645-6945-7
- Paris For Dummies
  0-7645-5494-8
- RV Vacations For Dummies
  0-7645-5443-3
- Walt Disney World & Orlando For Dummie
  0-7645-6943-0

GRAPHICS, DESIGN & WEB DEVELOPMENT

0-7645-4345-8

0-7645-5589-8

Also available:

- Adobe Acrobat 6 PDF For Dummies
  0-7645-3760-1
- Building a Web Site For Dummies
  0-7645-7144-3
- Dreamweaver MX 2004 For Dummies
  0-7645-4342-3
- FrontPage 2003 For Dummies
  0-7645-3882-9
- HTML 4 For Dummies
  0-7645-1995-6
- Illustrator cs For Dummies
  0-7645-4084-X

- Macromedia Flash MX 2004 For Dummie
  0-7645-4358-X
- Photoshop 7 All-in-One Desk
  Reference For Dummies
  0-7645-1667-1
- Photoshop cs Timesaving Techniques
  For Dummies
  0-7645-6782-9
- PHP 5 For Dummies
  0-7645-4166-8
- PowerPoint 2003 For Dummies
  0-7645-3908-6
- QuarkXPress 6 For Dummies
  0-7645-2593-X

NETWORKING, SECURITY, PROGRAMMING & DATABASES

0-7645-6852-3

0-7645-5784-X

Also available:

- A+ Certification For Dummies
  0-7645-4187-0
- Access 2003 All-in-One Desk
  Reference For Dummies
  0-7645-3988-4
- Beginning Programming For Dummies
  0-7645-4997-9
- C For Dummies
  0-7645-7068-4
- Firewalls For Dummies
  0-7645-4048-3
- Home Networking For Dummies
  0-7645-42796

- Network Security For Dummies
  0-7645-1679-5
- Networking For Dummies
  0-7645-1677-9
- TCP/IP For Dummies
  0-7645-1760-0
- VBA For Dummies
  0-7645-3989-2
- Wireless All In-One Desk Reference
  For Dummies
  0-7645-7496-5
- Wireless Home Networking For Dummie
  0-7645-3910-8